SLAVERY
AND FREEDOM

SLAVERY
AND FREEDOM
Expanded Edition

Willie Lee Rose

Edited by
William W. Freehling

OXFORD UNIVERSITY PRESS
Oxford   New York   Toronto   Melbourne

Oxford University Press

Oxford London Glasgow
New York Toronto Melbourne Auckland
Delhi Bombay Calcutta Madras Karachi
Kuala Lumpur Singapore Hong Kong Tokyo
Nairobi Dar es Salaam Cape Town

and associate companies in
Beirut Berlin Ibadan Mexico City Nicosia

First published by Oxford University Press, New York, 1982

First issued as an Oxford University Press paperback, 1982, with
an additional chapter, which was originally published in Great
Britain as a pamphlet under the title, "Race and Region in
American Historical Fiction: Four Episodes in Popular Culture"
(Oxford: Clarendon Press, 1979), © Oxford University Press
1979; in the United States it was first published in J. Morgan
Kousser and James M. McPherson, eds., *Region, Race and Re-
construction: Essays in Honor of C. Vann Woodward* (New
York: Oxford University Press, 1982), copyright © 1982 by
Oxford University Press, Inc.

Library of Congress Cataloging in Publication Data
Rose, Willie Lee Nichols, 1927–
  Slavery and freedom.
  Bibliography: p. Includes index.
  1. Slavery–United States–Addresses, essays,
lectures. 2. Afro-Americans–History–To 1863–
Addresses, essays, lectures. 3. United States–
Race relations–Addresses, essays, lectures.
I. Freehling, William W., 1935– . II. Title.
E441.R79 1982 973'.0496073 82–18773
ISBN 0–19–503266–7 (pbk.)

Printing (last digit): 9 8 7 6 5 4 3 2 1

Printed in the United States of America

For C. Vann Woodward
and William George Rose

Preface

Neither the author nor subject of the following essays demands introduction. A writer celebrated for delicate renderings of the American experience here reconsiders a celebrated episode in our history. But two perspectives may illuminate the nature and shape of these pieces. The essays should be seen as a beginning turned by the fates into a culmination. Mrs. Rose's essays should also be read as beginning from—and yielding a fresh culmination of—a generation's writings about black bondage.

The subject of slavery and freedom has long been Mrs. Rose's prime professional preoccupation. Her interest grew out of her first book, *Rehearsal for Reconstruction*.[1] Her preliminary essays for this volume, written shortly after *Rehearsal* was published, were nurtured by close relationships with other historians preoccupied with antebellum southern slavery. Her ambition was to take these pieces, penned before others wrote their books, and expand her words, in the light of friends' publications, to synthesize a generation's findings.

Mrs. Rose's generation, like all others, began with the preceding generation's conclusions. The pivotal volumes, for those beginning research in the early 1960s, were Kenneth Stampp's *The Peculiar Institution* and Stanley Elkins's *Slavery*.[2] The two studies, while different, had much in common. Stampp and Elkins both portrayed harsh slaveholders. Neither saw benevolent paternalists. Elkins likened slaveholders to Nazi concentration camp guards. Stampp saw them as hardfisted capitalists.

Both additionally shared a sadness about how much human potential such masters could warp. Elkins called the Sambo stereotype of shuffling, childlike dependents all too true. Stampp, while denying that most slaves were Sambos and stressing day-to-day resistance, also emphasized black losses. North American slaves, he wrote, were by and large robbed of African culture and not permitted a white man's sensibility. They fell "between two cultures" into a pit of culturelessness.

Stampp and Elkins also shared a timeless view of slavery. Neither saw the institution as evolving and changing. Elkins, significantly, saw the shock of the voyage from Africa as so lasting as to warp slaves living generations later. Stampp, no less significantly, wrote as if the thirty years from 1830 to 1860 were a model for the way slavery had been generations before. Neither saw much variation, over time or space, in an institution peculiar not least for being so constantly oppressive.

In the years when Mrs. Rose was working out her views, her generation was disavowing this inherited viewpoint. The master, no longer SS guard or remorseless money-grubber, was reportrayed as a patriarch, sometimes harsh, sometimes benevolent. The slave, no longer Sambo or cultureless, was redescribed as a cunning conniver, sometimes culturally creative, sometimes mastering the master. The institution, no longer unchanging, was redescribed as evolving toward a rather self-serving paternalism above and remarkable achievement under adversity below. The combination of masters becoming more scrupulous and slaves becoming more autonomous added up to an institution becoming significantly less dismal.

Mrs. Rose considered the stress on change to be the most important revision. In this respect her generation never seemed to her critical enough of past writers. Her insight into slavery's evolutions went with the territory she made her own in *Rehearsal*. The story of the Sea Islands of South Carolina, where slavery first collapsed during the Civil War and Northerners first imposed a new order, had to be told as a drama of becoming. In the process of relating that evolution, Mrs. Rose became aware of possible earlier and later changes. "Almost never," she noted over a decade ago in an unpublished fragment, "has the institution of slavery been treated as an evolving institution, very different in the seventeenth century from what it became in the eighteenth, and eventually in the nineteenth century. In fact most studies of slavery are static in their conception, resting squarely upon the one period where most of the evidence survives, the thirty years preceding the Civil War. Somehow the idea of the passage of time and the sense of change must be interjected into this history if it is to become meaningful history, as opposed to sociology."[3]

Mrs. Rose's attempt to take the history of slavery beyond sociology led her to project a time frame of unprecedented scale. She planned to begin earlier than most historians of mid-nineteenth-century slavery and to end later than any of them, eliminating arbitrary division between centuries and between antebellum and postbellum history. *Rehearsal* was partially premised on the conviction that the first moment of freedom threw much light on slavery. She would now lengthen the perspective by studying the freedmen's participation during every moment of Reconstruction.

An insight into masters as something akin to "fathers" also came naturally to an historian of the transition from slavery to freedom. In *Rehearsal*, Mrs. Rose traced out how unreconstructed southern masters and reconstructing northern missionaries shared tendencies to patronize blacks as childlike. She suspected that such paternalistic thought and behavior must be a key to an understanding of slavery no less than of Reconstruction.

An historian alive to change necessarily saw constant paternalism as constantly changing. She intended to explore how benevolence grew to fruition and thereby made slave treatment more patriarchal. She would investigate how emancipation frustrated patronizing planters and thus led stymied "fathers" to bring Reconstruction on themselves. She would describe how the act of playing children during slavery both evolved toward and partially limited the success of freedmen after the war.

Her essays on these evolutions, presented to historical conventions and passed on to her colleagues for comment in the mid and late sixties, paralleled the way others were moving. While she was reconsidering her essays, historians such as Eugene D. Genovese, James Roark, and Leon Litwack were completing massive publications on similar conceptions.[4] It was not a question of her influencing them or them influencing her, although influences flew both ways. More centrally involved was the tendency of an entire generation to move, more or less together, toward a fresh conception of historical truth.

If, on the question of evolution over time, Mrs. Rose was moving further than her generation, on the question of how much slaves were servile children she was moving more cautiously. Her essay on servility in *Rehearsal*, viewed in the context of her later writings on bondage, rehearsed what was to come. Although she emphasized, as the post–Stampp-Elkins generation inevitably emphasized, black creativity, culture, and refusal to be patronized, she could not go as far as Genovese, Lawrence Levine, or Herbert Gutman in minimizing psychological dependency.[5] Her blacks, while hardly Elkins's Sambos, necessarily *had* to be a little damaged by such overweening patronizers.

It was all so ironic. As slavery grew more benevolent in the 1800–1840 period, it also grew more closed; slave treatment became better as slave emancipation became more difficult. No less ironically, as slave treatment ameliorated, servile dependency worsened; heavy-handed patronization could suffocate human autonomy as easily as could heavy-handed lashings. Mrs. Rose believed that her friends, when softening the Stampp-Elkins view of unrelieved oppression from above, had missed the irony of better becoming partially worse for those below. In her big book, she meant to help her generation see that even creative and resourceful dependents could not emerge from slavery *totally* independent.

Her book was destined to assume a shorter form. On August 5, 1978, Mrs. Rose suffered a severe stroke. Despite her remarkable recovery, ambitious new research and writing were, at least in the immediate future, no longer feasible. But what could be done, what she desired to help accomplish, was to prepare already written essays for publication. For once, her generation would offer a small new book on slavery.

The paradox is that this little collection of pieces is being published at an appropriate moment to exert a large impact on slavery studies. In the several years since Mrs. Rose lost power to further her evolving ironies, fellow historians have been evolving toward her preliminary positions. Ira Berlin, who won Mrs. Rose's praise for telling the history of free blacks in changing terms of time and space, has recently applied the same technique to enslaved blacks, just as she believed everyone must.[6] Stanley Elkins, who Mrs. Rose thought had hold of an unbalanced fraction of the truth, has recently moved from an emphasis on damaged Sambo to a call for a model balancing servility and creativity.[7] Kenneth Stampp's recent reformulations also move toward that more balanced view of victimization and resistance.[8] Eugene Genovese too has been publicly excoriating those who accuse him of celebrating black counterculture at the cost of minimizing stifling oppressiveness.

The next assignment, for the next generation, may well be to trace out, in still more subtle forms, the evolving dialectic between patronization and dependency, damage and resistance, Sambo and Nat Turner. That assignment may well be carried out best not by ideologues who would formulate unchanging abstractions but by scholars of multiple decades and locales, sensitive to changing nuances of time and space. Such new localists may avoid the current balkanizing trap of local history. They may instead mine local archives in the spirit of *Rehearsal for Reconstruction*, always relating local and specific findings to national and general arguments.

If so, those who follow will find Mrs. Rose's essays the ideal starting place. She will relish future advances. For an historian so alive to irony and evolution, there can be few more satisfying publications than a collection of essays, written precociously early, published inadvertently late, which point out fresh ways to continue traveling.

The Johns Hopkins University   William W. Freehling
April 15, 1981

Acknowledgments

It is with gratitude and affection that I acknowledge the help and encouragement of my friends and colleagues Perra Bell, Mary Allen, Faith Holland, Elborg and Robert Forster, Patricia Romero, Patricia and Orest Ranum, Ronald Walters, and John Baldwin.

I especially wish to thank William Freehling, dear friend and colleague, for his constant support and encouragement in addition to his efforts in editing this volume.

Mr. Freehling and I are grateful to Andrea Mattei, our mutual graduate student, who drafted much of the editorial material, checked every word in my drafts, and made numerous important suggestions. We are all grateful to The Johns Hopkins University for providing Ms. Mattei's help. We all remember William Harris's initial contribution. We all appreciate William W. Abbot's, Sheldon Meyer's, and C. Vann Woodward's advice. Finally, none of us can adequately thank William Rose. This book is the least of what he has made possible.

Willie Lee Rose

Remarks on Editorial Procedure

Although I have never met Don E. Fehrenbacher, and although he knows nothing about my editorial work, he has unintentionally aided in editing this volume. Professor Fehrenbacher's publication of David Potter's manuscripts has served as a model of collegial responsibility. He has also elegantly indicated how troubling difficulties in that responsibility should be resolved.

When working with a manuscript by an author who could no longer apply helpful finishing touches, Fehrenbacher defined the editor as the author's "surrogate in the publication process." The author, if given the opportunity, "might have decided to revise or even rewrite." But as editor, Fehrenbacher confined himself "to minor corrections and alterations of the kind that constitute refinement rather than revision of a text."[1]

Fehrenbacher's crisp distinction between refinement and revision established for me a salutory line between small matters of style and large matters of substance. Accordingly, my pen has only occasionally intruded on Mrs. Rose's drafts, and only to accomplish those small deletions, little reorganizations, and slight rephrasings a manuscript receives in the final publication process, so that the argument emerges more clearly. I am aware that Mrs. Rose might have somewhat changed certain arguments in unpublished essays written years ago on subjects about which much has subsequently been published. But I have been at pains to maintain the integrity of the argument as the author drafted it.

In the process of final retouching, I have had one advantage denied Professor Fehrenbacher. He was working with a deceased colleague's papers. I could consult an author wonderfully alive to nuances of language. Mrs. Rose herself suggested some delicate improvements when I or Andrea Mattei read her the original drafts. She also corrected some indelicacies in my alleged improvements. She was, in short, partly her own editor, and her original draft is the better for her latest efforts.

One essay required a variation on my editorial role. Mrs. Rose projected for this volume an essay on ex-slaves during Reconstruction to parallel her piece "Masters without Slaves." Three versions of "Blacks without Masters," all written in the 1960s, survive in her files. All make the same points. But no one draft presents the argument as efficiently as do the best parts of all three versions, taken together. I have accordingly linked the three essays into one. To ease linkages, I have added transitional sentences here and there. Still, "Blacks without Masters" is 95 percent of the time word for word from Mrs. Rose's pen. And the analytical framework is entirely as she sketched it.

W. W. F.

Contents

Contents

V   Views on the Sources

I

Slavery

1

The Impact of the
American Revolution
on the Black Population

This essay began as a lecture at the University of Utah, Salt Lake City, and at Weber State College, Ogden, Utah, during 1975–76, as part of a bicentennial series assessing the American Revolution. A revised version was published in Larry Gerlach, ed., Legacies of the American Revolution *(Logan, Ore., 1978), pp. 183–97. The essay is here reprinted with only a few slight verbal changes.*

When I was first asked to give my impressions of the impact of the American Revolution on the black population, I must admit that I wondered what might be said, silently confessing to myself the doubts implied by an editor of a prominent black magazine who recently asked me, bluntly, whether there was any good reason why blacks should celebrate this bicentennial. I reflected that once, long ago, in 1852 to be precise, the famous black abolitionist Frederick Douglass had been asked to speak on the Fourth of July in Rochester, New York, and that he had mused aloud why he, of all men, should have been asked to do any such thing. "Fellow citizens, pardon me," he begged; "are the great principles of political freedom and justice, embodied in that Declaration of Independence, extended to us?"[1] Speaking as an escaped slave, in a period when slavery was still alive and thriving, Douglass in asking the question was suggesting the answer.

Considering the intervening 200 years, the slow development of the promise of the Declaration, and the incomplete realization, even now, of that promise for black America, the editor's question of me seemed not unreasonable, and Douglass's answer of 1852 not entirely inappropriate, even these 124 years later. But it then occurred to me that if this were true, that blacks still had no reason to celebrate, then perhaps nobody has a reason to celebrate. By such a standard American liberty would have failed the test of twentieth-century problems.

Laying that question aside for a moment, I began to think further about the meaning of the entire Revolutionary epoch for slaves, and indeed for all those left out on the first round of freedom. In the most general terms, the answer is simple: ideas long circulating in the Western world were given a concrete reality in a new government, ideas that moved slowly but very surely toward a great enlargement of human freedom, at first for a few, later for many, as our ideas of the relationship between freedom and property slowly changed. But that would be to defer too much to the future, beyond doubt, and my task is to assess the more immediate effects of the Revolution.

What convinced me that something might be said to good effect was the sudden thought that this was really the question Chief Justice Roger Brooke Taney felt obliged to answer back in 1857, in the famous Dred Scott case: whether a black man, even if free, could really be a citizen of the United States, endowed with the right to bring his case into federal court. It must be believed that Justice Taney thought he understood the frame of mind of the Founders and their world when he came out with a thumping "no," and declared that our government was formed by white men, for whites only, and that such rights as even free blacks enjoyed were mere courtesies, and further, in the line that angered so many of his contemporaries, that "they had no rights which the white man was bound to respect," and further yet, that "this opinion was at that time . . . universal in the civilized portion of the white race. . . ."[2] He spoke less than a hundred years after the Declaration of Independence, and sixty-nine years after the Constitution was formed. Although he was, of course, interpreting the Constitution, his generalizations apparently refer to the dominant attitudes of the entire Revolutionary generation, and it has not been hard for historians now, or indeed for lawyers then, to show that the Chief Justice was mistaken in so summarily dismissing the impact of Enlightenment ideas, natural law, the concept of the essential worth of man, on both whites and blacks in the late eighteenth century.

Justice Taney lived in a period when a reaction against natural rights had affixed to southern blacks a more difficult legal position than they had had in the Revolutionary period. There were restrictions on free blacks that had not existed earlier, and for slaves the chances of becoming free had become much dimmer. It is true that there were also laws requiring masters to provide decently for their chattels, and restraining them from cruel punishments and other barbarisms that marred the laws of the eighteenth century. No doubt these laws were frequently ignored, but the owner who did so was scouting public opinion, and there seems little doubt that life in a physical sense was becoming more bearable for most slaves in the nineteenth century. A new position for slaves was crystallizing, so that a slave might be regarded with more benign paternalism, almost *because* he could no longer hope for eventual emancipation.[3]

Ironically, an age of expanded liberties for whites had witnessed the rationalization of the slave system, making it harder for slaves to become free (even if their masters desired to emancipate), to learn to read, or open their minds in any way. It would almost appear to be a historical trade-off, in which the society at large indicates by law a will to secure decent order and some humanity on the plantations in return for some assurance that slaves would not become free men and trouble society at large. Roger B. Taney, victim of his own time-frame, failed as a historian in sensing the very different spirit of Revolutionary times, no matter how ambivalent attitudes on race in that earlier period can be proven to have been. Might not the passage of another century, with new views of property and freedom, allow a clearer perspective on how blacks were involved in the Age of Revolution, and what it meant to them?

This might be an appropriate place to recite the exploits of black men and women in the Revolution—Crispus Attucks and the

Boston Massacre, Phillis Wheatley's poems about liberty, the black soldiers who served in various sectors of the war—to tell of the black men who served as spies, scouts, pilots, sailors, laborers for the patriot's cause, or perhaps to tell of the Battle of Rhode Island in August of 1778, where a black regiment figured prominently and served bravely.[4] No. We shall hear a lot about these matters, no doubt, in the coming months, and much that we hear will of necessity be speculative, perhaps pious and therapeutic. Black participation is hard to assess, for a reason that indicates why Justice Taney's period is so very different from the Revolutionary era. In the Revolution blacks were for the most part integrated into white units, because they were freely accepted as substitutes, and accepted by many of the colonial governments as volunteers on the same basis as whites, and also, one supposes, because blacks were less alarming to the whites of that period when not concentrated in units.

No, the real meaning of the Revolution for America's black people was more subtle, and rests more on the vigorous circulation of the idea of freedom, the new opportunities the general disruption of society afforded, and most particularly on the important social and demographic changes that came out of the struggle between the British and their obstreperous colonials. Yet it is interesting to note in passing that, just as the combatants did eighty-five years later in the Civil War, both the British and the Americans were increasingly ready to call on blacks as soldiers, and hazard the possibility of an insurrection, as the going got rough. By Taney's time men apparently had forgotten what part black soldiers played in the Revolution, and three years after the Dred Scott decision a war began in which black men were ultimately asked to prove themselves as fighting men in special separate units, sometimes, alas, as cannon fodder. The black man of the Revolutionary era was at least dignified by the assumption that he would be a regular fighting man. Reflecting on how poor a conception Taney had of the difference between the 1850s and the spirit of '76 has caused me to appreciate more the advantage of a 200-year perspective on the earlier period.

The most immediate and significant consequence of the Revolution for blacks was the formation during the Revolutionary epoch of a large free black community.[5] How New England, under the impulse of Revolutionary zeal, provided for emancipation is a well-known and praiseworthy chapter of our history. With only a blush or two for the hesitations of Connecticut and Rhode Island, where slavery was a larger economic factor than in its other states, New England had by 1790 only 3,763 slaves to report to the new federal census, out of a population of 16,882 blacks. By 1810 the number of slaves remaining was just 418, in Rhode Island and Connecticut, which had taken gradual measures.[6] The urgings of blacks themselves, the interpretations of courts favorable to freedom, the new constitutions—all these contributed to the success of the cause now actively pursued by an increasingly vigorous new antislavery movement. The Middle Atlantic states proved more hesitant to act, with New York and New Jersey entirely resistant to emancipation through the Revolutionary period. Pennsylvania joined Rhode Island and Connecticut as a gradualist state. There seems no reason to doubt that the great thrust of this movement owed its main impulse to the workings of the ideals of the Revolution on the minds of both black men and women and their owners.

But the black population of the North was numerically of small significance when compared to the thousands who lived and worked to the south in the tobacco colonies. Therefore it is to Maryland and Virginia that we must look to see the ideals of the Revolution in contact with the most stubborn economic facts of life. In these states the most important accomplishment of the Revolutionary era was the formation of a large free black community in the midst of slavery. Before the Revolution the number of free blacks in these states was negligible, and most of them were the mulatto offspring of mixed unions; surprisingly often they were the children of white mothers and black fathers, and therefore born free. White fathers who disliked seeing their black children grow up as slaves also contributed to this population, but less than one might imagine on the eve of the Revolution because a law of Virginia in force for fifty-nine years prior to its reversal in 1782 made manumission by will or deed illegal. Maryland, the only colony with a conveniently dated (1755) pre-Revolutionary census, had then only 1,817 free blacks, constituting only 4 percent of the black population. Eighty percent of those 1,817 were mulattoes. This picture can serve reasonably well for other southern states. Ira Berlin, in his excellent book on the subject, produces convincing evidence that the number of free blacks was small in each state and that of these a very few were of purely African extraction.[7]

Over the three decades from 1770 to the end of the eighteenth century, the free black population increased at a remarkable rate, not only in New England, where we have seen general emancipations, and in the Middle Atlantic states, where the pattern of gradual emancipation prevailed, but even more remarkably in the Upper South, where the black population was actually concentrated. Virginia and Maryland accounted for well over half of all the slaves owned before the Revolution. Feeling the impulses of the Revolution early, they showed an increase in manumissions before the war started, and showed approximate percentage increases in free blacks before 1790 of 609 percent and 340 percent respectively. By 1810 over 23 percent of Maryland's slaves were free. Virginia, holding so many thousands of slaves, could count only a 7 percent increase of free blacks by that time, but this percent amounted to a larger number of free blacks than in any other southern state except Maryland, and came numerically to 30,570 souls; Maryland had over 33,000. This growth represented in Virginia, the overwhelmingly largest slave state, a surging growth in the free black population, rising from the year 1782 when the liberalized manumission law was passed (overturning a law and a policy of fifty-nine years' duration prohibiting private manumission). Free persons of color increased by 1790 to 12,766, to 20,124 by the end of the century, and to 30,570 in 1810.[8]

Leaving aside for the moment the circumstances, and by whose volition these blacks became free, we should mention that these figures cannot include the tens of thousands of slaves who fled to the British, many thousands of them never returning. When the center of the war shifted to the South after 1778 the British systematically took off slaves in groups of hundreds at a time. Benjamin Quarles estimates that the British carried away in their final evacuation perhaps 4,000 or more from New York, the same number from Savannah, from Charleston 6,000 and from Yorktown, before the surrender, 5,000. He estimates that as many as 5,000 had already been carried away during the fighting.[9] The fate of the evacuees was various, some going to Nova Scotia, many freed, some sold without conscience in the West Indies. Some remained the slaves of their loyalist masters who departed at the same time.

It is difficult to assess the full reaction of a largely illiterate black population to the ideas of the Revoluton, but slaves who seized opportunities to escape were speaking with their heels. Their vigorous response to Lord Dunmore's policy of offering freedom to those who would defect and join the British spoke reams, especially when the Americans began to counter with proposals to emancipate slaves who bore arms for the patriots. Those who took their chances with the colonials may have reasoned as did a slave named Saul, who had served as a double spy, and asked the legislature for his freedom after the war. He was, he said, "taught to know that the war was levied upon America, not for the emancipation of Blacks, but for the subjugation of Whites, and he thought the number of Bond-ment [sic] ought not to be augmented."[10] To their credit, most petitioners received their freedom. By a Virginia law of 1783 "all who had served in the late war" were liberated, the law itself being tacit admission that many slaves had served the American armies in spite of Virginia laws restricting service to free blacks.[11]

Perhaps more important than the struggle between the British and the colonials was the general disruption of the times, which permitted slaves to escape their owners and declare themselves free at some distance from home. The depressed condition of agriculture worked hand in glove with the ideas of the Revolution, making many masters who were disposed by conscience to free their slaves more willing to do so. When Richard Randolph freed his slaves by will in the wake of the Revolution, he did so, as he wrote, "to make retribution, as far as I am able, to an unfortunate race of bond-men, over whom my ancestors have usurped and exercised the most lawless and monstrous tyranny, and in whom my countrymen (by their iniquitous laws, in contradiction of their own declaration of rights, and in violation of every sacred law of nature, of the inherent, inalienable and imprescriptible rights of man, and of every principle of moral and political honesty) have vested me with absolute property. . . ."[12]

Estimating the effect of the Enlightenment upon the emancipators when counting up the expansion of freedom in the Revolutionary era is just as puzzling as understanding how much the slaves understood about the same ideas. Yet the problems are quite different. With the black population one has to distinguish between the urge, which must have been present always, to break free, and the special form it would take under the impulse of new ideas of natural right; with the slaveowning class, one would have to distinguish between stated motives and economic facilitators. Exploring this point would extend beyond the scope of this paper, but it seems reasonable to assume that the greatly enlarged free black population resulted from impulses from both sides of the color line, eased by the economic fact of reduced value—as it proved, a temporarily reduced value—of slave labor, and the enlarged possibility of an escaped slave's escaping detection, once there were more free blacks with whom to merge one's identity.

Not only was that free black community enlarged, but in the Upper South, where it was growing so fast, it was also changing significantly in color composition. Ira Berlin has pointed to the significance of the nondiscriminatory nature of the emancipation of the period: where owners had once chosen to emancipate only a few light-colored blood relatives, for special reasons, they now emancipated wholesale on grounds of conscience, which meant that the free black community began to receive large numbers of blacks with pure African ancestry, and thus to reflect more perfectly the entire range of the black population.[13] He regards this condition in the Upper South as being an important difference between the free black communities there and in the Lower South, particularly Louisiana, where lightness of color remained a distinguishing feature.

After the Revolution, in Maryland and Virginia, one could no longer use blackness of complexion as prima facie indication of slave status, which greatly increased the probabilities of escaping detection for such slaves of any shade of complexion as decided to run off the plantation. These circumstances generated a wholesome restlessness in the slave population, and there is considerable evidence that the advertisements for runaways register a marked increase in the 1790s of those who are described as being black or African.[14] The talented, skilled, light-colored population that Gerald Mullin describes so well in *Flight and Rebellion* were now joined in flight by those who were black, and not particularly skilled.[15] With the development of towns in the post-Revolutionary period blacks had an increasingly improved chance of escaping detection, and the seaport cities became a favored target.

The attitudes of blacks who sought freedom are best registered in words through the petitions they made for freedom. These petitions often pointed to the inconsistency of the ideals of the Revolution and the maintenance of slavery. Freedom suits were "invariably won," according to Benjamin Quarles, who appears in this instance to be referring primarily to cases arising in Massachusetts. There one group presented themselves as "a Grate [*sic*] number of Blacks . . . who . . . are held in a state of slavery within the bowels of a free and christian Country." Although "a free-born people who had never forfeited that natural right," they had been "stolen from the bosoms of our tender Parents, . . . to be made slaves for Life in a christian land." A group of blacks in New Hampshire urged that a law be passed to free them (1779), "that the name of slave may not more be heard in a land gloriously contending for the sweets of freedom."[16]

Liberal decisions in some key court cases also contributed to the expansion of freedom. In many instances blacks petitioned for freedom, especially in Maryland, on grounds of descent from a white woman. The famous case in that state of the Butler family illustrates the point, and its multiplier effect. William and Mary Butler claimed descent from a white woman's union with a slave sometime between 1664 and 1681, when a law operated to enslave the woman along with her children in such instances. The law's object was to discourage such alleged "shameful matches." Although the Butlers did not win their suit in 1771 when they opened litigation, their daughter, Mary, was more successful sixteen years later. Soon the name of Butler appears regularly in such suits, and for the same reason that Shorter and Toogood family names appear.[17]

Sometimes slaves bought their freedom, but larger numbers

gained it by flight, suits for freedom, and general emancipations. Thus the free black community emerged, and its importance through the entire slave era would be hard to exaggerate. Not only did its existence inspire flight in slaves, but also it became a center for the development of institutions very important to the entire black population after 1863 and the Emancipation Proclamation. Here the black church experienced its first vigorous semi-independent growth, and in the free black communities the fraternal organizations flourished. The African church became the significant social unit, beyond the home, of the free black community, and at least one able scholar has concluded that blacks had a higher proportion of church membership in the antebellum period than whites did.[18] One function of the church was educational, for nearly all the churches conducted Sunday Schools, and through the churches came the largest cadre of black leadership that was to become so significant a resource in the Reconstruction that followed the Civil War. Had there been no substantial free black community the transition in 1863 from slave to freedman, to free men and women, would have been infinitely more difficult.

Almost as significant in its consequences for the condition of the slave population was a second result of the Revolution, the suppression of the African slave trade. The origin of the movement that culminated in the prohibition of 1807 came with the pre-Revolutionary nonimportation agreements among the colonial legislatures. Massachusetts acted in 1774, as did Connecticut. Rhode Island, the colony most heavily involved economically in slave-trading, restricted the traffic sharply, stating that "those who are desirous of enjoying all the advantage of liberty themselves, should be willing to extend personal liberty to others."[19] The Middle Atlantic states worked variously to the same end. As in the case of emancipation, economic circumstances eased the course of Revolutionary rhetoric and idealism. Glutted slave markets and overstocked, underpaying plantations in the middle colonies and the Upper South, and the need to hurt British commerce, eased the path of conscience. Virginia, North Carolina, and Georgia acted in 1774 and 1775, and three months ahead of the Declaration of Independence the Continental Congress acted in the name of the thirteen united colonies to end the international slave trade to America.[20]

The limited nature of this commitment is a familiar story to all students of American history. How Jefferson's harsh and uncompromising charge against King George for allegedly forcing the colonies to participate in this "piratical warfare" was struck from the Declaration of Independence at the insistence of the Deep South representatives is part of a predictable backdown. Later, in the Constitutional Convention at Philadelphia, South Carolina could easily point out that Virginia had more slaves than she needed, while South Carolina had fewer, and suggest that economic motives prompted this liberal view on the part of Upper South representatives who were anticipating a rise in the value of their property. This intra-South debate marked subsequent discussions through the Constitution-making era.[21] And yet the magic words were out, that men, all men, were endowed with "inalienable rights" that included "Life, Liberty, and the pursuit of Happiness." As Bernard Bailyn has pointed out, such ideas are weapons. The inconsistency pervading the American fight for liberty and its denial forced itself forward at every turn.[22] The British were, of course, prompt in their derisive reminders; but England's continued status as a slaveholding polity limited the effect of her laughter to embarrassment only. The most telling thrusts came from within, with the development of the first serious attacks not only on the slave trade but on slavery itself.

Levi Hart in 1775 cried that it was now "high time for this colony to wake up and put an effectual stop to the cruel business of stealing and selling our fellow men," and asked, "what inconsistence [*sic*] and self-contradiction is this! . . . When, O when shall the happy day come, that Americans shall be *consistently* engaged in the cause of liberty?"[23] The Americans' use of the word "slavery" to sum up their position in the British Empire was bound to have the result of associating the Revolution with the slavery question where it meant *most*, and for that reason it seems altogether natural that the first organized activities for emancipation began with the Revolution. The work of Anthony Benezet and John Woolman and others like them, the Quakers and other religious sects, did not bear the fruit in their own lives that they could have wished, though they doubtless inspired many to free their slaves in the interest of a clear conscience and consistency.[24] But their work was remembered past the time of reaction against what they had stood for, and inspired a new generation of abolitionists in the next century. The ideas of the Declaration moved blacks deeply, focusing their thoughts on their own emancipation. Truly, they held themselves to be, in Quarles's very appropriate phrase, "heirs of the same promise."[25]

A generation of black and white abolitionists taunted slaveholders and their abettors among the politicians with the language of the Declaration, eventually forcing the most ardent defenders of slavery to denounce the document altogether. The abolitionists claimed blacks were included in the promise of the Declaration and made a fierce distinction between the grandeur of its faith in mankind and the United States Constitution, which many of them ritually burned for its wordless but real sanction of slavery in federal law. When John Brown organized a black congress in Canada for his coming push on Harper's Ferry in 1859 the congress made its own constitution and endorsed the Declaration.[26]

One final act of the Revolutionary generation should be mentioned because of its ultimate significance in the sectional struggle. When individual states ceded their western land claims to the new Confederation, they invested the government with the responsibility of determining the laws that would govern territories. The Northwest Ordinance of 1787, devised for the purpose, prohibited the introduction of slavery in the territories north of the Ohio River, and became the first positive articulation in law of the policy of containing slavery. It also became the most significant legal precedent for the Free-Soilers after 1848, and later for the new Republican Party in the 1850s when it argued that Congress itself had the duty and right to prohibit slavery in the territories acquired from Mexico. As William W. Freehling has pointed out, "containment" was the road that ultimately led to the end of slavery in the United States, and he places Thomas Jefferson, the author of the Ordinance, very close to Abraham Lincoln in his thinking on the subject.[27]

These, to conclude, are my notions of the impact of the Revolution on black Americans: the development of a free black community of size and strength to become a guardian of cherished institutions and an aid in the struggle for general emancipation and to provide leadership; the suppression of the African slave trade, an event that meant better physical conditions in the nineteenth century for the enslaved population; the rise of the first abolition movement; and the emergence of a policy of containment of slavery in the Confederation period, a policy that had its ups and downs, to be sure, but eventually became the rallying point for the emergent Free-Soil movement and the Republican Party, and the sticking point for Lincoln's government in the secession crisis. Containment in time became the precipitating cause of the Civil War and emancipation.

In all this the gains surely were greater than the detrimental side-effects, but these last should be mentioned, for they are thickly entangled with the reaction that followed the passing of the Revolutionary generation. The rise of the free black population in the crucial Upper South region, where the course of the first emancipation stopped in its tracks, frightened a vulnerable slaveholding society who recognized it as a threat, especially after the black revolution in St. Domingue in 1794 and even more after the disruption of Gabriel Prosser's attempted revolt in Virginia in 1800. Virginia's black population was over 40 percent of the whole at this period, and heavily concentrated in the eastern counties. The suppression of the African slave trade created a stronger determination to retain in bondage those who were slaves, and contributed in some measure to the restrictive laws on manumission appearing in the early nineteenth century. No doubt some of the cruel strength and vigor of the interstate slave traffic is owing to the rise in value of slave property, which also owes something to reviving agricultural profits. Attempting to answer the unanswerable arguments of the first abolitionists readied the defenders of slavery for the greater onslaught to come. They learned to do better than Patrick Henry, who when asked why he kept slaves, said he would not, could not defend it, and held as his only, very limp excuse "ye general inconvenience" of doing without them.[28] The policy of containment wobbled badly before it struck the iron resistance of the white South, in deep dread of being contained *with* the blacks as a race along with the institution, and then brought on a great war over the question, a war that exacted one life for every five slaves emancipated by the conflict. Surely this was a costly emancipation, even when one joins in the noble meaning of Lincoln's words, when he asked in the Second Inaugural, just on this very point:

> Shall we discern . . . [in "this terrible war"] any departure from the divine attributes which the believers in a Living God always ascribe to Him? Fondly do we hope—fervently do we pray —that this mighty scourge of war may speedily pass away. Yet, if God wills that it continue, until all the wealth piled [up] by the bond-man's two hundred and fifty years of unrequited toil shall be sunk, and until every drop of blood drawn with the lash, shall be paid with another drawn with the sword, as was said three thousand years ago, so still it must be said "the judgments of the Lord, are true and righteous altogether."[29]

Lincoln had God; moderns have Marx. Explaining such costs and the nature of social change is never easy. But who would criticize Lincoln at such a moment for failing to mention the less exalted forces of sectional economic interest and partisan political requirements that had accompanied the spirit of the Declaration of Independence so much cherished by the Republican Party down the long road to war?

Lincoln's sense of America's mission, and its derivation from the spirit of the Declaration, justify him, as does the burning sense of suffering in the process of learning that suffused his words. Perhaps for this reason more than for all others the suffering nation could identify with its leader. In all events, his humility contrasts most agreeably with Chief Justice Taney's Godlike confidence in his own understanding of the literal nature and the historical background of the Revolution and the Constitution. And who can doubt that Lincoln would have been most pleased had he lived to read the opening clause of the Fourteenth Amendment to the Constitution, designed most specifically to set right the omission that had eased Justice Taney's decision that Dred Scott could *not* be a citizen, a new clause extending the blessing and protection of citizenship to *all* persons born in the United States?

As all men know, setting things right in law does not accomplish all it ought, and the road to realization of the full meaning of the Revolution is far from its goal. That thought might lead to pessimism, but might it not lead as easily to renewed understanding of a generation who had a view of the relationship of property to freedom at considerable variance from our own, and to gratitude for the words they articulated but only partially implemented in their time? All things considered, I take heart, and vote for the words. Their promise, though imperfectly fulfilled, is no longer denied. If Frederick Douglass could conclude his Fourth of July oration to the Rochester Ladies' Anti-Slavery Society by drawing encouragement from "the great principles" of the Declaration, "cheered by the obvious tendencies" of his own age, then surely we may, after this long journey and the developments of our own time, do as well.

2

The Domestication
of Domestic Slavery

The presentation of this paper as the William P. Cardoza Memorial Lecture in American History on April 23, 1973, was the highpoint of Mrs. Rose's tenure as Visiting Professor of History at Yale University, 1972–73. The lecture at Yale is also the linchpin of this book. For in this previously unpublished essay, Professor Rose traces out what she conceived to be the greatest of all evolutions in a history she saw as badly in need of a sense of historical change.

Soon after Christmas in the year 1847, an aging Virginia planter named John Hartwell Cocke left his estate, Bremo Bluff in Fluvanna County, Virginia, to journey to his distant plantation in Alabama. He was off to check on his interesting human experiment involving preparation of certain chosen slaves for self-government and colonization in Liberia. Cocke was a staunch colonizationist, a religious evangelical, and a late child of the Revolutionary era. More important for our purposes, his life interests span the most crucial generation in the evolution of slavery in the United States.

By late January, 1848, General Cocke's journey ended at his estate near Greensboro. In his private diary, Cocke revealed dismay at the state of affairs on his plantation and described measures taken to mend matters. The entry reveals much about Cocke and much about his class in the late antebellum era:

A few days looking into the state of my plantation . . . disclosed a shocking state of moral depravity. . . . Two of my Foreman's

Daughters had bastard white children. A state of almost indiscriminate sexual intercourse among them—not a marriage since I was last there—3 years ago. The venereal disease has been prevalent—And to crown this mass of corruption—my Foreman with a wife and 10 living Children was keeping a young girl on the place. While his eldest daughters were the kept mistresses (there was strong reason to believe by his consent) of two of the young Southern Gentlemen of the vicinity—Another man hitherto regarded as next in respectability to the Foreman also with a wife and 10 children, had had the venereal—and these two both members of the Baptist Church. . . . My School for ultimate Liberian freedom had become a plantation Brothel headed by my Foreman. . . .

I now commanded, that which I had formerly requested and advised—"that they should be married forthwith or be punished and sold"—they chose the first alternative. I allowed one week for them to make matches among themselves—but what was not agreed upon, at the expiration of that time—I should finish by my own authority—until every single man and woman were disposed of and united in marriage. The consequence was nine couples reported themselves as willing to marry forthwith. And I commenced building 4 new rooms required to accommodate the parties—which requiring two weeks afforded time to procure and make up a dress for each bride and some articles of simple furniture for the Chambers. To give solemnity to the matter—I engaged a respectable Baptist clergyman . . . to preach a Sermon upon the marriage relation—and unite the Nine Couples in the holy State of wedlock. . . . On Saturday the 12th of March the Ceremony was performed, . . . [preceded by] suitable corporal punishment inflicted upon the Foreman and his brother of the Baptist Church. Having received abundant promises of amendment and confessions—I left with the hope of doing better in the future.[1]

Such concern for slaves' domestic relations may surprise some readers. But I'd like to dispose of one question right away. Even if a scholar is latitudinarian in his definition of hypocrisy (and I am not), and wishes to question the sincerity of even material in the privacy of a diary, Cocke *was* sincere in his experiment. As long as the law had permitted, he had maintained a northern schoolteacher in residence at Bremo Bluff, charged with instructing his slaves to read and write. He had sent slaves to Liberia at his own expense and had sent them funds on request after they arrived. Knowing his religious views of the sanctity of "domestic relations," as well as his hostility to alcohol and tobacco, it seems most *improbable* that the desire to foster slave family life was prompted primarily by the consideration so often expressed by more acquisitive planters, that monogamous families were "favorable to increase" and promiscuity was not.

No, Cocke sincerely wished to elevate the character of "his people" to the presumed standard of Liberia, a word meaning, significantly, the land of freedom. Hundreds of planters who had no notion of freeing human property were also concerned, for whatever reasons, to establish among their slaves their own religious and social views, especially their view of domestic life. In fact their domesticating mission became for planters who bothered to justify slaveholding in the nineteenth century the main excuse for retaining what they very significantly entitled their "domestic institution."

It is a fascinating sidelight on slavery and on nineteenth-century ideas of domestic morality that when slaveholders, travelers, or abolitionists attempted to assess slaves' social "progress" they tended to gravitate sooner or later to the subject of sex on the plantation and the regularity (or lack) of family stability. But this was distinctly a nineteenth-century phenomenon. Until the late eighteenth century, planters and their womenfolk seldom referred either to slave marriages or to slave religion. Nothing better illustrates the folly of treating an institution that existed for nearly 250 years as the same institution from start to finish. Slavery had to *become* "the Domestic Institution." How this took place requires a backward look.

Even the word "domestic," when applied to chattel slavery in the eighteenth century, carried a non-nineteenth-century connotation. In 1794, for example, St. George Tucker, a distinguished Virginia jurist, made careful use of the word when writing a disquisition on emancipation. Tucker distinguished between three types of bondage: political, civil, and domestic slavery. Merely political slavery Tucker illustrated by the example of the American colonial relation to England before the Revolution. Civil slavery he illustrated by the example of blacks freed but lacking such civil rights as power to vote. *Domestic* slavery was the legal position of enslaved blacks. Domestic slavery, then, was political slavery, plus civil slavery, plus the "numerous calamities" involved in one man being "subject to be directed by another in all his actions."[2]

Whether this pleasant little word "domestic" came into style during the Revolutionary epoch as a means of avoiding the blatant contradiction that property in human beings implied for the natural rights philosophy, and/or from the need to distinguish between black chattel servitude and lesser forms of political servitude, is not clear. It is nevertheless a supreme irony that the phrase "domestic slavery" should have become in the nineteenth century the most frequent designation of an institution that was supposed, then and now, to have had a particularly devastating effect on family life—on homes of enslavers as well as the enslaved. Certainly in time defenders of slavery had so distinct a preference for the term "domestic slavery" that when they referred to their "domestic institution" the phrase absorbed the color of a euphemism, and was more often enunciated with pride than apology. Proslavery philosophers intended to suggest a benign institution that encouraged between masters and slaves the qualities so much admired in the Victorian family: cheerful obedience and gratitude on the part of children (read slaves), and paternalistic wisdom, protection, and discipline on the part of the father (read master). An organic world was implied, the world of St. Paul's twelfth chapter to the Corinthians, in which feet, head, hands, and heart performed distinct but essential functions in the ongoing good of the whole. So, in the nineteenth century, the phrase "domestic institution" came to mean slavery idealized, slavery translated into a fundamental and idealized Victorian institution, the family. Of the hundred paradoxes set by the contradiction of property in man, none more teases the imagination.

Even in the eighteenth century some masters liked to think of themselves as "fathers." As early as 1726 William Byrd of Westover gave an engaging domestic picture of life in Virginia in a letter to the Earl of Orrery: "I have a large Family of my own," he wrote. "Like one of the Patriarchs, I have my Flocks and my Herds, my Bonds-men and Bond-women." He had to "take care to keep all my people to their Duty, to set all the springs in motion, and make everyone draw his equal share to carry the Machine forward."[3]

But Byrd's attempt to identify himself with Father Abraham is somewhat vitiated by accounts in his famous private diary of times when his lady took a hot poker to an obstreperous maid, or when he made his eighteen-year-old slave Eugene (to use Byrd's inimitable language) "drink a pint of piss" as a correction for chronic bedwetting.[4] Even in a day when parents occasionally horsewhipped their offspring, Byrd's "corrections" torture his analogy. Compared to their nineteenth-century descendants, eighteenth-century planters were decidedly poor patriarchs, if patriarchs at all. Even the enlightened Robert Carter of Nomini Hall was accused by his children's tutor, Philip Fithian, of feeding his slaves inadequately, an accusation which has the ring of sincerity because the young teacher had otherwise favorable judgments on the character of his employer.[5]

For the most part planters of eighteenth-century Virginia appear to have been more concerned with the state of their crops than with paternal relations with their chattels. George Washington, though opposed to slavery, was under no illusion about the essentially exploitative nature of "domestic slavery." He was a notably rigorous manager of slaves. No small details escaped his eagle eye. Once he learned how many shirts his seamstresses could make per week, he instructed their supervisor to inform them that "what *has* been done *shall* be done," adding ominously, "by fair means or foul."[6] Certainly Dr. Benjamin West, traveling in the back country, seeing slaves half-clothed or naked, and noticing that white women took no more notice of naked male adults than if they had been horses, had no idea that eighteenth-century Virginia slaveowners thought of themselves as patriarchal providers.[7] Nor could the Reverend Francis LeJau, sent to South Carolina by the Society for the Propagation of the Gospel in Foreign Parts, have been favorably impressed by his experience with masters who would castrate their slaves or invent diabolical punishment for trivial offenses. LeJau reported that these non-patriarchs denied slaves religion either because they wished labor on Sunday, or because they were afraid that slaves who became Christians might fancy themselves free men.[8]

Of course instances of such abuse could be found throughout the slaveholding period. But the very frequency and casual nature of these eighteenth-century revelations indicates more pervasive suffering and brutality. There was neither sentiment nor sentimentality in eighteenth-century slaveholding. Slave codes were unspeakably harsh, permitting punishment by dismemberment and allowing anyone to kill slaves declared outlaws by masters. Slaveholders had no specific and enforceable obligations for housing, food, or clothing. Few appeared to have taken pride in physical arrangements for chattel property. Most never underestimated slaves' capacity or desire to resist and were distinctly frightened of what these "children" might take it into their heads to do. One seldom finds mention of slave marriages in early eighteenth-century accounts, and there is a great deal of hostility to the idea that religion could mean anything to slaves.

Developments of far-reaching importance occurred by the third decade of the nineteenth century. These changes are clearly registered in personal letters and diaries and in the legal system that protected slaves. The meaning of these changes has been much harder for historians to assess than identifying them has been. The easiest and most fashionable course has been to assume that there could be no improvement in the physical or moral condition of victims of so barbarous an institution.[9] The horror was too absolute to admit of changes in degrees. But to do this is to overlook the evolutionary nature of all institutions. It is to denounce history as unnecessary.

The northern legal scholar James Codman Hurd, writing in the 1850s of southern laws on slavery, observed that every legal responsibility assigned to the master tended to establish the slave as a legal person. Every legal recognition of slaves' "rights, independent of the will of the owner or master, . . . diminishes in some degree the essence of that slavery by changing it into a relation between legal persons."[10] These tendencies were gaining ground in all southern states in the first decades of the nineteenth century.

In time slave codes were altered to require decent provisioning by slaveowners, and to curtail once-unbounded power to chastise slaves. Dismemberment and other cruel and unusual punishments became illegal. Killing a slave with malice was murder, and slaves were defined as persons at law, in spite of crippling civil disabilities. Humane judges extended by interpretation laws defending slaves' right to life and limb. Life assumed greater regularity, as the frontier retreated further to the west. Travelers in slavehold-ing states seldom reported seeing slaves half-clothed and underfed. Reports of witnessing outrageous beatings are also much less fre-quent. Undoubtedly there was much, very much, that travelers did not see, on remote plantations where strangers never came. But remembering that in the eighteenth century planters had taken small pains to hide from view pitiable conditions of planta-tion life, it is apparent that in the nineteenth century a new social ideal, however imperfectly realized, had taken root. The new law, even if merely window-dressing and unenforceable, had become, as always, a social artifact, a kind of cultural fist-hatchet indicating what a majority believed to be correct or desirable or necessary at the given time.

What was left undone in law was also significant. Aside from the responsibility for decent care and a limitation on indecent punishment, no part of a master's awful power was reduced. He could buy or sell slaves at will without regard for their family connections or wishes. Only social opinion could control him. He could punish, short of life and limb, as he saw fit. In fact society at large seemed bent on forcing the master to assume ever *more* responsibility to police a population that could, if not carefully watched, create grave public danger. Tighter provisions were enacted for patrol duty, and laws restricting the association of slaves with free blacks became a regular feature of the new codes. Harsh punishments were still assigned to rebels against the system. To prevent the master from shielding the slave from the law be-cause of personal financial interest, the master was in most states awarded part or all of the cost of any slave the state condemned to death. Even meetings of slaves for religious exercises and fu-nerals were tightly regulated.[11] These opposing tendencies in the changing slave law produced equivocal results, and one more fascinating paradox. They caused abolitionists to assert that slavery was becoming harsher with each passing year, and enabled south-ern apologists to state, with equal confidence, that slavery was be-coming milder.

In fact, both sides were right, and both were wrong. As physi-cal conditions improved, the slave's essential humanity was being recognized. But new laws restricting chattels' movement and eliminating their education indicate blacks were categorized as *a special and different kind of humanity*, as lesser humans in a dependency assumed to be perpetual. In earlier, harsher times, they had been seen as luckless, unfortunate barbarians. Now they were to be treated as children expected never to grow up.

The changing position of the nineteenth-century free black completes this portrait of a regime becoming tighter as it became softer. Manumission was made vastly more difficult, and petitioners all over the South made known their wish to keep freed blacks at a distance from their slaves by getting them out of the state wherever possible. Adult freedmen did not fit into a new scheme for humanizing treatment of perpetual children.[12]

The Old South was actually engaged in a process of rationalizing slavery, not only in an economic sense, but also in emotional and psychological terms. The South was "domesticating" slavery, taming it, so to speak, for the new century. Of course domesticating laws were always flouted by passionate, sadistic, insane, or miserly masters. But the evolving attitudes and the changed law register an important choice made by the white South at the turn of the nineteenth century.

To explain how this change was brought about requires an understanding of the intellectual challenge slavery posed for the Revolutionary generation, and the eventual solution, partly progressive, partly reactionary, to that crisis. It also requires a look at the demographic changes among the slave population resulting from a liberalized emancipation policy in Virginia, the suppression of the slave trade, and from the increasing proportion of slaves born in America.

How close the older South came to general emancipation during the Revolutionary epoch is not a settled question. Considering all economic and social factors, it was probably not very close.[13] And yet strong ideological pressures toward emancipation existed. An appreciable number of slaveowners were ready to take that step, either because they sensed that for the time slavery was no longer as profitable as it had been before the Revolution, or because slaves were dangerous, or because the Revolution had taught them that all men should be free.

Certainly important changes were called for even if the change from slavery to freedom should be rejected. If slavery should remain, it had to be made safe; and bondage did not seem to be safe at all, largely because bondsmen too seemed to be deciding whether slavery should remain. The prolonged struggle of Haitian blacks to be free had raised alarms that had not yet subsided when the mammoth plot of Gabriel Prosser, involving possibly thousands of Virginia slaves, was uncovered. Newspapers were peppered from this time forward with demands that black watermen's free movement on the Chesapeake Bay and up the rivers be curtailed. The black population had mounted steeply in proportion to the white through the eighteenth century, and by 1790 had come to constitute nearly half the total population. Blacks were recognized as a dangerous element.

This fear was further enhanced by the process of Afro-American acculturation. Newly imported Africans had been less able to resist slavery because of their ignorance of English and of regional geography. As they gained knowledge of their owners, however, and especially if they became skilled artisans, opportunities to resist or run away vastly enlarged. Many were able to escape slavery altogether by passing for free men in towns.[14]

The phenomenon was the fruit of a serious dilemma eighteenth-century planters had faced. They had felt compelled to train slaves to diversify their economy. But steps taken to develop slaves' skills and to acculturate ex-Africans had made the captive population more dangerous.

The rise of *free* blacks in proportion to slaves during the Revolutionary era greatly increased this sense of danger. Laws were passed emancipating slaves who had served in the Revolutionary army. In 1776 a law was enacted forbidding further importation of slaves and emancipating those entered illegally. And in 1782 a policy in force for over fifty years prohibiting private emancipation was overturned. Emancipation was made as simple as a master's willingness.[15] The response was enthusiastic, and before this policy was effectively neutralized by a law of 1806 requiring manumitted slaves to leave the state, the free black population rose from 2,000–3,000 in 1782 to over 30,000 by 1810.

Popular reaction to this increase in free blacks was almost immediate. Petitions objecting to emancipation by will or deed poured into the legislature. The discovery in 1800 of Gabriel Prosser's plot for insurrection gave force to this reactionary trend. Whether fear of free blacks or the economic motive of conserving slavery after the close of the slave trade was more important in this development is still a question. But the result was the same. The Virginia legislature opted, in the first twenty years of the new century, for a course designed to make slavery a safe and profitable institution, and one that did the private conscience of slave owners as little violence as possible. Other southern states followed suit. The domesticating process was on.[16]

Domestication proceeded to feed on itself. New laws consolidating the regime, by reducing society's fears allowed masters to heed those other new laws requiring more humane treatment. The result was a more regular and systematic labor system, obtained more often by the threat of force than its employment. On well-managed plantations, just as in the home or in school, the use of violence was considered to be a failure of diplomacy. Selling slaves apart from their immediate families incurred a social stigma, and masters when they did this had to find a reasonable excuse for doing so, if they meant to save face. To retain the reputation of a good master, a "patriarch," as he liked to call himself, had to provide decently for "his people," as he liked to call them. To be known as a Christian master, he had to provide religious instruction for his slaves.

The role of evangelical religion in the South was an important element in planters' changing notions of familial responsibility. It was as though, once having made the decision to retain slavery (by means of the hundreds of small constituent decisions that comprise class movements), they required some omniscient plan on the part of the deity to explain it to themselves. Slavery, most of them were ready to admit, was an evil system, but God has His purposes. In this instance His purpose was the extension of Christianity to the slave population. Some even joined John Hartwell Cocke in reasoning that intelligent slaves would and should then be returned to Africa as missionaries.

It is an interesting and significant sidelight on the religious influence that most attacks launched later within the South against laws forbidding anyone to teach slaves to read were based on the

Protestant idea that to save their souls men had to read and interpret the Bible for themselves: salvation was an individual matter. The same religious reason was advanced by those who wanted slave marriages to carry the same civil effects as marriages among whites. Neither drive won numerous converts, however, because each flew in the face of social control and endangered foundations of the social order.

Even with its many hardships and its total injustice, the plantation system had become a "domestic" institution, with the economic and social divisions of labor that suggest a patriarchy that could be benevolent or cruel, according to the disposition of the patriarch. As master, the slaveholder presided over not one, but three interlocking domesticities—his blood family, the slave families, and the larger family of the plantation community. The effects of each of these upon the other two has been the subject of endless speculation and too little dispassionate inquiry, but it is important, because it is as clear a register as historians have available of what the new domesticity was like in practice and of how white "fathers" and black "children" saw "familial" roles.

The master gave himself star billing at the apex of this domestic hierarchy, and he had the same self-indulgent vision of his role in the lives of his retainers that many novelists and some historians have thought he had. With the help of a virtuous and industrious wife, whose price (in the Old Testament phrase) was "above rubies," he strove to create on his plantation an orderly world, where slaves were well-fed and properly cared for, and to see that they worked hard enough to raise his crops, keep him solvent, and provide the entire plantation with essentials of life. He was stern, but not unnecessarily so. In her inimitable diary that records this world collapsing under the impact of the Civil War, Mary Boykin Chesnut turned a beady eye on her aging father-in-law, a stately old man who was, in her words, "partly patriarch, partly *grand seigneur*," a ruler of men, under whose "smooth exterior" lay "the grip of a tyrant whose will has never been crossed."[17] He might have stood for a portrait for George Balcombe, the fictional creation of Beverley Tucker, who is given to say, "I am well pleased with the established order of things. I see subordination everywhere. And when I find the subordinate content with his actual conditions, and recognizing his place in the scale of being, . . . I am content to leave him there."[18]

But the domestic world men like Chesnut ruled and Tucker described was more complex than a "patriarchy," despite the planter's awesome legal power. The planter's blood family was actually more of a matriarchy, because of the paramount role of his wife in child-rearing, in household management, and in religious and social matters. Dispensing medicine and comfort, the matriarch kept the keys to the larder, insisted on order and morality at the quarters, and kept a sharp eye on the deportment of her growing sons in the seductive ambience of her nubile maids.

To make the "domestic institution" still more complicated, while the plantation community was a patriarchy and the planter's family a matriarchy, the domesticity in the enslaved cabin at the quarters was, ironically, about as close an approximation to equality of the sexes as the nineteenth century provided. An androgynous world was born, weirdly enough, not of freedom, but bondage.[19]

Actually each human creature was involved in an economic and social way in at least two of these conflicting domesticities. Such an interlocking system of colliding conceptions of "family" invited love-hate relationships, a certain nervous stability, a discernable atmosphere of tension, and a pervading sense of incongruities locked in interminable suspension. Witness the many instances where slaveholders were thrown into conflict between demands of their blood families and the plantation family's welfare. These conflicts were not always resolved in the interest of the planter's pocketbook, or even his own family's affluence. Every decision to emancipate, or to enable a slave to purchase his own freedom, was a decision of this sort, and so would have been any decision not to deprive slaves of some customary or anticipated treat.

But because the slave and not the slaveholder had the most to lose when domestic arrangements became tense, the "dependent's" ambivalent attitude toward the "familial" regime more challenges the imagination. Ambivalence about "patriarchs" is registered in every category of the source materials of slavery, from the planters' private records to the songs and stories of slaves, their narratives, and travelers' accounts. Former slaves told about how sometimes old mistress's kindness helped when master was mean. Sometimes travelers told how it worked the other way. Harriet Martineau, for instance, learned of the young bridegroom whose new wife was so cruel to the house servants, and so reluctant to curb her temper and reform, that he sent them out of the house and helped her do the chores himself.[20]

Very often slaves complained to the master about the abuse they received from overseers. Sometimes masters sided with their "people" rather than overseers. The result, slaves' sometime sense of living in a caring domesticity, helps explain the rarity of organized political revolt on southern plantations. Hard as life was, it appears that few slaves really wanted to massacre the entire white domestic establishment.

There were even stronger supports for the domestic system within the slave family. Undoubtedly many a slave parent put off running away interminably because of attachment to wife, husband, or children. In this sense complex interdependencies of the plantation "family" became a most significant bulwark of slavery as a working system, even for slaves who wanted desperately to be free.[21]

Some historians have futilely tried to deny the significance of slave treatment. But it obviously makes the greatest difference to slaves, prisoners, and children *how* and *whether* the necessities of life are provided. It makes a difference in physical security, personality development, emotional health, and in interpersonal relations. Because the plantation was indeed a personal affair, examples can be found of every conceivable kind of handling of slave property, from outrages to relative order and kindness. It is almost too obvious to mention that the same spectrum exists in the behavior of parents to their children, or prison guards to their inmates; it is also obvious that there are more kind parents than prison guards or plantation owners. But logic demands that historians face squarely the problem of assessing the kind of plantations *most* slaves lived on, for this would have had approximately everything to do with the result for most slaves, for the slave family, and for the eventual prospects a slave had as a successful free citizen.

Judgments are fraught with hazards. Some matters may in time yield to statistical analysis: provision of clothing, food allowances, hours of work, even the extent of family disruption resulting from the interstate slave trade.[22] Punishment and discipline probably never will, unless they may be deduced from other care provided. Nor will subjective and affective human relationships. But until further developments on the statistical front are brought to bear on this problem, the historian will have to deal with the evidence he has, with all the common sense he can command.

Because the slave had the same human emotional needs and biological urges all others have, the historian has got to remember that if these needs had not been met at least halfway, irreparable damage would have ensued, and disorder would have proliferated. Some historians have tried to have it both ways, describing a totally dehumanizing institution that dehumanized nobody. This won't do, logically speaking. Then the historian has got to stop undervaluing the role of the Christian religion in the lives of slaves and masters alike, and recapture its dominant influence on nineteenth-century people, especially rural people. Then he must consider overriding facts. The rate of the black population growth in this country almost kept pace with the growth of the white population, one of the most phenomenal population explosions in world history. No other slaveholding country in the Western Hemisphere could show anything like this record. There was less slave suicide in this country by far than in Brazil, Carl Degler tells us in his comparative study of the two slave societies.[23]

There was also relatively little overt resistance to slavery in the American South, as compared with other nations. Most running away, the most common form of resistance, was short-term, and to the nearby woods and swamps, and it was most often a work-strike, or a demonstration against unwanted or unjustified discipline. When opportunities developed during the Civil War for organized revolt, those who expected insurrection were disappointed.

There can be little doubt that most slaves, nearly all, one assumes, deeply desired to be free. But their typical forms of resistance were passive rather than violent, individual rather than organized, involving malingering much more than murdering. Such resistance was usually provoked by slavery perverted, by domestic bondage become undomesticated by some outrageously anti-familial instance of treatment or by some master's breach of un-spoken patriarchal obligation. Such resistance successfully lived up to one of its key objectives: it forced masters to live up more regularly to prevailing standards. Unless one employs theories unconnected with demonstrable facts of behavior, one is forced to conclude that the "domestic institution" had more regularity than current portraits would indicate, and that most slaves thought they had something to lose by slaying patriarchs.

Most intelligent planters attempted to see that slaves *would* have something to lose, by introducing some incentives and ac-commodations into a system that was at bottom based on force.[24] Most intelligent masters, whether harsh or liberal, understood that although force was the basis of their system, it had distinct limits in application. The slave had too many annoying means at his disposal to pay the master back. Let us note some of those slave reprisals. In the effort to discredit a bad overseer, slaves on an Alabama plantation got together to cover up the weeds in the cotton instead of chopping them out. The object was simple. Lose the crop, and see that the overseer is fired.[25] In South Carolina six brothers threatened to run away in a group when one was threat-ened with a whipping. None of these brothers was whipped.[26] Of two men who appeared well enough, but who were claiming to be ill, the master said in his diary, "I give up; they will have their time out."[27] A master in Mississippi enjoined his overseer to give his slaves all they needed to eat, lest they steal.

Perhaps a closer examination of an extended crisis on a planta-tion that has enjoyed no very good reputation for "paternalism" may prove illuminating.[28] Ever since Fanny Kemble denounced her husband's South Georgia estate, in a published form of her diary that came out during the Civil War, Butler's Island and its overseer, Roswell King, have been synonymous with hard use.[29] In fact this little world of overseer King and absentee owner Thomas P. Butler and Sambo and Sampson and all the other "people" was a difficult family circle, controllable, if at all, only by a master diplomat.

In 1829, a slave preacher and plantation fiddler named Sampson put overseer King's diplomacy to a severe test. Sampson accused King of killing Sampson's son, Emanuel. Emanuel had allegedly been given a "cold shower" either for punishment or as treatment for an ailment. On this point King is rather vague, but he had secured the plantation doctor's note assigning the cause of death to worms, a grave affliction among the island's child population.

Sampson was angry. We must suppose that he really believed the overseer to be an unfamilial tyrant, responsible for his son's death. But Sampson was also engaged in a more elaborate political maneuver. With the aid of another influential plantation leader, an African named Icy, Sampson wanted to undermine the influence of the head slave driver, a man named Sambo.

Overseer King had himself at first distrusted Sambo. He remembered that Sambo's father had in his term as head driver organized a combination of slaves against King's father, when the elder King had been overseer for Pierce Butler's father. But after a period of watchful waiting, King understood that Sambo was as loyal as a man named Sambo ought to be. The overseer then did everything he could to bolster the driver's authority.

Before the dispute was settled, Sampson had attacked Sambo with an axe, and was threatening to run off with more than thirty slaves. Explaining his difficulties to Butler, far away in Philadelphia, and excusing himself for failing to punish Sampson for his violence on Sambo, King also illuminated some basic plantation strategies. "It would not do," King wrote, "to have" Sampson "taken by our people. Years hence it would be a source of dispute, between family connections and friends on either side, which must be avoided on a plantation." Sambo at last outgeneraled Sampson by calling the constable, who took the culprit to jail. King told Butler that Sampson remained the "most awful fellow in the country, who can play forcefully on the minds of others."

Throughout his service King showed the same caution before punishing those who could influence others. "The great art of managing negroes is to outmaneuver them," he said. Explaining to Butler why he had not followed instructions to sell a pair of troublemakers, King wrote that "unless done in such a way as to be productive of good, it would be an injury." As a manager of men and women as distinct from animals, King saw fit to consult public opinion in the plantation community. During the extended struggle with Sampson and Icy nothing disturbed King more than the charge Sampson circulated that he (King) and Sambo had divided between themselves the money raised from a part of the rice crop that was traditionally used to buy dried fish for the slaves themselves.

Over this point, and Sampson's assertion of his responsibility for little Emanuel's death, and other alleged ill use of the plantation people, overseer King eventually offered his resignation as manager of Butler's estate. It appears that the word of a slave could in some instances mortify a white man by endangering his reputation. Whether Sampson or King and Sambo were telling the truth is not the point here. It is not even the point whether King was the beast he appeared to be in Fanny Kemble's diary, or the good neighbor he seems to be in the Charles Colcock Jones family papers (published as *The Children of Pride*), or simply the harassed driver of men he reveals himself to be in his letters to Butler.[30] The point is that plantation life was populated by people, not animals. Slaves had leaders who had to be negotiated with, allied with, cajoled, or isolated. King ultimately hung onto Sambo because he considered that driver the most useful slave on the entire place, clever enough to do anything from helve an axe to mend a rice mill. It also appears that family relationships would ultimately determine the side a person took in a quarrel, that people's memories were long, and that punishment when applied was supposed to have constructive purpose.

King's story also reveals considerable variety in slave talent and that this particular overseer liked to develop divergent abilities. Perhaps one reason why modern writers have difficulty seeing past the very real monotony and drudgery of agricultural labor, and particularly slave labor, into the complexity of that life is that we tend to associate it with modern mass production. In any event, even the most cursory list of slaves on any inventory reveals a wider variety of training and function than we have been ready to recognize. This complexity was not just a characteristic of good or bad plantations, but a plantation characteristic.

Still another characteristic of a domesticated regime was that plantations less harmful to the body could be more afflicting to the soul. Much can be learned about the patriarchy by examining what was left once it was destroyed. During the Civil War a young teacher who was working with freedmen in South Carolina, an area of high concentration of slaves, observed that all slaves in the neighborhood knew who the good masters were, and who were the cruel ones, and that they all agreed. The teacher offered his own opinion that slaves who had been harshly treated had many "faults" of character, being licentious, dishonest, irresponsible, and hard to work with, but he thought they were more independent, on the whole, than those who had had extremely benevolent masters.[31]

If we grant the teacher his insight, we may also note that he observed, in the first moments of freedom, an unconscious reaching backward on the part of his more pliable students and their parents for the order of the plantation world, in which master was ultimately responsible for all manner of provisions and decisions for which nobody now seemed responsible. There must have been very few freedmen who regretted the passing of slavery. But many were discontent with the disorderliness of freedom, which took a little getting used to. By their subconscious efforts to thrust teachers and new plantation superintendents into old master's role, they revealed something of the part the patriarch had played in their lives.

It would appear that the time has come when historians of slavery should be more inquisitive about interpersonal relations in individual communities to determine what "normal" conditions were during the era of "domestic" servitude. Such an approach provides a way to determine some matters that quantifiers may never disclose, and may serve better to explain some matters they do disclose. The "domestic institution" must be studied in its full social, legal, religious, and material context.

Further advances also dictate that we approach slavery from the historian's true perspective, which is evolutionary, chronological (if you will), changing. In time we may know the relative weight to assign to social and religious factors as compared with material ones in the changes that gradually occurred in the nineteenth century: the way slavery became "domesticated," in the forlorn hope of the master class that it might be retained to their profit and as a social control. Such an evolutionary approach can illuminate as well how a strong and resilient people survived an institution designed to retain them in a perpetual state of childhood—how they endured and understood that slavery was a wretched institution, whether they were beaten and abused every day or not. The study of slavery can illuminate the spirit of freedom, which is of the mind as well as the body. I suggest we do not drop it.

3

Childhood in Bondage

This celebrated piece, never before published, was first tried out in public at the Annual Meeting of the Organization of American Historians, Los Angeles, California, April 17, 1970.

A few years before the Civil War, deep in South Carolina, a crisis occurred in the life of a small black boy named Jacob. Colonel M. R. Singleton, who owned Jacob, also owned a stable of fine racing horses. Jacob was being trained for special duty as a jockey. Jacob remembered himself as not a particularly good little boy, meaning perhaps that he was not tractable, and difficulties of a grave kind immediately developed between Jacob and the trainer of horses, who had him in charge. The trainer fell into the habit of beating Jacob on a regular basis, for no reason the child or his parents could understand. Jacob's father, to the astonishment of his son, coolly advised him to try harder: "Go back to your work and be a good boy, for I cannot do anything for you." Although Jacob's mother remonstrated, she was cuffed about for her pains, and grieved though she was, learned to hold her tongue. The suddenness of this change in his life circumstances, the abrupt awareness of his parents' impotence, impressed itself so strongly in his memory that Jacob Stroyer recalled the episode with extraordinary vividness when he wrote his memoirs in later life.[1]

Before this time, only his parents had spanked Jacob, and his first confrontation with the ubiquity of plantation authority was almost more than so small a child could bear. Matters became worse before they became better. The child sustained a serious injury. Numerous consultations in the intimate family circle concerned how best to spare the boy. The mother's instinct was to complain to master, who had been a special childhood friend when they were growing up as "equals." But Jacob's father warned that the overseer was a friend of the horse trainer. She would be blamed for the implied rebuke to the horse trainer, if Jacob were removed from his charge. As a field slave, she might be the eventual target, through the overseer, of the horse trainer's resentment. It was decided therefore to do nothing but pray, which Jacob's father did.

The child expected the freedom Jacob's father prayed for to appear in a few weeks. It took six years. In that time little Jacob found out how to live under slavery. He learned to ride Colonel Singleton's fine horses. He did not run away, at least as far as his account indicates, nor did he attempt to do so. He lived with the hope of freedom.

The story illuminates a distinct social process, one that must have taken place for nearly every slave child, but one that differs so sharply from certain prevailing ideas about plantation life that its special features deserve consideration. It is worth noting that the mother and father consulted each other through the crisis, and that the father made the ultimate decision, while at the same time comforting the mother tenderly in her distress. Though she was but a field slave, the mother resisted the trainer to the point of being struck herself. But she ultimately followed her husband's wisdom. One gains the impression that the mother was more rebellious, but that the father was the stronger character of the two, and had the more lasting influence upon Jacob. The father did the praying; and he not only prayed for freedom, but stated his expectation that liberty would come in Jacob's lifetime.

Few slave narrators described so perfectly the point in time when the slave child stepped beyond the immediate domestic circle, and became subject to plantation authority, as did Jacob Stroyer. But most blacks who wrote of their childhood in bondage remembered such a traumatic moment.[2] The resolution of these crises, and all that prefigured that moment of resolution, were probably of very serious consequence for slaves' future pattern of response.

The disturbing truth is that we know much less than we ought to know about childhood in slavery, although nearly every planter's diary, almost all travelers' accounts, and practically every fugitive slave narrative refer to the condition of children, often at length. In spite of the significance psychologists and sociologists attribute to experiences of infancy and youth in development of personality, few historians have stressed this aspect of slavery, or described it adequately. An investigation of this subject could reveal interpersonal relationships of great complexity and illuminate mechanisms of the slave's response to his condition. For in childhood, the slave acquired lifelong patterns of response to bondage—including how to accommodate and when to resist.

Patterns of accommodation and resistance, as learned in childhood and carried out in adulthood, must be studied with scholarly detachment, within a framework that allows for diverse personal responses. Generalized conclusions must not be isolated from individual cases. Conclusions must also squarely face the facts as we know them: there was less overt resistance to slavery in the antebellum South than in certain other Western slaveholding societies, and yet there was a very great deal of not-so-overt resistance, perhaps even more effective, under North American circumstances, than violent resistance.

The controversy over the nature and extent of slave resistance, and the concomitant issue of the nature and extent of slave accommodation, has arisen, predictably enough, out of contradictory facts. In the course of a highly eclectic trip through the conflicting and polemical literature on the slave experience, I have reached the conclusion that the reason so little agreement exists on these highly charged questions is that making generalizations about slavery is a very difficult business. However uniform the brute legal facts of bondage were, slaves were born, brought up, lived, and died under a considerable variety of physical and social conditions, and scholars have been reluctant to take this fact into account. These differences in conditions of life existed between plantations in different areas, between large and small plantations, and between regimes in different decades. No scholar has yet attempted a comprehensive historical study of bondage as it developed from its seventeenth-century origins down to the Civil

War, although few have been unaware of the way legal, demographic, and social changes affected master and man.[3]

If historians, when considering slave resistance, have erred in supposing a greater uniformity of condition than actually existed, they have also erred in focusing exclusively on adult resistance. Why should we not boldly assume that slaves were exactly like free people in one important respect, that basic attitudes toward their world were formed early in childhood, and that personalities and modes of adjustment were fixed by parental teachings and by childhood experiences? This does not permit us to escape from problems imposed by diversity, nor does it bring absolute answers to questions of accommodation and resistance. It may assist us, however, in discovering *patterns* of behavior and thought that are associated with resistance and accommodation respectively. It may also help us to identify lifelong patterns of accommodation that were broken only by severe challenges or by radically new knowledge or by experience encountered later in life. Even a casual reading of fugitive slaves' narratives usually reveals some traumatic experience or deep disappointment immediately behind the decision to break with accommodationist patterns learned in childhood. As a result of some injustice, graver than all those that ran before it, or at least more deeply resented, a slave decided, "This is too much. Now is the time."[4]

Jacob's story tells us that slave parents, in ways different than slave owners, acculturated slave youngsters in processes of "getting along"; and so a consideration of training for bondage must begin by analyzing the slave family. Historians have often generalized that family life among slaves was to all intents and purposes nonexistent, that the father's role in his children's lives was severely limited, and that frequent separations among slaves meant that no real sense of family survived. Although considerable evidence supports this view, a very great deal of evidence refutes such easy generalizations. In fact, all over the South, the most *typical* domestic picture is of a father and mother living together in a humble cabin with their children. That in all too many instances enforced separations meant that the picture had to be redrawn again on another plantation does not alter the standard portrait at a given moment in time.

If the father was not directly responsible for minimal needs of survival, he shared with the mother the burden of nearly every material comfort beyond that crude level of subsistence. Even for slaves, good things could be provided by resourceful and energetic parents. Many planter records, as well as many fugitives' recollections, indicate that fathers shared with mothers the working of a little vegetable garden, usually attached to the cabin. Whenever possible, the slave fathers' custom was to raise a hog, to fish, even in some areas to hunt in order to supplement the family diet.

Occasionally, the father's skill yielded other small comforts. He could make a better chair or bed for the cabin, or could turn his manufactured products into enough cash to buy some small luxury. James W. C. Pennington reported that he worked with his father at night, when he was a boy, making straw hats and willow baskets, "by which means we supplied our family with little articles of food, clothing, and luxury, which slaves in the mildest form of the system never got from the master."[5]

The established pattern in coastal South Carolina and Georgia on the many plantations using the task system was for a strong slave to finish his field work by two o'clock in certain seasons. The rest of the afternoon could be spent in familial enterprises.[6] In this way the father's care came to be institutionalized in a modest way. Even unauthorized appropriation and summary execution of plantation livestock appears to have been primarily a male slave's function.

In instances where the father was living on another plantation, he could do little for his children. But numerous instances are recorded when the father, even in such circumstances, brought small gifts to his wife and children on a neighboring plantation, and took part in discipline of children.

Unfortunately, the effort to overturn the prevailing monolithic view of family life under slavery offers a temptation to exaggeration. Clearly there were limits placed upon the father's role in the family. The historian must recall enforced separations and the father's pitiful ineffectuality to protect his family in the face of plantation authority. These problems bore in upon both parents.

Still, not every area of family life was impinged upon directly by knowledge of the possibility of separation, or of the master's intervention. The Civil War revealed strong family feeling among freedmen. In 1865 freedmen all over the South were seeking former wives, husbands, children, and parents.

Perhaps the sanest evaluation feasible at the present state of research is that fathers had less influence than mothers on the development of the child's personality, but that both mothers and fathers of slaves were involved in the same business parents are always engaged in: the process of socializing their children for the world they know, and in making the child conformable to the general peace. The difficulty posed for the slave parent was that training a child for survival under slavery was simply more difficult than educating him for freedom. Essential challenges were reversed.

Mother and father shared a further handicap in preparing off-spring to cope with plantation authoritarians. Parental roles were not so strongly differentiated, the one from the other, as has been the custom in the dominant free white world. The black father's role took on some *traditionally* feminine characteristics under the necessity of showing the child how to resist without seeming to resist. Meanwhile the black mother's role was surely on occasion more aggressive than the black man's, because she sometimes got away with manifestations of hostility when a black man could not. These partially reversed roles, while exaggerated by white nineteenth-century observers accustomed to extremely dominant males and extremely shrinking females, were in the nature of things bound to exist.

Victorian observers of slavery, black and white, were tempted to underrate the importance of the father, because of their own frame of reference. In their world a dominant father seemed most natural. But by our own contemporary standards the role of the black father does not seem so regressive as it did then, and no more unnatural than that of the suburban father who sees little of his children except on weekends.

If it can be agreed that a sense of family existed in some strength among slaves, then surely it may also be agreed that the family helped prepare the child for the predictable future—life-time bondage. When men and women survive on the precarious raft of another man's good will, they teach children arts of survival. They do not normally teach them to break their necks, or their hearts. It is arrogance in posterity to expect them to have done so. Given the circumstances, it is remarkable that many exceptional parents did lead children, subtly or overtly, to think of freedom, and even of how it might be won in the child's lifetime.

In order to apply what limited knowledge we have of child-rearing in slavery to the specific problem of slave resistance and accommodation, it is well to search for particular patterns of childhood, with the object of drawing tentative conclusions between these patterns and the future product of these patterns. We may well ask what life was like on large plantations, especially for children. Here, as in other situations, the father was more *likely* to be present than otherwise, living in the cabin with the mother. One would also be *likely* to discover less differentiation in work roles of parents, for both were probably field slaves.

What were the majority of mothers like? Knowing the mind and heart of the average mother may prove forever beyond the reach of the historian. But her condition has often been described in general terms by sympathetic travelers and reluctant plantation mistresses like Fanny Kemble. Charges against the black mother for improvidence concerning her children, and even licentiousness, are to be found readily enough in the literature. Yet her hardships were legendary, and can be found anywhere one looks; they included sexual abuse, hard work unsuitable to maternity, lack of privacy, and lack of proper food. But as an individual personality this woman remains obscure; she was written about nearly always in a collective sense. It may be possible, however, by reasoning from her condition and known difficulties, to establish a portrait, even if a severely limited one.

We know that on most Lower South plantations, the mother returned to the field approximately four weeks after the birth of her child, but that infants were usually not weaned for a year or more. When the mother returned to the field, the baby was placed in the plantation nursery for the daytime, where some elderly plantation woman took charge. The effects of this early break in regular contact between mother and child varied no doubt with persons, plantations, and time. But the importance of nursing upon the child's evolving personality seems too well established to be ignored. Certainly if one thinks of the affectionate play associated with a relaxed nursing period and compares it with the tension that must have accompanied the worst nursing situations for the most exhausted slave mothers, the importance of the matter for slave children would seem very great.

Even plantation masters understood in a dim way the connection between the mother's relaxation at nursing time and the physical well-being of the infant. Certain slavemasters were very specific about the time allowed the mother for nursing the baby, the length of time she should wait (after coming in from the field) before beginning to nurse, and the precise regimen she should follow in weaning her infant.[7] It is highly improbable that any plantation master understood psychological implications, however, and the child's trauma at weaning time must have been severe. At that time the child was removed from contact with its mother entirely for a period of several weeks, and we have no reason to suppose that it was cared for by the same friendly hands as the baby's white counterpart up in the Big House.

On some plantations, or at times when the work was far from the quarters, the mother carried her child with her, leaving it, as Frederick Douglass remembered, at "the turning row" or in the corner of the fences. Sometimes older children brought babies out to mothers.[8] These matters, however managed, allowed little time for the affectionate play between mother and infant that Dr. Spock so heartily recommended to modern mothers.

Nor were slave nurseries on large estates to be thought of as antebellum versions of Israeli kibbutzim, where child training is managed by those presumably best able to train children. Reams of testimony could be called out on this point. Being the nurse was a favorite assignment for an old woman, who had far too many children in charge to allow much time for individual needs. It requires but small effort to imagine her probable handling of what we call the "No!" stage of infant development. Fredrika Bremer, a Scandinavian woman of considerable insight who visited the South in the 1850s, said she had seen "sometimes as many as sixty or more [small children] together, and their guardians were a couple of old Negro witches who with rod of reeds kept rule over these poor little black lambs, who with an unmistakable expression of fear and horror shrank back whenever the threatening witches came forth, flourishing their rods." An ancient slave survivor recalled how as a child in such a "nursery," she ate peas from a clearing made on the ground.[9]

Brought up by force themselves, living under conditions of enforced labor, slave mothers believed that sparing the rod spoiled the child. "What the Lord Almighty make trees for," inquired one experienced Mamma gravely, "If it ain't fur lick boy chillen?"[10] Adult slaves often assumed community responsibility in chastisement of misbehaving children, and a sympathetic northern schoolteacher at work in the South during the Civil War objected that children were "invariably spoken to in harsh and peremptory tones" and "whipped unmercifully for the least offense."[11]

What lessons were enforced? Most often they were lessons of accommodation and adjustment, which we should call, under slavery, lessons of survival. Obedience and good manners would head any list, based on a fair sampling of recorded incidents of chastisement. "Mind yo' manners, child!" was a constant refrain. Mothers knew, no doubt, without much thinking about it, that self-reliance would not be necessary, but that being agreeable could save one a licking, or win favors, or even a promotion to the Big House, and maybe an easier life.[12]

Rigors of childhood in bondage did not end with the nursery. When the child was old enough, he was returned to the cabin, usually overcrowded, and to the care of parents who had more than their share of troubles. The psycho-social implications of the absence of privacy require little elaboration; adult slaves' severity toward misbehaving children did not mean that children were unloved, and that too should require no explanation.

As a means of setting a typical plantation child's accommodationist lessons in negative relief, let us turn to children who learned the opposite lesson. Slaves who later published accounts of their experience offer an easily identified group distinctive for learning not dependency but independence. We may be confident that men broken to extreme dependency do not often write books!

I have been able to authenticate, reasonably well, thirty-three narratives of former slaves. How striking it is that only four mention having had the collective upbringing in nurseries associated with large plantations. Twenty of the thirty-three narrators fled from bondage; the other thirteen merely outlived the institution. How striking it again is that all but four of the thirty-three writers mentioned their father, that every one of the twenty fugitives recalled his father, and that in four fugitive cases the father influenced the child to think of escape.[13]

Mothers of fugitives were of two kinds. Mothers were either nonexistent, in that they disappeared into the shadows early because of death or separation, leaving the child open to other nonconformist influences; or they were matriarchs, strong females whose impact upon the child was not forgotten. They sometimes counseled children to resist. The mothers of Frederick Douglass and Charles Ball seem to have been of the first sort. Other fugitives' mothers were women of authority. They often occupied a special position in the plantation hierarchy: cooks, seamstresses, or nurses.[14]

Other plantation sources reinforce the impression that slave women independent of the average field-hand role were more likely to raise independent spirits. A South Carolina "Mauma" brought up six strapping sons for her master. Though these men became field slaves, they never were "Sambos." They let it be known that they would allow no one of their fraternity to be whipped, and would take to the woods in group protest if any one of the six happened to be threatened. The seamstress on the same plantation brought up a son who appeared to be "Sambo" at first, so adept was he at executing his master's will in such matters as trapping runaways and polishing boots in general. But in the end Archie Pope turned out to be a rebel himself. He deserted his master's service because his master whipped *him*.[15]

Surely the character of female influence was not the absolute determinant of the development of a rebellious streak in the child, but still another example suggests a correlation. Robert Smalls was a South Carolina slave who spectacularly escaped from Charleston Harbor with his master's ship and all his own family aboard. His mother was another slave woman with an unusually independent position. Smalls's mother knew that Robert had seen only the milder side of slavery, because he was a privileged house servant, as was she. So she made him witness the punishment of a slave woman in the town jail in order to impress him with harsher realities.[16] In numerous instances of slaves brought up with minimal male influences in early childhood, such strong-willed females undoubtedly did much to inculcate resistance. These women were performing a traditional male role. They were also unusual women, in all probability, even within the somewhat mother-focused childhood of slaves.

It would be foolhardy on the basis of so small a sampling to make conclusions about the kind of background a rebellious or fugitive slave would certainly have come from. But even so crude an accounting seems to suggest that many refractory bondsmen came from circumstances that included experiences and relationships very different from those supposed to have prevailed on the largest plantations. We are speaking of probabilities, of course. Rebelliousness of one kind or another existed everywhere, and so did accommodation. The multitude of forces acting upon the human personality may be constrained, but they cannot be obliterated by any system of social organization. When we come to consider conditions conducive to rebelliousness and accommodation, we must remember that the concepts are statistical only.

If fugitives tended to come from different environments than those better educated in accommodation, they experienced the same initial accommodationist trauma. Some of the most painful incidents in recollections of former slaves are associated with the entry of the child into the larger world of the planter's authority. This could be the first time a slave was officially disciplined for imperfect performance of some set task, or the first time he saw an adult slave severely whipped.[17] On large plantations the formal process of induction into the working world began with an assignment to the "trash gang," composed of children who had KP duty, tending house and grounds. Then the youngster went to the field, and by regular stages took on increasing duties until he had the full field job of a man or woman, under the watchful eye of the overseer.

Fugitives' accounts are filled with traumatic recollections of being inducted into the work force, and the sudden realization that authority had become more impersonal and that it was everywhere. Luck undoubtedly played an important role in what happened at this point, but no amount of luck could have altered the basic pattern of this sudden change. The delight, for example, one small boy felt at getting into a fancy house servant's uniform was suddenly dashed in the realization that he was on duty almost around the clock. A slave named Henry Bibb, seeing his young mistress with whom he had been a playmate go off to school, was distressed when *he* went to work to help pay for *her* education.[18] These kinds of things could happen even if one were *not* going to the field.

Through experiences such as Henry Bibb's and Jacob Stroyer's, and those of countless others, the slave left the world of childhood, bleak and cheerless for the most part, a world of few toys and practically no "constructive play," for the full-time service of his master. How the slave would now respond to his fate depended on circumstance and mother wit, but also in large measure upon lessons of survival learned in childhood. If many thousands of slaves, especially those on the large plantations, learned a non-revolutionary adaptation to slavery, this did not mean that they were nonresistant. A strong case could be made for the general healthiness of such modes of protest as pretended illness, sheep-stealing, short-term running off to the woods (called "lying out"), and deceit in all its interesting forms.

Whether many slaves came to believe in the reality of their response is a metaphysical question. Most learned survival, and the family was an important factor in that process. Indeed family affection was one of the most important single deterrents for many slaves who contemplated escape. One is somehow reminded of the words of the grandfather in his deathbed scene from Ralph Ellison's remarkable book, *The Invisible Man:* "Live with your head in the lion's mouth. I want you to overcome 'em with yeses, undermine 'em with grins, agree 'em to death and destruction, let 'em swoller you till they vomit or bust wide open."[19] If that isn't resistance, one may well ask, "What is?"

4

The Old Allegiance

This essay, first published as Chapter Four of Professor Rose's first publication, Rehearsal for Reconstruction, *coincidentally fits in most comfortably as Chapter Four here. The quirky similarity in chapter numbers is the least. connection between Professor Rose's earliest and latest offerings. Established in this essay, as throughout Professor Rose's initial venture, was a method of making a provincial corner of South Carolina illuminate a national concern, of cherishing the localistic integrity of documents, in all their concrete specificity of time and place, while still squeezing out broader significance. Everywhere in this volume, Professor Rose will be seen exemplifying and publicizing that methodology, whether instructing beginners in how to use documents or advising professionals on how to temper generalizations. "The Old Allegiance" is here published in somewhat abridged form. Some passages connecting to issues elsewhere in* Rehearsal *are not relevant to, or are repetitious of, material elsewhere in this volume and have accordingly been excised. Mrs. Rose and I have also occasionally been tempted to lay hands on occasional passages bearing phrasings and interpretations grating on her latest sensibility. But Professor Rose's approach has dictated that the temptation be repudiated. For to allow a later interpretation to change an earlier position would be to deny that "The Old Allegiance," like all human documents, must be preserved in all its specificity of time and place.*

I. THE BACKGROUND[1]

Fall came late to South Carolina in 1861. October made way for November, and the gentility of Charleston drifted to lowland plantations. In this sequestered region lived Heywards, Barnwells, Elliotts, Coffins, and Fripps, along with Negroes without surnames upon whose broad backs and nimble fingers rested the cotton culture and the well-ordered but static society of the islands. In 1861 slaves comprised nearly 83 percent of the total population.

Fall of 1861 was no ordinary time for master or man. On November 7, at 9:25 in the morning, the Union war fleet, under command of Samuel Francis DuPont, approached the entrance to Port Royal Sound. It was fired upon; and the bombardment began. Soon the Confederate flag came down, and Negroes streaming in from the fields found white people hastily preparing for flight. Slaves left behind were, in terms of current practice, neither slave nor free but "contraband" property, subject to seizure by federal authorities.

Secretary of the Treasury Salmon P. Chase bore responsibility for collection of abandoned property. Because of his antislavery convictions, the Secretary seized the opportunity to foster the first important experiment with newly released slaves. On the twentieth of December, Secretary Chase wired a young Boston antislavery attorney named Edward L. Pierce, requesting him "at once" to report on Port Royal.

Pierce's ensuing report on the "contrabands," February 3, 1862, omitted reference to his project of sending ministers and teachers to preach and to open schools for Negro children. Pierce only asked Chase for permission for teachers to travel South. Chase approved. Pierce found enthusiasm in Boston for his plan. Within two weeks, fifty-three men and women were in New York preparing to leave for South Carolina.

Pierce's little band laid claim to a militant zeal to make war on evil. Derisive soldiers would quickly nickname them "Gideon's Band." Like the "Puritans" of old, the missionaries considered derision an accolade. As Gideonites, they moved forward to another battle between freedom and slavery.

By April of 1862 a steady stream of teachers and superintendents began to arrive on the islands. From Philadelphia a ship carried southward a large store of provisions and a special representative, Miss Laura Matilda Towne, whose duty it would be to oversee their distribution. Miss Towne moved to the Pierce headquarters on St. Helena Island soon after her arrival, little dreaming that she would call no other place home for the rest of her life.

The Boston-area teachers whose commitment and sympathies Laura Towne shared included Edward Philbrick, his wife Helen, her friend Harriet Ware, Harriet's brother Charles Ware, and Arthur Sumner of Cambridge. Although they would not join fellow New Englanders until later, William Allen and Elizabeth Botume would also teach at Beaufort, South Carolina.

II. THE OLD ALLEGIANCE

On the veranda of Dr. Jenkins's plantation house on Station Creek, looking across the salt flats to the distant point where the blue waters of Port Royal Sound narrow and flow past the straits of Bay Point and Hilton Head Island, St. Helena planters had converged on that Thursday back in November to watch the battle of Port Royal. They had hoped to see their sons and relatives in the Beaufort Volunteer Artillery drive off the invading fleet, but although they possibly were too far away to hear the victorious strains of "Yankee Doodle," they had realized early in the afternoon that the forts were falling. Hastily mounting their horses, the planters had ridden away to spread the alarm.[2]

For the few confused hours that followed, every plantation had its own special story. A few planters had succeeded in quickly driving their slaves and livestock to the Beaufort ferry, but for every one who had succeeded in this, there were a dozen who failed. The Negroes too had heard the guns, and some had hidden in the swamps and in the fields, crouched low between the corn rows. Others had sensed their power for the first time and had stubbornly stood their ground before their masters, impervious to cajolery and threats that the Yankees would sell them to Cuba. Master Daniel Pope's seamstress, Susannah, had asked her master when he urged and threatened, "Why should they [the Yankees] kill poor black folks who did no harm and could only be guided by white folks?"[3] The majority of the Negroes showed the shrewdness of a certain Dr. Sams's man Cupid, who recalled that his master had told his slaves to collect at a certain point so that "dey could jus' sweep us up in a heap, an' put us in de boat." The Negroes had taken to the woods instead. "Jus as if I was gwine to be sich a goat!" commented Cupid. According to Pompey of Coffin's Point Plantation, some Negroes there would have been duped by the Cuba story but for the fact that the "poor whites" of Beaufort had made the slaves "sensible" to the fact that their own freedom was at stake in the conflict.[4]

Not every planter had even tried to remove his slaves. There were perhaps a few others who followed the course of Captain John Fripp of St. Helena Island. This remarkable man, who was at once one of the richest landowners in the district and a Union sympathizer, called his slaves together and explained the situation. He warned that they would probably starve if they followed him to the interior and advised them to hide until the Confederate soldiers had passed through the island. They should then keep together, work their provision crops as usual, and forget about the cotton. It was late in the day when Henry, the cook at Coffin's Point, sounded the alarm on the northern end of St. Helena. He excitedly informed the overseer that he had better be off, for "all the Yankee ships were 'going in procession up to Beaufort, solemn as a funeral.' " The overseer left, but Henry did not.[5]

Had DuPont's gunboats occupied Beaufort immediately, they would probably have intercepted almost the entire white population embarking for Charleston on a steamer that was docked conveniently at the town landing.[6] Such action would also have frustrated the enactment of a most instructive morality play on the true character of slavery. In the few days that elapsed before federal authority was consolidated throughout the island region, the social and legal bindings of the peculiar institution unwound with the speed and ferocity of a coiled wire spring.

The sack of Beaufort probably began with the motive of plunder. But in a short time crowds of field hands descended upon the town and took it apart, presumably for the satisfaction of doing it. Whatever manorial pride the field hands may have felt in the country estates of their late owners, it did not encompass the elegance of the family town houses. Over the protests of the house servants who had remained, plantation Negroes broke up furniture, loaded valuables onto boats to carry away, and helped themselves to the wine.[7] Thomas Elliott, who returned to his Beaufort house the day following the November 7 attack on the forts, reported that he discovered "Chloe, Stephen's wife, seated at Phoebe's piano playing away like the very Devil and two damsels upstairs dancing away famously. . . ." They were all plantation Negroes who had come into town. The houses had little furniture left and had been "completely turned upside down and inside out. The organs in both churches were broken up," Elliott reported, "and the churches themselves robbed of many articles which were deposited there for safe keeping."[8]

The correspondent of the New York *Tribune* described the destruction that DuPont and his landing party found when they went up to Beaufort on November 12. "We went through spacious houses where only a week ago families were living in luxury, and saw their costly furniture despoiled; books and papers smashed; pianos on the sidewalk, feather beds ripped open, and even the filth of the Negroes left lying in parlors and bedchambers." The destruction had been "wanton," and much of it could have served "no purposes of plunder" but only a "malicious love of mischief gratified."[9] Nothing that happened illustrated better the frustrated hostilities of generations than the desecration of the stylish houses in the east end of town.

DuPont heard other, darker things as well. The planters and overseers were in some cases shooting down rebellious slaves who would not leave the plantations with them.[10] In a panic to retrieve the most portable part of his evaporating fortunes, each planter had, in his own way, borne witness by action to his private conception of chattel slavery. For every man like Captain John Fripp, who thought first of his slaves as people, there was another who thought of them first as property. When Thomas R. S. Elliott returned to his plantation and found the Negroes idle, he attempted to force them away with him. He was unsuccessful and commented grimly, "I think we will have to make a terrible example of many of them." Although Elliott's meaning is not precise, it is clear that many "terrible examples" were made.[11]

William Elliott had once written, in a candid defense of slavery, that masters were usually kind and that slavery served the interests of civilization. "Against *insubordination alone,* we are severe."[12] That was precisely what the masters had been obliged to deal with when the islands were invaded. The only eyewitnesses of these atrocities were the Negroes themselves, but their accounts were complete in many cases with names and places and were sufficient to convince the naval officers who questioned them. Commodore DuPont was horrified to hear from an army officer, whose information had come "from reliable testimony," of recalcitrant slaves being burned to death in their cotton-houses. George W. Smalley, the New York *Tribune* correspondent, concluded that "the horrible fact stands out with appalling clearness and certainty that the murder of slaves who cannot be compelled to follow their masters is a deliberate and relentless purpose." His informants too gave names and places. A responsible Negro named Will Capers told of thirty Negroes who were shot for resistance.[13]

When all possible allowance is made for exaggeration, understandable mistakes, and even for the possibility that Negroes met death by accident while hiding in burning cotton-houses, the sheer weight of the evidence leads to the belief that many white men were willing to go to extreme lengths to retrieve their human property. James Petigru, following the Port Royal story from Charleston, heard of a planter who had burned all buildings on his plantation, including all stores of corn and cotton, "and by so doing compelled his negroes to follow him, as they were on an island without food and shelter."[14]

Masters who owned slaves on the periphery of the territory held by the Union forces were faced with the possible loss of all their slaves through running away. John Berkeley Grimball, who owned slaves and plantations in Beaufort and Colleton districts, recorded in his diary for the early days of March 1862 the gradual depopulation of his estates. The forty-eight slaves who stayed, including the old and sick, had their reward at the end of the season in being sold for the round figure of $820 each.[15] Some masters relied upon severe punishment to discourage running away. When Ralph Elliott frustrated the escape of his father's slaves from Oak Lawn, he had two of the leaders sold in Charleston, and "the others were punished by whips and hand-cuffing."

Every night they were chained and watched while Elliott waited for the danger to pass.[16]

But the danger did not pass. To William Elliott the Negroes seemed "utterly demoralized" by Yankee propaganda. The missionaries saw it differently. The streams of Negroes were coming out of the interior as a result of their total dissatisfaction with the "patriarchal institution." Generations of servitude had not stamped out of these people the desire to do as they pleased, although any real understanding of the responsibilities of freedom must have been, for most of them, very remote. E. L. Pierce wrote, in a moment of insight, that "the slave is unknown to all, even to himself, while the bondage lasts."[17]

He might have added that the moment of freedom revealed the essence of ownership. The barbaric behavior of certain masters was probably no surprise to Negroes who had been their slaves. A slave's life was one long lesson in accommodation. There were plantations where nearly every Negro's back showed marks of whipping, and Negro testimony against certain old owners was remarkably consistent. Missionaries heard again and again the same condemnation of certain cruel men and virtually unanimous praise of others.[18] While concluding that the majority of slaves had been treated decently, Arthur Sumner reported that all Negroes agreed that a number of planters had been "devils in cruelty." The fact puzzled Sumner, for he had thought that "wherever the country belonged to old families whose plantations were hereditary property," masters had been generous and kind.[19]

That Sumner was ill-prepared for what he saw indicated that the young teacher's conception of slavery had been conditioned, perhaps subconsciously, by certain tenets of the proslavery argument. Perhaps Sumner had read *The Hireling and the Slave*, the poetic contribution of a bluff St. Helena planter-poet named William J. Grayson. In eight hundred heroic couplets, Grayson had presented an idyll of plantation slavery, where labor was "safe from harassing doubts and annual fears" and "unassailed by care." The happy slave was spared those conditions of unlucky northern workers, where

> Labor with hunger wages ceaseless strife,
> And want and suffering only end with life.[20]

A native son of Beaufort also had contributed to the theological defense of slavery. The Reverend Dr. Richard Fuller had written in 1845 a series of letters to the Reverend Dr. Francis Wayland, in which he developed a battery of scriptural justifications for slavery. That some masters behaved sinfully toward their slaves the minister was not prepared to deny; but he emphasized the benevolent aspects of servitude in his part of the country, where "the slaves are not only watched over with guardian kindness and affection, but prefer to remain with their masters. . . ."[21] A northern visitor had been so much impressed by the conditions of life on the William Joyner Smith plantation just south of Beaufort that he had written *A South-Side View of Slavery;* he had gained the never-ending contempt of all good abolitionists by the favorable impressions he conveyed.[22]

Other visitors had not seen the "south-side view" at all. Certainly the European visitor who witnessed in Beaufort the sale of a handsome young slave woman and her sad separation from her young husband when she left Beaufort in the possession of a slave trader had not been favorably impressed. Fanny Kemble, the famous English actress who married Pierce Butler and went in 1838 to live at his plantation on St. Simon's Island, was made miserable by what she saw.[23] Fanny Kemble disdained one supposedly "most admirable circumstance in this slavery: you are absolute on your own plantation." Each plantation reflected the essential character of its owner, acting within the extremely liberal bounds allowed him by the slave law of South Carolina.

Even Dr. Fuller had washed his hands of the attempt to vindicate certain of the "oppressive and wicked" slave statutes, for South Carolina statutes regarding slavery had offered the owners every facility for the exploitation of their human property and denied the slave any personal rights whatever.[24] The fundamental code, enacted in 1740, underwent no important changes between its enactment and the outbreak of the Civil War. In an important 1812 decision, the case of the *Executors of Walker* v. *Bostick and Walker*, a South Carolina court said that the slaves of the southern United States were in their condition more analogous to the slaves of ancient Rome and Greece than to the villeins of medieval Europe, and that for precedent and authority the Roman civil law rather than the English common law must be consulted. Slaves were, "generally speaking, not considered as persons but as things. Almost all our statute regulations follow the principles of the civil law in relation to slaves. . . ." This position was stated even more strongly as late as 1847, when the court placed the slave well outside the protection of common law and Magna Carta. Of the slave it was said, "In the very nature of things he is subject to despotism. Law is to him only a compact between his rulers. . . ."[25]

That compact decreed that a slave was a slave for the rest of his natural life, that he could be hired out, sold, or disposed of by deed or gift. He could not bring action in his own name in court but was obliged to seek a white man friendly to his cause, even when his own freedom was the question. A slave's testimony was neither sought nor accepted. His marriage had no legal standing, and families could be separated by sale or bequest. In this last respect slavery was more severe in the United States than in Latin America, where the Roman Catholic Church was an established institution. The Church required masters to respect Christian marriage and the relations of mother and child, husband and wife. No such institution operated in any slave state except Louisiana to ameliorate the conditions of bondage or to stay the hand of individual owners in making use of chattel property.[26]

The harshly unreciprocal law helped make the sometimes reciprocal relationship between master and man very hard for Gideon's Band to understand. Upon occasion Susannah, in charge of the kitchen at The Oaks, urged Laura Towne to accept gifts of fresh fish and other native delicacies for the table, explaining firmly that she did not want *pay*. Susannah said "she always gave such things to her old massas, and then they in return gave a little sweetning or something good from the table. It was give and take, good feeling all around." By this time Miss Towne was well aware that Master Dan was not the gentlest of men, and she sniffed to herself, "All giving on one side I should think, all taking, nearly, on the other, and good feeling according to the nature of the class, one only content in grasping, the other in giving." How was William Allen to understand old Captain John Fripp's charm? Praised for his kindness and generosity by all his slaves, and called by one "the best man on the island—from Coffin's Point to Land's End," the old patriarch in his daguerreotype looked forbidding to young Allen. He had "sharp and restless features" and looked as though "there might be vinegar in him." There was a whipping post within twenty feet of the big house. And he did whip his slaves, as one of them, Dick, told Allen, but mildly, "jes like a young chile whippin'." Evidently, the aspect of personality could transcend even the worst aspects of the peculiar institution.[27]

In his defensive writings on slavery, Dr. Richard Fuller, who had also been a very popular man not only with his own slaves but with all those to whom he preached, liked to compare the master's role to that of a father to his children. He had enlarged upon the "painfully responsible situation" inherited by the Christian master, whose duty was the moral and spiritual elevation of his bonds-men.[28] But how many such men had taken their responsibility seriously?

In 1860, Beaufort District contained 939 property owners of landed estates. The Negro population for the same district, including a negligible sprinkling of free Negroes, numbered 33,339. An average based on these figures would place every owner of land and slaves in the great planter category. But three fourths of the slaveholders owned fewer than twenty slaves each, and only 19.9 percent owned more than fifty. Even in the heart of the Carolina low country the typical planter was a small planter. This did not prevent the typical *slave* from being a field hand on a great plantation, for most of the slave population was concentrated in the hands of the large owners.[29] There was clearly one stubborn fact damaging to Dr. Fuller's picture of slavery: most patriarchs had too many "children."

At the very summit of the social and economic life of the low country were such men as William Elliott, head of a large family whose widespread holdings throughout the entire rice and long-staple cotton region were only partly indicated by their acres in Beaufort District. Among the other great landowners of the area were William H. Trescot, paying taxes on an estate valued at $40,000, and Micah Jenkins, whose lands were valued at $34,600. Captain John Fripp and Mrs. Mary Coffin held more than two thousand acres each on St. Helena Island. The Reverend Dr. Fuller was himself a large owner of land and slaves.[30]

It would have been impossible for such men to come into direct contact of any depth with many of their slaves. Not only were the Negroes too numerous, but many of the great planters were away from home a great part of the year. Dr. Fuller had since 1847 been the minister to the Seventh Baptist Church in Baltimore, and only visited his plantations on vacations.[31] Because of the prevalence of fevers during the hot months, planters who could afford to do so left the islands completely or settled in some healthy locality nearby.[32]

When the William Elliott family issued an invitation, they found it necessary to say first where they would be. They called the Oak Lawn plantation on the Pon-Pon River their "winter quarters," but toward the end of February "the gayer portion of the family" visited Charleston, returning to Oak Lawn only a short time before leaving in May for Beaufort, "our residence during the summer months." Sometimes Elliott took his daughters to the North, where at Newport, Boston, and Saratoga Springs they met their New England counterparts in the social world. There was an occasional European tour.[33]

For these great planters much time was consumed in the pursuit of culture, politics, and the amusements of sport. The handsome collection of rare volumes in biography and history belonging to the Beaufort Library Society was ample testimony to the cultural interests of these gentlemen planters. William Elliott had found time to write a widely known book, *Carolina Sports by Land and Water* (New York, 1859); and his estate, Oak Lawn, became a mecca for prominent anglers who wished to experience the thrill of fishing for the giant drum, or "devilfish." The English journalist William H. Russell described a fishing party organized for his benefit in the spring the war began. A swift boat approached his landing, "pulled by six powerful Negroes, attired in red flannel jackets and white straw hats with broad ribands. The craft itself . . . lay deep in the water, for there were extra Negroes for fishing, servants, baskets of provisions, water buckets, stone jars of less innocent drinking, and abaft there was a knot of great planters —Elliotts all—cousins, uncles, and brothers."[34] It is probable that for the great planters most of their personal contacts with slaves other than house servants occurred on such pleasant sporting occasions, almost as jolly for the Negroes as for their master. This may go far to account for a fact that the missionaries duly noted: plantation Negroes tended to exculpate their masters from responsibility for overseers' harsh policies.[35]

If the wealthier planters had fewer direct contacts with field slaves than did their poorer counterparts, they frequently provided superior physical accommodations. The housing of slaves could become a symbol of wealth and status for the master. Dr. Milton Hawks, an agent of Pierce stationed on Edisto Island and a man who would have preferred to see the worst in slavery, thought the cabins on the island were "as good" as the homes of poor white people in Georgia and South Carolina. Fredrika Bremer, a fair-minded Scandinavian visitor to the region in the decade preceding the war, was pleased to see on some plantations "small, whitewashed wooden houses, for the most part built in rows, forming a street, each house standing detached in its little yard or garden," surrounded by flowering peach trees, and kept in neat and clean condition. The volume of the evidence, however, evolves into a different picture, one of comfortless little two-room puncheon cabins about twenty-five feet square, with wooden chimneys, and without glass in the windows.[36] J. Miller McKim spoke in withering contempt of the homes of the "happiest of all peasantries," pronouncing them "indescribable and incredible." A great deal depended upon the eye of the beholder, but it is worth noting that Nehemiah Adams was himself put on the defensive about the slave cabins, admitting that they would "strike everyone disagreeably at first."[37]

Closely related to housing was the matter of slave health. We may assume that it was ever in the planter's best interest to see that his human property was kept in good condition, and the mention of the expense of having doctors in attendance upon slaves appears frequently in the records of the period. Planters also became adept at home remedies and quickly learned to perform routine vaccinations.[38] Despite the enlistment of the planters' interests on the side of good health, there was a depressing prevalence of disease and suffering. The symptoms are not always easy to identify, and specific diagnoses are seldom given. Fevers and pulmonary diseases were the most common afflictions, but there were certain ailments that seem to be directly related to hard labor, poor living conditions, and bad social attitudes. Among these were swollen and sore feet and joints, abdominal pains, syphilis, rupture, and prolapsed uterus.[39] The latter problem, wrote Fanny Kemble, affected nearly every other woman on her husband's plantation and was directly attributable to severe tasking and the return of female slaves to the field too soon after childbearing. It frequently incapacitated the slave completely.[40]

Housing and health varied more from plantation to plantation than did the rations and clothing supplied to field Negroes. The weekly peck of Indian corn, with occasional allotments of approximately three pounds of salt pork, supplemented from time to time by fresh beef and vegetables in season, made up the bulk of the diet. There was a regular issue of salt and molasses. The Negroes ground their own meal with a stone hand mill and varied their diet with crabs and fish caught on their own time. Clothing was provided at the rate of one outfit twice yearly, at the change of the seasons, and was usually issued by the yard. Shoes were included in the fall distribution, and a new blanket might be issued once every three years.[41] Such issues were highly standardized; the Negroes stated them as clearly as did any planter's manual when they knew the federal fleet was coming and they went singing down to Hilton Head to build the fortifications they hoped would be inadequate:

> No more peck o' corn for me, No more, no more; . . .
> No more driver's lash for me . . .
> No more pint o' salt for me . . .
> No more hundred lash for me . . .
> No more mistress' call for me, No more, no more . . .
> Many thousands go.[42]

The real significance of the song lay in its simple unaccented statement of the conditions of slavery. The slave did not understand that he received his peck of corn and the pint of salt in *return* for his labor; it was rather a condition of his life, a regular issue. It was by no means the reward of superior service, for all received the same allotment. The slave's inducement to work was the negative one of evading the "driver's lash," another hard condition of life.

For those in the field the hard work stretched around the year, with the only slack season occurring in midsummer before the picking began. Plantation activity was at its zenith in the fall when the crop was brought in, and the tension mounted steadily. Owners anxious to save their crops from possible hurricanes urged their slaves to greater exertion than at any other time, and they often resorted to the lash. John Fripp (not the benevolent Captain John) reported with impatience that he "gave nearly all of them a poping [sic] . . . they should go over more ground or bring in more cotton." Chaplin thought of his slaves who were picking slowly that "a little cowhide will make them do better." Edgar Fripp, a wealthy and arrogant man, sometimes made his slaves work all night by the light of the full moon during the heaviest part of the season.[43]

Pickers were obliged to exercise the greatest care in freeing the cotton of dirt as they picked, as well as in the final operations of ginning and packing. These last tasks were not finished before the hardier hands reported to the fields again to prepare ground for the next crop. The fertility of the fields was maintained by transporting "salt marsh" grass or mud to the fields, a step that was absolutely necessary to the production of the fine staple. No job, however, was hated more by the slave than this cold, dirty, and wet midwinter duty.[44]

The most grotesque aspect of plantation paternalism lay in the fact that if a planter took *too* complaisant an attitude toward the performance of field work, he courted financial failure, and with failure would come the sale of his slaves to pay his indebtedness. If a planter managed badly or was the victim of extravagant tastes, he had to endure the bitter experience of Thomas Chaplin, forced in 1845 to sell ten prime field hands to clear his debts:

> Nothing can be more mortifying and grieving to a man, than to select out some of his Negroes to be sold—you know not to whom, or how they will be treated by their new owners, and negroes that you find no fault with—to separate families. Mothers and daughters—Brothers and sisters all to pay for your own extravagances—People will laugh at your distress—and say it serves you right—you lived beyond your means. . . .[45]

The Negroes of the islands, wrote Edward Pierce, "had become an abject race, more docile and submissive than those of any other locality." Nowhere else had "the deterioration from their native manhood been carried so far. . . ." Pierce was by no means alone in this conclusion, for all the missionaries were struck with certain childish qualities manifested by many of the Negroes.[46] Elizabeth Botume described a class of young adults:

> They rolled up their eyes and scratched their heads when puzzled, and every line in their faces was in motion. If any one missed a word, or gave a wrong answer, he looked very grave. But whenever a correct answer was given, especially if it seemed difficult, they laughed aloud, and reeled about, hitting each other with their elbows. Such "guffaws" could not be tolerated in regular school hours. They joked each other like children; but, unlike them, they took all good-naturedly.[47]

A superintendent concluded that the Negroes were entirely dependent, lacking in initiative, and that they needed "the positive ordering that a child of five or ten years of age requires." The sum of these observations added up to a picture of the personality known in American literature as "Sambo," the plantation slave, "docile but irresponsible, loyal but lazy, humble but chronically given to lying and stealing."[48]

But it is well to remember that although "Sambo" finds many illustrations in the observations of the teachers on the islands, he remains a *statistical* concept, and the record contains as many stories of protest, disloyalty to the late masters, and manly independence as of servile acquiescence. The extent to which the personality of the common field hand had been fundamentally altered by the experience of slavery finds a good test in his response to the opportunities offered by the new order inaugurated in the wake of the northern occupation. The first reaction can be found in the large numbers of slaves willing to risk severe punishment and even death by running away from their masters. The wild sacking not only of Beaufort but of plantation houses, as well as the complete destruction of cotton gins, show a bitter and long dammed-up hostility that, if perhaps childish in its discharge, is yet remarkably similar to the venting of spleen demonstrable among more "civilized" peoples.

A more probable explanation of the obsequious and infantile behavior of the majority of slaves who demonstrated childish traits is that playing "Sambo" had its rewards and that failing to play him incurred many risks. That the role could be one of conscious hypocrisy is illustrated by the case of Elijah Green. This ancient veteran of slavery remembered with rancor, many long years after his freedom came, having been obliged to give an affectionate endorsement of the new brides and grooms who joined his master's family, whether he liked them or not.[49]

The main effect of slavery was a thick residue of accumulated habits and responses that a slave child learned early in life. It was a culture, in short, that invested its members with a number of character traits useful in slavery but unbecoming in free men. The extent to which these traits developed in an individual slave depended in part upon the class to which he belonged. It has been a general assumption that more enlightenment and self-respect were to be found among house servants and the Negroes of the towns than among field slaves. The common corollary, however, that these "Swonga" people, as they were denominated by the field hands, also possessed a greater spirit of *independence* is, at the very least, a debatable point. They had merely absorbed more of the white man's culture, and they paid for it in daily contacts with the "superior" beings whose very presence was a reminder of their own inferior status. Sometimes the loyalty of a well-treated house servant could make war on the very notion of independence. There is considerable evidence to support the idea that, while the Swonga people had perhaps more self-esteem and were better dressed, the field hands had more self-reliance.

For many a servant, a close personal tie with a good master or mistress could go a long way toward reconciliation to a dependent condition. Henry, formerly cook for Mrs. Thomas Aston Coffin, spoke affectionately of his former mistress to Harriett Ware and readily seized upon Miss Ware's offer to write to Mrs. Coffin for him. He had hesitated to make the request himself for fear "they wouldn't think it right to have anything to do with the old people—'but she's a Nort' lady, you know, Ma'am,'" he said to Miss Ware, "'a beautiful lady, I would serve her all my life.'" When Thomas Chaplin's slave Anthony died, Chaplin wrote, perhaps a little self-consciously, "he is regretted by many—white and black—I miss him more than I would any other negro that I own," and added, "Peace be to his soul."[50]

Anthony had belonged, as a "driver," to the uppermost rank of plantation life. These foremen and the skilled laborers enjoyed an even more exalted position than the house servants. The driver held the most responsible position a slave could occupy. His job included maintaining order in the quarters as well as calling the Negroes to work, assigning the daily tasks, and seeing that the work was well done. That the driver was sometimes a cruel despot, as he was frequently portrayed in abolition literature, is undeniable; but there is little evidence in the Sea Island story to indicate that he was commonly such. If the driver developed a fine knowledge of farming and enjoyed his master's confidence over a period of years, their relationship could become one of mutual esteem and friendly respect, contrasting most favorably with the often unstable and transient connections between plantation owners and their overseers.

Isaac Stephens, "master servant" to William Elliott, was able to keep his master informed of the condition of the crops on Elliott's numerous estates while the latter was on extended trips from home. He had been certain enough of his own standing to pass judgment on the relative qualities of the white overseers at the several plantations and to exchange social information with his master about the family at home:

> Old Mistress and Miss Mary are quite well. I was quite sorry that some of my young mistress and masters wear [sic] not in Beaufort to enjoy some of the fine dinners and Tea partys [sic] old Mistress has been giving for her grandchildren. . . .
>
> Master will be so kind as to give my love to my wife—all her friends are well—and say howdey to her and myself just like an old Buck—hearty and prime. . . .[51]

There must have been few Negroes on the islands who had enjoyed so relaxed a relationship with their masters, or who had had such opportunities to develop judgment and leadership. The evangels could count on these few, however, to provide an example for the rest in making an adaptation to freedom.

There had even been a few opportunities for slaves to develop special talents outside the economic hierarchy of the plantation. Religious leaders enjoyed special standing with their fellows, and women sometimes achieved status as midwives. For all the slaves there was a small economic venture open in the raising of poultry and a little garden crop, or perhaps a pig. The surplus was sold to the master for cash; occasionally, it was sold outside the plantation by the slave himself. Although a statute against trading with slaves existed, it was usually ignored.[52] Outside these limited interests, there was nothing for most slaves but the dull routine of the cotton field. The real trouble with slavery as a "school" for anything was that the institution provided so few directions in which to grow and so much necessity to conform.

The Negro child on a large Sea Island plantation began learning how to be a slave almost from the moment of birth. In view of the generally acknowledged impact of early childhood experiences upon personality, the restrictions of a slave's childhood may go further than institutions or laws to explain certain of "Sambo's" failings. When the slave mother emerged from her confinement and returned to the field at the end of the third or fourth week, she saw her baby in the day only long enough for feeding and had very little time for the affectionate caressing so important for the development of the child's personality and security.[53] On the other hand, the mother herself could not experience the happiest aspects of motherhood when the child was merely an additional drain upon a tired body. The missionaries frequently observed that numbers of mothers on the great plantations appeared to demonstrate very little affection for their offspring. Arthur Sumner complained that the children were "invariably spoken to in harsh and peremptory tones" by adult Negroes and "whipped unmercifully for the least offence." A stern system called for stern discipline. But the numbers of tender stories of maternal love show that, even among the victims of such a severe regimen, the human instincts served to soften the general harshness of the lives of children.[54]

When the mother returned to the field the child usually went, on the large Sea Island plantations, to a nursery, where he joined too many other children under the supervision of too few and too harassed superannuated "Maumas" or grannies. More fortunate slave children came to a time when they might, as the chosen playmates of the master's children, be able to take a part in the free country life about them. Sometimes the white parents objected that "the little negroes are ruining the children," but sooner or later the democracy of childhood broke down parental resolutions. Mrs. Thomas Chaplin might complain of the "badness" little Jack was teaching her son Ernest, but shortly she would see the two riding off on the same horse to gather wild plums or mulberries. The slave child's formal education would consist of learning the catechism, on plantations where that was deemed important, and he was instructed that his duty to his master was faithful work and that he was responsible to God for a good performance.[55] An important lesson most small slaves learned early was their relation to the white race in general and to the master in particular. Little Jane, of the Robert Oswald household, learned it the day she objected to calling her mistress's small son "Marse" and was sent around to Wilcox's store for a cowhide switch.[56]

The plantation child quickly grasped other things also. He learned how the slave enjoyed life a little more at his master's expense. Thomas Chaplin wrote with some sense of resignation:

More robery [sic]. —discovered that my little rascal William, who I had minding the crows off the watermellons [sic] had been the worse crow himself, and does the thing quite sistematically [sic]. He turns over a mellon, cuts a hole on the under side large enough to admit his hand, eats out the inside, when he finds a ripe one, then turns the mellon back again, not breaking it off the vine, there it lays, looking as sound as ever. No one would suppose it hollow. In picking some—we found no less than 23 or 4 in this fix. *Cunning*, very.[57]

It is not surprising that the missionaries should have found the former slaves irresponsible. At no point in his passage to adulthood did the slave youth have the experience of learning to accept responsibility. The peculiar circumstances of his life became most apparent at the time of marriage. Nehemiah Adams was usually blind to the worst aspects of slave life, but even he saw clearly that slavery was inimical to the family as an institution, and he wrote particularly of "the annihilation . . . of the father in the domestic relations of the slaves. . . ." The master supplied the necessaries of life, and what else there was to receive was far more likely to be in the power of the wife to dispense than in that of her husband. The cabin was regarded as hers, and the small poultry and garden operations were usually her primary responsibility. She converted the yard goods into clothing for herself and her family and did the cooking. Even the children were acknowledged to be the mother's and were usually known by her name, as in the case of "Binah's Toby" or "Moll's Judy."[58] Unless he had a friendly alliance with some good-natured woman, the male slave did without many conveniences. Laura Towne commented drily that the liberated Negro men were better satisfied about being released from domestic tyranny than about any other aspect of their freedom. It is worth mentioning that the family picture under slavery was actually a reinforcement of the West African family pattern, arising, as it had there, from the polygynous household. The individual wives in the African community no doubt had to bow to the will of the husband; but within her own hut, and to her own children, the mother had been the omnipotent reality. Rivalry for preferences and honors to her children had provided the African woman with political outlets not unknown in the courts of Europe.[59]

Despite the legal and social obstacles, marriage had a reasonable chance of lasting if it was honored and respected by the owners of the principals. Thomas B. Chaplin complained of the "tomfoolery" of his wife, who took care to make a special occasion of the double wedding of her two maids, Eliza and Nelly. The girls were married by Robert, the spiritual leader of the plantation, and the party was provided with "a grand supper." "They had out," Chaplin complained, "my crockery—Tables, chairs, candle-sticks, and I suppose everything else they wanted." Then there was some of Chaplin's "good liquor made into a bowl of punch" for the guests. Twenty-seven years later, Chaplin penciled into the margin of his diary that the two girls were still alive, well, and still married to "the very same husbands." Many owners did not devote this much interest to their slaves' marriages, but some element of formality was usually present.[60] Without legal protection, however, marriages suffered real stress under the conditions of slavery, which often promoted transient unions and easy partings. The religious leaders among the slaves complained often of unchastity and tried, sometimes without good effect, to bring moral suasion to the aid of family stability.[61] An understanding of this situation requires only the remembrance that the social and legal forces at work to bind together unhappy nineteenth-century white couples were largely inoperative with the slaves. One major problem for the evangels would clearly be to strengthen the Negro family, encouraging the fathers to assume hitherto unknown responsibilities.

So many of the faults of the slave had been perversions of laudable impulses, impulses of protest; those who learned them best frequently comprised the most spirited people on a plantation. Even Master Chaplin had a species of respect for his small slave who had thought of a smart way to steal watermelons. Grown slaves learned how to gain a little time for themselves by idling or pretending illness, and as often as not the matter simply had to be faced with resignation. "Jim and Judge both lying up today," complained their master; "they will have their time out."[62]

When a man carried protest to the passionate length of running away, he had to be prepared for extreme punishment. Sweet must have been the knowledge to a "prime" runaway, even while reflecting on the bitter cost, that he was depriving his master of a week's hard work in the cotton field. Overt rebellion indeed existed, but it was for the few. Most slaves had learned to accept their condition, as one evangel said, just as "sand receives the cannon-ball, neither casting it off nor being shattered by it."[63] For the majority, the humdrum and safe satisfactions of a well-timed lie, petty theft, or feigned illness had seemed the appropriate defenses of reasonable beings. This mood permeates a folk story that was long told on St. Helena, of an old slave who had never worked in his life because his master was convinced he was a cripple. His master caught him one day, however, strumming his banjo to the words:

> I was fooling my master seventy-two years,
> And I'm fooling him now.

The enraged master prepared to whip the old man, but the timely magic of a "Negro doctor" intervened. "When his master started to whip him, none of the licks touch: And he had freedom."[64]

Fredrika Bremer wrote after her visit to the Sea Islands just before the war that she had not found a single plantation where the master was able to advance the social well-being of the slaves. Even the efforts of progressive men who tried to institute some means of self-regulation among the slaves had merely achieved a superior form of discipline. She concluded somberly, "In the darkness of slavery I have sought for the moment of freedom with faith and hope in the genius of America. It is no fault of mine that I have found the darkness so great and the work of light as yet so feeble in the slave states."[65]

There was hardly a plantation that had not a harsh old tale of abuse, and on many the abject fear the slaves had of all white men said all that needed to be told. In the final analysis, however, it was the institution in all its aspects, knowing and foolish, kind and cruel, that had created the prevailing problems confronting Gideon's Band: an exaggerated attitude of dependency; a weak sense of family; an inevitable tendency toward the classic faults of the slave—lying, theft, and irresponsibility. As one Gideonite clearly saw, the barbarism of exceptional slave masters did not really signify much in the total picture. "The real wrong in slavery did not affect the body; but it was a curse to the soul and mind of the slave. The aim of the master was to keep down every principle of manhood and growth, and this held for good and bad planters alike, and was the natural growth of slavery itself."[66] And that was why, despite the moving and testimonial exceptions of strength and character found among the slaves, the larger number of the liberated Negroes of the islands constituted, according to the missionary William C. Gannett, "a race of stunted, misshapen children, writhing from the grasp of that people, which, in so many respects, is foremost of the age."[67]

II
Freedom

5

Masters without Slaves

*The following piece has long enjoyed a larger under-
ground reputation in historical circles than other previously unpublished essays in this volume. The phenomenon owes most to
the quality of the essay but something to the occasion of its de-
livery. For "Masters without Slaves" came into the public domain
as something of a happening.*

*What happened was that one of the profession's most promising
newcomers, two years past winning three coveted prizes for her
first book, came to the American Historical Association Convention in December, 1966, to indicate where her new work was
tending. The largest ballroom in New York City's largest convention hotel could not accommodate all who wished to hear.
The crowd heard what it took to be the beginning of a major
new work on Reconstruction. Dr. Rose seemed to be assaulting
Eric McKitrick's celebrated thesis on President Andrew Johnson's
responsibility for Reconstruction.*

*McKitrick had lately urged that President Johnson, beset by
personal neuroses, had failed to lead the southern ruling class to
make those symbolic gestures of surrendering the old slave order
which might have satisfied the North and made Reconstruction
unnecessary. Mrs. Rose seemed to be spreading neuroses more
sensibly across the South. She seemed to be making the psychology of an old class, not the leadership failings of a new President,
chiefly responsible for the way an intransigent elite symbolically
resurrected its old order and brought Reconstruction on itself.*

The audience missed the speaker's other intent because it was

*trapped in confining categories of periodization. A paper osten-
sibly about Reconstruction could only be about, well, Reconstruction. Few then thought of capturing the essence of bondage
by studying the moment slavery turned to freedom. Few even
now think that a history of slavery must begin no later than the
eighteenth century and end no sooner than 1876. In the context
of this book, for which it was always intended, "Masters without
Slaves" emerges as Mrs. Rose's first step after* Rehearsal *toward
making the phenomenon of change and continuity over time
critical to studies of slavery no less than of freedom.*

In the current process of reconstructing the history of the
American Reconstruction, there is no more bemusing role the historian must play than that of psychoanalyst, the good doctor who
invites the main participants, individually and in collective stereotype, to lie upon his couch and tell dreams. Much has been gained
from this process. Although main personages have not always received a clean bill of health, or been "made whole," posterity can
at least understand them a little better for the treatment. The
war-weary northern citizen who needed psychological vindica-
tion for this stupendous loss of blood and treasure is better justified in his demand that the white South be "sorry," and "re-
pentant," and in his eventual option for a radical reconstruction
of the recalcitrant section that denied him the necessary symbolic
satisfactions. President Andrew Johnson's troubles are set in clear
relief when his susceptibility to the flattery of being sought out
by the late master class of the South is fully understood, and
shown in its bearing upon the President, "poor white," and
"racist" to boot.[1] Numbers of scalawags (those not of the Old
Whig variety at least) can be fitted neatly into this pattern tai-
lored to Andrew Johnson's dimensions.

The freedmen and the radicals have to this time been somewhat
resistant to analysis. But signs indicate that when the last synthesis
is written, the historian will be in a better position to render justice with mercy when he accounts for racial strains within Republican ranks, and for Republican abuse of public office. At the
least, that unstable constellation of power will be truly understood as being made up after all of real human beings who some-

times confused means and ends, and behaved, when caught up in our greatest internal conflict, as human beings always will in times of high idealism and political corruption . . . sometimes idealistically and sometimes corruptly.

But one character has not reached the doctor's office yet. He is still waiting, very much in the manner of a certain Dr. Clarence Fripp, seen by the reporter for the New York *Nation* on his way home from the war, "a person who had the easily distinguishable appearance and manners of a South Carolinian . . . dressed tolerably well in a suit of grey clothes, with a large display of crumpled linen at the collar and cuffs of his coat . . . sitting before the stove smoking, and talking very freely about his present poverty and his plans for the future."[2] The southern planter did, indeed, in his own time talk freely of his trials, and so did his children and his children's children. So much so, in fact, that it appeared for some decades early in this century that he was about to talk his way into having won the Civil War. Certainly the contemporary historian, who has to observe that a few textbook writers have not even yet gotten past the magnolia legend of the Old South, has left the myth's hero, the southern planter, to be last to benefit from the doctor's treatment.

Nevertheless, the time has come that we should begin to consider some sources of the planter's irrational political behavior in 1865 and early 1866, when he so mismanaged his chance to reconstruct his own society that he doomed himself to Radical Reconstruction. Few will challenge the planter's guiding hand in such provocative acts as sending back to the national government the very men who had counseled destruction of the nation. Equally infuriating to Northerners was ex-slaveholders' role in framing Black Codes limiting ex-slaves' freedom. I suspect we have taken the easy way around a major hurdle when we assume that southern leadership was merely stupid, merely blind, and merely selfish when it reached out to control its new environment. We shall not have a mature history of Reconstruction until failings of the planter elite are accounted for with more sophistication.

The planter showed every indication of astonishment at the outraged northern reaction to his Black Codes. Is it fair to assume that the patriarch was merely cynical in protestations that he regarded these codes as being effected in large measure for *protecting* "his people"? As one close student of Reconstruction has observed, whites North and South felt the ex-slave needed protection in his first experience in freedom. The difference was that the Northerner thought the freedman needed protection from his late master, and the Southerner thought he needed protection from *himself*.[3] Granted that planter political behavior must now be assessed as unenlightened, and probably selfish, the ex-master was no cynic. His record, as it appears in private letters and diaries, reveals him to have been a man undergoing severe trauma. Not only were his finances in chaos. So was his superego.

The southern planter's failure to take into account the extent to which radical measures and aspirations had won a popular following in the North partly resulted from preoccupation with his own internal conflict. The extent to which he had become victim of his own proslavery argument before the war may be open to question.[4] In general, however, the planter endorsed the antebellum polemicist's view of the slaveholder as benevolent paternalist, the Biblical patriarch at the center of a stable and orderly agrarian world. Now at last, after years of isolating this image of himself from outside attack, the planter was suddenly obliged to re-think that role, to re-think slavery, to re-think race relations. Nothing less than his own significance in the only world he knew was at stake. As a member of a self-conscious elite that had had more than three decades to bolster its psychological defenses, the great planter felt himself to be discredited; his values were not only defeated in war, but under the indictment of the civilized world. Distaste for slaves, he thought, had led to English and French refusal to intervene in behalf of the South during the Civil War. Indeed, his government had been willing at the end of the war to consider some form of emancipation as a desperate gambit to win foreign support.[5] It would also appear that the planter had to pick up the check within the South, as well as whatever moral bills the North and Europe had to present. He was even discredited, at least for the time being, in the eyes of the many poorer whites who had once considered his leadership infallible. They now held him responsible for bringing on the war.

The planter not only had to accept judgments passed at home

and abroad. He had some reason to suppose that God had condemned him too. In a society where the religious defense of the peculiar institution had assumed such importance, it is not surprising that in intimate revelations most planters who thought deeply about the meaning of the war expressed belief that the conflict had been God's means of ending slavery. In fact wherever the will of God is mentioned in connection with defeat, it is in that sense. "For myself," wrote a lawyer-planter of North Carolina, "I have become thoroughly convinced that the great design of Providence in this war is to exterminate our system of Slavery[,] as it is not the slavery of the Bible; and that this war will continue until that end is obtained. If we be wise, we may respect his wishes and save our country; otherwise he will use our enemies to effect his purpose."[6] Usually these wartime self-examinations assumed that slavery as it had existed in Biblical times had not been morally evil. But the South had erred, many men confessed, in using external antislavery threats as an excuse to gloss over evils peculiar to southern slavery. When clergymen spoke of these matters to their congregations during the war they urged reforms in the slave codes, reforms making it impossible, for instance, to break up slave families, and to make it possible for masters to teach slaves to read without breaking the law. How otherwise, they asked, could slavery be made the school for civilization and the vehicle of uplift its supporters claimed that it was?[7]

With these considerations behind them, most planters accepted northern victory as God's judgment. When William Henry Ravenel was coping with the widespread labor disorganization under the occupation of northern white and black troops, he cried out that "I cannot avoid the conviction that a righteous God had designed this punishment for our sins." He noted that most of the black troops who struck fear into the planter's heart had come from coastal South Carolina, where the master was so often absent, abandoning duties as patriarch, leaving slaves without spiritual instruction. "This is not the form of 'Slavery,'" Ravenel wrote, "that we can justify. . . . It may be that God has seen fit to deprive us of our stewardship."[8]

That God and the nineteenth century had spoken against him was painful to consider. But of more immediate concern was the riddle the mind of the emancipated slave now posed for his old master. How would the black man, now that he was indeed a man, regard that old stewardship? Coming to terms with freedmen would be the first challenge. At its best, which was the way the displaced master liked to remember it, his "stewardship" had been the source of generous impulses. Whether the lost stewardship had been conscientiously administered or cruelly betrayed, most slaveholders had justified their position in the center of the plantation-universe upon the conviction that they were necessary to the health, happiness, and welfare of their slaves, dependent beings whom they much preferred to call their "people." But nothing guaranteed that the slave of yesterday would remember his owner as benevolent paternalist, or picture him in the mind's eye of a Christmas morning, at the door of the Big House, dispensing gifts and favors. Who could say that the slave's recollection of every quarrel, every discipline, might not be stronger? One had to consider what the slave's idea of slavery had been.

Just as yesterday's slave watched the old master carefully for evidence that the planter recognized and accepted the passing of the old order, just so did the displaced master watch the new-made man hungrily to catch some sign that he, in turn, recalled benefits as well as hardships of their dying relationship. One would be unfeeling not to recognize the pathos in the gratitude many a displaced paternalist expressed at every encouraging sign from blacks. Ex-slaveholders, on many pages of their diaries and letters, betray hunger for recognition and the need to be needed again, made all the sharper for the sense of being discredited in the world's eyes. When the Chesnut family heard that the plantation nurse wanted to come home after having run off with Yankees, they felt vindicated: "Poor old Myrtilia, after the first natural frenzy of freedom subsided, knew well on which side her bread was buttered; and she knew too, or found out, where her real friends were. So in a short time old Myrtilia was on our hands to support once more." And then there was the elderly freedman who said to his ex-master, "When you'all had de power you was good to me, and I'll protect you now. No nigger nor Yankee shall touch you. If you want anything call for Sambo. I mean, call for Mr. Samuel—that's my name now."[9]

On the other hand, signs that freedmen planned to take full advantage of the new liberty were often alarming. The planter's apprehensions were deeply related to the often unspoken antebellum fears of slave insurrection. It is ironic that northern radicals had anticipated—indeed many had hoped for—a militant response from southern blacks as a consequence of the Emancipation Proclamation, and yet dismissed this as a plausible cause for concern once the war was well over. The southern white, on the other hand, had loudly (almost too loudly) deprecated the possibility of insurrection *during* the war, and (while taking a certain number of precautions) had boasted that southern blacks had behaved admirably, standing beside *their* people in the crisis. But *after* the war was over, fears of racial conflict gripped southern whites in direct proportion to the amount of freedom blacks were actually enjoying.

The historian has tended to side with the Northerner of yesteryear and to dismiss postwar fears of racial conflict as unrealistic. The judgment is partly based on hindsight but more on ambivalence in the planter's own record.[10] That record swings with special circumstances in any given region from expressions of fear, to confidence, to fear again. But the most consistent fear came in the months between the end of the war and Christmas of 1865, when many white persons in all sections were apprehensive that freedmen might take matters into their own hands, if the government failed to redistribute lands. These fears were understandably acutest in regions where black soldiers were stationed.[11]

The trouble was that, in spite of his tone of assurance, the planter had no more idea what the one-time slave would do than the freedman's new white friends of the North had. Nothing makes this plainer than those initial impressions entered into private letters and diaries at whatever point consequences of the war came home to any individual. As early as the spring of 1862, for example, when Sarah Morgan and her family beat a hasty retreat from Baton Rouge in front of Benjamin Butler's attempt on the city, the young girl commented upon the friendly slaves who joined the exodus. "White and black were all mixed together," she wrote, "and were as confidential as though related." And again, "Negroes deserve the greatest praise for their conduct. Hundreds were walking with babies or bundles; ask them what they had saved, it was invariably, 'My mistress's clothes, or silver, or baby.' Ask what they had for themselves, it was 'Bless your heart, honey, I was glad to get away with mistress's things; I didn't think 'bout mine.' "

Nevertheless, when the question came up of Butler's proposal to *arm* the freedmen, Miss Morgan was not amused. She pronounced the scheme worthy of a "Coward, Brute or Bully," and "enough to strike terror in the hearts of frail women." No wonder that Miss Morgan triumphantly recorded every instance of loyalty. One cannot escape the sense of relief that informs every such entry. In this, Sarah Morgan was typical of her class.[12]

It is not so much from the individual character of such comments that the planter's concern over racial conflict is made plain. Rather, the sheer volume of references to the subject displays the anxiety. Wherever federal armies passed through a region and left chaotic social and agricultural conditions behind, anxiety was especially keen. Along the march of Sherman's army, disorganization of labor was complete, and numbers of well-meaning men complained, in the words of one of them, that ". . . now all is confusion, disorder, anarchy. If those who uprooted the old order of things had remained long enough to reconstruct another system in which there should be order restored, it would have been well, but they have destroyed our system and left us in ruins."[13] Slavery had depended upon order, and it was small comfort to planters to reflect that they were undergoing a revolution that they had done much to precipitate. One does not expect logic from a society under attack any more than one expects it of individuals.

Like other ailments, mental stress is often studied most profitably when it is manifest in acute stages. For that reason, the historian who would pinpoint southern attitudes toward the social crisis could do much worse than follow the accusing finger of William T. Sherman after he had finished his famous trip through Georgia and was ready for South Carolina. In a rough and disquieting analogy, the General paired Massachusetts with the Palmetto State, blamed them equally for bringing on the war with their much-talking, and suggested it would be well if both were cut off from the mainland and hauled out to sea.[14] Whatever the justice of the insult to Massachusetts, Sherman had a point about South Carolina's having had a particularly severe case of slavery and secession. The General was not alone in blaming South Carolina for starting the war. Certainly South Carolina was destined to undergo a prolonged case of Reconstruction, and her fever was considerably elevated by two factors: the black population was greater than the white, and in no state were interests of the former slave placed in such distinct opposition to those of his former master. After all, planter and slave had always shared one common interest; they were both farmers. A farmer's requirements are land and labor. At the close of the war the freedmen of the South Carolina low country had *de facto* possession of both. The planter had control of neither.

This state of affairs resulted from unusual circumstances surrounding the occupation of the Sea Island country between Charleston and Savannah as early as the fall of 1861.[15] By 1865 sufficient time had elapsed to permit the federal confiscation acts of 1861 and 1862 to become operative in large areas of this rich cotton- and rice-producing region. Land confiscated for back taxes owed the federal government had been resold to private purchasers. Former slaves had bought some small plots; some acres had been reserved for military purposes; and the rest had passed into the hands of private purchasers from the North, who were employing freedmen to cultivate it on a wage basis.

These transactions had taken place in the absence of former owners. Planters had fled the district with the first arrival of the Union forces. They had lived in exile until the spring of 1865. By that time the government had also instituted confiscation proceedings for most remaining real estate along the South Carolina coastal estuaries, and all of it was being administered by the Freedmen's Bureau. Land in this latter category was being farmed at the close of the war by blacks who had followed Sherman's armies out of Georgia. Believing that their "promissory" titles were valid or would be made valid by the United States Congress, the freedmen of the coast considered themselves with some justice to be landowners. So did some Congressional radicals, who reasoned that the only way to democratize the South was to revolutionize landholding. South Carolina was a reasonable place to begin.

Blacks' hope of a new beginning, with forty acres and a mule, hardly stemmed only from federal authorities. In fact, blacks had gleaned the idea from their former owners, during the war, that under the confiscation acts rebels' land would be seized and given to slaves. Planters had regarded this as the best reason to fight to the last ditch.[16]

And yet masters had not convinced themselves, it would appear, that loss of land was irrevocable. They returned to the island country after the war determined to recover their hereditary real estate, and to employ the erstwhile slave to cultivate it. In this hope some planters, those who had owned property in districts first occupied by federal forces, were disappointed. Their land had been sold to private purchasers, and the federal government never revoked the sales. But most of the dispossessed, were, in fact, reinstated in their property in the late fall and winter of 1865–66, when President Johnson's policy betrayed freedmen's hopes and reduced them to the painful necessity of choosing whether they would leave the land or work for one-time owners.[17]

But this moves ahead of the story. The outcome should not obscure the fact that nobody knew for sure how conflicts over land would resolve themselves until Congress had convened and failed to verify freedmen's claims. Throughout the summer and fall of 1865 the former owner and the former slave gravely eyed each other in an atmosphere of mounting tension that more than once threatened to break into armed conflict.[18]

The most dramatic encounter between master and man occurred in a country church on Edisto Island, South Carolina, in October of 1865. Major General O. O. Howard brought a number of former owners together with freedmen who were in *de facto* possession of old estates. In his capacity as head of the Freedmen's Bureau, Howard had the impossible task of finding a just settlement between conflicting claimants. A New England teacher who lived on the island reported that blacks and whites alike showed personal emotion when they met, and that with the "Howdys" exchanged there were also a few tears. Sometimes the planter's outstretched hand was rejected, however, and tears solved nothing. The planter was unalterably opposed to selling land to blacks, and almost as dead set against leasing it to ex-slaves.[19] Every inch in the direction of releasing land to blacks was a hard-fought inch. Freedmen fully understood the significance of the struggle.

The ultimate resolution was the same solution reached elsewhere: freedmen worked for a share of the crop. Many pressures went into this resolution, and not the least of these was the planter's lack of capital to pay wages. Only the more affluent could do this, but it did offer the master more control over the day-to-day activities of his employees, and over land use. It would have been owners' preferred way of planting after the war. Blacks, however, preferred cropping on shares to wage labor, if they had no chance to buy or rent land, and their reason was precisely the same reason why sharecropping was less attractive than wage labor to the planter.[20] The cropper could be less easily mastered than the employee.

The planter could accept emancipation, but he was unprepared to accept the black man as an independent agent disposing of his own time. In the mind of the former master such a solution was an invitation to chaos; he believed that blacks would only work under close direction.[21] Few masters had ever seen them working under other circumstances. "From all I can see of this free labor system," wrote John Fripp, "I am not pleased with it. It takes three to do the work of one before the war." But he hoped that "time and experience" would improve the freedmen.[22]

The conflict over the land had also caused the low country planter to distrust the black as a responsible party to a contract. In 1865 many ex-slaves from surrounding districts had indeed abandoned agreements undertaken with old owners in more remote districts, in order to come down the coast and take up land. Many others refused to contract because they did not want to be at a disadvantage when lands were distributed, as they almost universally believed they would be.[23] One could hardly blame the freedmen for wanting to be free to take advantage of anticipated opportunities. But the planter thought unwillingness to contract proved one thing he had believed about blacks for a long time: that they were lazy.

The master also frequently complained that black soldiers created havoc on plantations. Black soldiers did sometimes threaten ex-slaves with dire consequences if they continued to work for their old master, regardless of how generous his terms were.[24] But the presence of the black army was also symbolic of former bondsmen's new freedom, and was hotly resented and blamed not only for trouble on plantations, but for what the freedman as a soldier stood for. The black soldier had indeed rejected the past, both manor and master, in the most conclusive way—by abandoning one and fighting the other.

Here again the Sea Island country offers a microcosm of a tension common all over the South—and again because of the special circumstances. Wherever the master class retained the land, the freedman whose attachment to home, family, and friends was strong had to accept the old owner too, and to reach an accommodation with him. In the Sea Island country, tables were turned. Here the master was often in the position of courting the favor of his one-time slave. Massa returned to the islands penniless, and was frequently a suppliant for whatever crude comforts the land itself could offer in such trying times—shelter, or firewood, for instance, sweet potatoes, or blackberries in season. Sometimes the impoverished master was not above asking for and accepting small cash loans from his erstwhile slaves.[25] In this region the freedman was in a position to offer favors, to affirm purely personal bonds of the old relationship without endorsing its economic and exploitative aspects. His relative freedom from coercion makes his response more meaningful. The master, for his part, had few advantages in his drive to return to his position of primary influence in the former slave's new life.

In fact, the one-time owner had a formidable rival in that arena. During the war numbers of northern men and women of antislavery conviction had come into the South Carolina islands to teach blacks and to supervise their first efforts at farming for wages. These missionaries had had by 1865 several years of contact with Sea Islanders. By a not-so-surprising but nevertheless ironic twist of fate, they had often, if somewhat unconsciously, slipped into the planter's old paternal role. It looked very much, to use a psychological expression made famous in the historiography of slavery by Stanley Elkins, as if the freedmen's most significant "significant other" was not old master at all, but the

"Everlasting Yankee," who appeared in many guises, as the school-teacher, the plantation superintendent, or the Freedmen's Bureau agent. His was now the power to provide aid, security, advice.[26]

Under the circumstances the planter's situation as the symbolic father whose children have rejected him was particularly painful. One is therefore hardly surprised to discover that the earliest and most consistent complaints registered by the master were of the one-time slave's *ingratitude*. When Thomas Chaplin returned to St. Helena Island, he found his property had been divided and sold to his slaves. But what he singled out for special comment was the disloyalty of his faithful retainer, Robert: "I left everything in his hands and he never saved a single thing for me and has always kept out of my way since peace. He might have saved something if ever so little." He thought fondly of a favorite rocking-chair that he had some reason to suppose the estimable Robert had appropriated to his own uses. Reflecting further upon how upside down the world had become, Chaplin remembered a terrible time in his youth, when he had been forced by the sheriff to sell ten slaves to clear his debts. Chaplin took belated comfort. He should not have "felt bad about it," he wrote, for "in truth the Negroes did not care as much about us as we did for them." With the benefit of hindsight, he ought, he declared bitterly, "to have put them all in my pocket."[27]

The Thomas Chaplins had not anticipated such rejections. When one respected coastal planter returned to his old home, his former slaves went out to welcome him, with the familiar "Huddy," and took him in. According to the northern teacher who wrote about the incident later, the master then made the mistake of telling the freedmen that he expected to get his property back soon, and he wanted to know how many would work for him for wages. Nobody was willing. "Even if you pay as well, sir," said the foreman, "we had rather work for the Yankees who have been our friends."[28] Stephen Elliott's slaves also took him in "with overflowing affection," and according to Elliott, they treated him "as before," serving "beautiful breakfasts and splendid dinners." But there were limits. "We own this land now," they informed their old master. "Put it out of your head that it will ever be yours again."[29]

Complaints of ingratitude were invariably amusing to northern observers. Stephen Powers gives an account of the South Carolinian who was appalled at the behavior of his slaves when Sherman's army had come through. Even while the white family were shuddering for their very lives, slaves were "singin' and shoutin' praises." Even though he had been, at least in his own estimation, a kind master, and even though his wife had nursed them when ill, this planter's slaves had deserted him. "The last one of 'em showed me their heels, like a passel of colts, and away they went, though they left all the old women and children on my hands." Oh yes, he continued, "they was so ongrateful. They didn't even ask my advice about goin' away."[30]

It was but a short step from this kind of indignation to embitterment. Complaints of ingratitude may have been ever so amusing to outside observers. But they were made in all earnestness. They are accurately read as signs of what the planter understood the human relations of slavery to have been. The complaints also make it clear that freedmen did not always endorse the planter's interpretation of the peculiar institution.

Cast in this perspective, the master's repeated predictions that the black could not survive on his own take on new meaning. Dr. John Bachman, a man who had more reason than most to be embittered at consequences of the war, fumed that "black thieves are dying out with smallpox and loathsome diseases, a nation of 3 million of negroes must now be doomed to perish in compliance with the infamous prejudices" of their new leaders. Dr. Bachman had never, in the days when he contributed to the proslavery argument, denied blacks membership in the human race—he had stuck to his reading of the Holy Scripture on that point—but he had always maintained that the black needed slavery and its guidance and protection in his struggle for existence with superior Anglo-Saxons. He was therefore reaffirming former theories when he predicted untold hardship and death for emancipated slaves. A North Carolinian complained that "the poor fool negro believes a dirty yankee soldier before he will a humane master and the soldiery . . . [out of] malice persuade them to evil."[31]

Sometimes the humiliation of having to ask the Freedmen's Bureau for assistance in getting laborers back to work created irrational resentment against an agency that was actually of great usefulness to the planter in persuading freedmen to contract. But having to consult an outsider as representative of former slaves' interests was galling to men who had learned to be masters. Their reactions were generally sullen, although the Bureau was occasionally praised for its service in the crucial period.

The extent of violent repression of the freedmen in areas where few federal troops patrolled will never be known with any certainty. The historian must deal with rumors without number, as well as a formidable body of fact. But many masters, beyond question, were abusive and unwilling to accept the one-time slave as a freedman until they were forced to do so. Such men, if paternalists, were not *benevolent* paternalists, even as many a Victorian papa was not. They ruled with the rod, just as before. The record is full of instances when resentment over emancipation was heaped upon blacks' heads instead of upon northern emancipators. A black waiter in Harper's Ferry told Edward Trowbridge that just knowing blacks were now free had caused many employers to treat ex-slaves "about as bad as could be." A South Carolinian was so stung by mass departure of his house servants that he "resolved never to have a Negro in our house again."[32]

The best planters were more rational. They sturdily faced facts and undertook new arrangements, no matter how difficult. William Henry Ravenel wrote that his servants would not leave the plantation, even when he told them that he was penniless and unable to pay them, and that "they had a right to leave if they wished and thought they could better themselves." When they made no demands, but stayed anyway, he shortly determined "to put the matter upon a different footing . . . so that they might have something to put up for clothing, shoes, blankets, taxes, sickness, etc. The condition is so new to both of us," he wrote, "that we find it awkward to manage. I have told them to consider it over and let me know what they will be willing to take, either by week or by month, either deducting lost days or not, and either paying their own doctor bills or not. All these matters have now to be considered, as they have had no experience taking care of themselves and providing for the future."[33]

But even such responsible and fair-minded men were as one

with their more exploitative and unreasonable brethren in the wish to retain a certain amount of control over the emancipated slave. They were also as one in their fear of black soldiers and of Northerners who seemed to be urging freedmen to assert rights.

Much of this fear was a rational response to racial conflict that certainly did exist in certain districts. Some of it was surely related to the unassuaged guilt that we must believe was inseparable from the sense that their system had been condemned by God as unjust. With the safe transit through the Christmas holiday of 1865, much of this fear appears to have subsided. There was no revolt, and Congress did not, after all, hold out for a revolution in landholding. The arrival of a new planting season invited the planter to try again. Freedmen now had little choice but to sign a contract. In the early days of Reconstruction planters often rendered a very sour version of "sour grapes," by privately and publicly protesting that slavery was a good riddance, one that they could never have achieved without the war. They could do without the former slave by replacing him with white labor, home grown or imported. Very shortly these remarks were heard no more. The white planter and black farmer had need of each other, after all, and would have to accommodate themselves to an altered version of the plantation system.

The old wish to retain paternalistic features of slavery remained strong with most planters. One of the earliest postwar spokesmen for a broader-based social paternalism was none other than George Fitzhugh, one-time champion of the peculiar institution. He urged the planter class to assume old obligations to blacks. He scouted the idea that white labor would ever replace blacks in the South. Fearing a general exodus of ex-slaves, Fitzhugh urged masters to consult interests if not humanity. Whites should modify laws unequal to blacks.

With the departure of federal troops and the Freedmen's Bureau, continued Fitzhugh, the ex-slave would be apprehensive. Those who had power must reassure the underclass. The planter had nothing to lose. He would merely resume ancient duties on a broader social base by instituting public agencies for the care of the old and infirm. The ruthless logic of the author of *Cannibals All: Slaves without Masters* held up to the end. Labor was capital, and labor was not free: "All laborers are alike slaves. The free, slaves to skill and capital; the slaves to individual masters."[34]

And so it was. After a decade of struggle to make freedmen truly free, the emancipating North withdrew, and the paternalism of the former slaveholding class was all the paternalism there was. It was the old, familiar mixture of exploitation and kindness, often enough within the mind of a single individual. The planter still trusted himself and his class as the best protectors of former slaves. How much the drive to continue in this role was a direct result of psychological needs is difficult to determine, and must be read between the lines, and by careful study of the context of the master's statements. But the importance of this force should not be denied. Many mistakes made between 1865 and 1867 were owing to the psychological defensiveness of a displaced elite whose world-view was shaken not only by their conquerors but also by their erstwhile slaves.

6

Blacks without Masters: Protagonists and Issue

This is a synthesis of three drafts, one untitled, one called "Black Leadership During Reconstruction," one entitled "The Negro American and the Reconstruction Experience: Protagonist and Issue." All three drafts were written in the 1960s; none has been previously published; and so far as the editor knows, none was presented in public lecture. For an explanation of the special editorial work on this chapter, see above, Remarks on Editorial Procedure.

The case has been made in the historical profession for the Afro-American as a central theme in American history. Much can be said for this point of view. Great areas of our history remain unrecorded because of the illiteracy of the slave and the powerlessness of the freedman. Yet as a goad and challenge to our society's democratic presumptions, nobody else's history has quite matched the black man's. His saga in the land of the free has exerted a kind of fascination for American historians best compared to the idea of original sin in theology. More than any other national failing, slavery seems to have been born out of some indigenous proneness to evil choices, to have been brought out of the Old World with the first-comers into a land we liked to call a Garden of Eden, to have been associated always with defeats and discouragements. Its acceptance was the price of the federal union. Its tendency to expand with the republic eventually caused the bloodiest war in our history, one from which, over a hundred years ago, we barely escaped with one nation.

To continue the theological analogy, the nation eventually cheated on God, if one will have it so—failed to live up to the covenant implicit in the emancipation of slaves during the war, voted in many northern states, even during the Reconstruction of the South, against equal suffrage, and in many ways evinced unwillingness to reach a moral solution to a national deliemma. In time white people North and South seized upon excuses to call off Reconstruction and to turn to other matters. As a consequence our guilt mounted at compound interest. Now, over a hundred years later, the debt arising from unsettled accounts has become again roughly equal to the price of our national existence.

Seen thus theologically, the part black America has played in the United States is indeed a "central theme" of no mean importance, and incidentally one reason why it is so supremely difficult to tell the Afro-American's story apart from the general history of the United States. It explains the intense moral overtones that the racial struggle has always evinced, the necessity of slavery being seen as immoral before it was abolished, the exalted and ferocious arrogation of virtue in the greatest of battle hymns, "as He died to make men holy, let us die to make men free!" and at last the sometimes crippling, often destructive, guilt that white America displays.

Yet this theological view has much less to say to *black* America. It is as much "about" blacks as the Trojan war was "about" Helen. The Afro-American is an issue and not a participant. White men quarrel, make war about him, and eventually make peace at his expense. And therefore when many people speak of integrating American history, teaching the whole story, they are speaking, consciously or unconsciously, of writing and teaching our history with the Afro-American relegated to a passive role. He is the issue, not the participant.

It is well, I think, to understand that not all of the reasons for this approach are attributable to stubborn limitations of the white mind. Historians must work with the evidence that they have. The slave's illiteracy, the new freedman's relative lack of power, the second-class black citizen's century-long exclusion from seats of authority and influence—all these weakened roles have conspired to deny black men that proportion of the written record that their numbers and contribution deserve. Not until recent times have historians made the effort to overcome this imbalance by searching for other kinds of evidence, oral tradition, folk stories, and songs.

There is yet another reason for difficulty in writing history from the Afro-American standpoint. The historian's craft is primarily narrative, and rests more upon art than many would like to believe. The frustrations and discontinuities in black experience, the exclusion from power, the continual broken hopes that seem to lead nowhere, all these make for less likely subject matter than the aims and hopes of those with more frequent opportunities to influence the course of human events.

These problems lessen somewhat when writing about black participation during Reconstruction. The decade stretching from the war years forward to 1877 afforded black Americans exceptional opportunities for a more vigorous participation in historic events than had been theirs in any previous period. The opportunities would not be matched for many years. In Reconstruction, one reads of black individuals and of their aspirations; one sees efforts made by black men to materialize aspirations; one reads of partial success and ultimate tragedy. One reads of cooperation between white men and black men, in politics and economics. But especially does the reader catch the authentic voice of blacks who have names, who are real people rather than an anonymous mass of humanity, abstractions about whom others are free to speculate. While the future of the emancipated slave was a great issue, the greatest probably of the epoch, the black man was also a participant in Reconstruction.

A study of Reconstruction organized and pursued from the vantage point of black participants is also an important means of understanding some important facts about slavery and its impact upon enslaver and enslaved. Southern blacks' response to opportunities offered by the Civil War revealed much about the essential nature of bondage, as well as giving an accurate indication of what black people wanted from free society. As those most closely connected with this transition from slavery to freedom clearly recognized, the slave could not be true to himself while still a slave. Only with freedom were his real views known.

Ex-slaves' participation in Reconstruction, then, is an important story and one easier to tell than the history of Afro-American participation in periods when blacks could make even less happen. Still, a focus on the black as protagonist during Reconstruction will plunge the historian into some of the most challenging problems of historical interpretation. At least two critical questions that can be evaded under some other system of organization must be resolved promptly. First of all, one has to reach some conclusion about the kind of revolution the Civil War and Reconstruction constituted, or indeed whether there was one at all, if one is to assess the importance of Afro-American participation in that revolution. Secondly, one has to find some narrative strategy for focusing on black participation when narrating a history where white participants had more power and deserve more of the spotlight in terms of making events happen.

From black participants' point of view, the Civil War was unquestionably a revolution of profound dimensions. Surely the difference between slavery and freedom is about the greatest difference in status we can imagine, no matter how kindly a view some historians might want to take of slavery, no matter how limited and curtailed freedom may have turned out to be.

But we must also grasp how very conservative the whole affair was by any standard of comparison with events in other countries during the same century. The development of the revolution disclosed features so seldom associated with the sudden emergence of a long-oppressed people that both friends and foes were surprised at the things blacks did not do. Unlike French peasants during the revolution of 1789, ex-slaves did not usually pillage and commit arson. When their time in the political sunlight came, they did not speak for elimination of the former slaveholding class, either physically, socially, or economically. They spoke instead of equal opportunities for themselves.

Unlike Russian peasants emancipated in 1862, the freedmen had to be satisfied working other people's land, although it is perfectly clear that for many slaves owning land was the absolute top priority after freedom itself. Where was there a nineteenth-century social revolution conceived of in such complete isolation from the economic basis of society? With the exception of a few isolated pockets, there was no confiscation of real estate in the American

South. The basis of power remained much as it had been before the war. The closest freedmen came to armed resistance was over this very point. But the entire epoch demonstrated little violence and much patient black politics.

Abolitionists who had thought a great deal about revolts in the West Indies often expected the black population to light a fire behind the Confederate army, a fire so hot that the war would have to be called off by the South. They spoke about this hope more often in private than in public, to be sure, for they understood that many northern supporters of the war were not so angry with southern whites as to wish upon them, as the phrase went, "all the horrors of a servile war." Instead of fulfilling this somewhat dubious hope of their friends, southern freedmen murdered exceedingly little. Rather, they escalated their traditional nonviolent forms of resistance: malingering, petty and not so petty sabotage, above all flight. In general, slaves behaved in accordance with a proper understanding of which army offered freedom. They assisted Union soldiers, spied upon Confederate movements, depleted the southern labor force by running to enemy lines, and finally, served in the Union army on every front.

Nevertheless, the four million slaves of the South did not behave in the way that servile populations are assumed to behave under the impact of revolution, in the crucible of war. It is a monument to the common sense of southern freedmen and their leaders that they did not in this way risk uniting whites engaged in deadly combat. Like American colonists in revolution against Britain, former slaves seemed more concerned to gain rights and privileges of citizenship than to alter terms of that citizenship in sweeping ways. This was made more clear in conventions held in numbers of communities after the war, conventions asking for the ballot and civil equality, and clinched later in constitutional conventions organized under Congressional Reconstruction. These revolutionaries were usually still in the Tennis Court Oath phase of the classic French Revolution, and not in the Reign of Terror and Virtue. In spite of acute racial and social tension during the entire period, there was no jacquerie, and much less specific animosity among freedmen toward former owners than there was reason to expect.

In writing about this period in later life, John R. Lynch, a prominent Afro-American leader in Mississippi, attempted to explain why many black Republicans abstained from voting for the Mississippi Constitution submitted by the radical convention of 1867. Lynch claimed that the clause disenfranchising Mississippi white citizens was disagreeable to blacks. He spoke of a bond of sympathy between the races, "a bond that the institution of slavery with all its horrors could not destroy, the Rebellion could not wipe out, Reconstruction could not efface, and subsequent events have not been able to change."[1]

This may well have been one of those generous sentiments that ripen and mellow with time. Yet a number of arresting examples of black leaders who behaved with extraordinary generosity toward conquered whites suggest that Lynch's sentiments may not have been altogether based on afterthought. Beverly Nash, a black representative to the radical convention in South Carolina, urged Afro-Americans to seek racial unity by petitioning Congress to remove white disenfranchisement. The talents of the best men were needed, Nash argued, regardless of color. Nash and his black associates W. J. Whipper and Francis L. Cardozo, also men of the highest qualifications, persuaded the convention to petition Congress to that effect. Few southern states went that far in the radical phase of Reconstruction, but there is strong evidence that in many states cooperation with former Confederates would have been possible had former Confederates been willing to accept black participation in politics as an accomplished fact. A few were willing, especially in Mississippi, where the old Whig leadership inclined to accept realities and join the Republican Party. But across the South there was a reluctance on the part of former leading citizens to cooperate across the race line.

For reasons why the white upper crust could not be colorblind, one does not have far to look. Inveterate racial hostility was undoubtedly a central factor for many, perhaps most. And yet poor whites, comprising the very class supposedly most prejudiced against blacks, cooperated with ex-slaves.

The problem for the dominant white classes seems to have been subtler. Throughout the private correspondence of the planting elite in the year following the war there is an undercurrent of partially suppressed fear of insurrection. But this theme gradually gave way to the typical resentment of the displaced paternalist, who finds himself dethroned from his former position of power and influence by outsiders, other "significant others." The aggressive self-assertions of being the "Negroes' best friends" alternate with an almost irrational denunciation of blacks' new friends, namely northern teachers and the Freedmen's Bureau. Having to go to Bureau agents for supervision of contracts with freedmen was galling to men who had ruled their little world so absolutely. Furthermore, the freedmen's open and undisguised affection for their teachers was an implied rebuke to the planting class for failure to do much toward educating slaves. Reactions took on the flavor of sour grapes: "We are more liberated than the slaves are"; "We're glad to be rid of the responsibility," and so forth. Assertions that black folk would now vanish, die out under freedom's challenges, were often dropped in as footnotes.

Freedmen seemed to understand former masters' minds better than former masters understood former slaves. Freedmen were reluctant to work for their own erstwhile owners, even if they had to go to the next plantation to work for somebody equally suspect. This was often true even when the relationship between master and man had not been one of excessive cruelty. To have been a slave was to have been obliged to understand the nature of power; to have been a slave was also to have been obliged to resort to flattery and deception upon many occasions. To have been a master was to have upon many occasions been deceived by that same flattery, and to have sunk often enough into a debilitating complacency about one's position in the world that was by no means realistic.

All these artifices erected to protect human beings from a full realization of the facts of bondage crumbled in the morning of freedom, and there were surprises for all, but more for the master than for the emancipated slave. Stephen Elliott returned to South Carolina to discover that his lands were now in the possession of his former slaves, and was doubly surprised when they treated him, as he reported, "as before," serving him his meals "with overflowing affection." But when conversation came round to specifics, his former slaves informed him, "We own this land now.

Put it out of your head that it will ever be yours again."[2] Another discouraged planter resented his former trusted servant for not taking pains to protect his property during the war, and commented bitterly that "in truth the Negroes did not care as much about us as we did for them."[3]

What the planting class ultimately discovered was that former slaves were ready enough to be friends, but that they were unwilling to resume relationships on the old basis. Freedmen understood politics well enough to see that the planters' interests were engaged in retaining as much of the old foundation as possible, while black interests lay with dismantling some of its essential features. Friendly enough in a personal way, the former slave tended to seek other mentors on political questions. Any effort on the part of the planting class to cooperate with blacks would have had to be based on an accommodation involving many black officeholders, much black educational opportunity, and perhaps a little land redistribution. Among the interesting might-have-beens is whether some such accommodation might have eventuated in more lasting and solid gains for the whole South, including the late masters, than the bitter history which flowed from upper-crust failure to make concessions. But the old regime offered only the terms of the old dependency.

Therefore, on the terms it was available to him, the freedman rejected the leadership of the former slaveholding class, often as much to the surprise of enemies of the slaveholding class as to that of the landlords. So great had been Republican fear that slaves of yesterday might be re-enslaved to the political leadership of former owners that even Thaddeus Stevens was hesitant to press for voting rights for blacks until "godly ministers" had been among freedmen, to propagandize a little and "make them truly free." It was clear very early, however, that there was little danger of this classic eventuality. Southern freedmen would not act the part of East Prussian peasants, whom Bismarck enfranchised with perfect confidence when he re-organized the German Empire in 1871, with the understanding that they would be a pillar of support for conservative interests. Blacks might not wish to smash everything. But neither would they settle for nothing.

If freedmen evidenced neither the militancy of French peasants nor the docility of Prussian peasants, but stuck somewhere in between, their nonrevolutionary resistance owed most to the paradoxical conditions of black participation in Reconstruction. That paradox can be stated precisely and never reiterated enough. Seldom in history has a people been so keenly and directly interested in the outcome of a contest and at the same time at such a sharp disadvantage in influencing that outcome. This inability to determine decisively the course of events meant that freedmen were obliged in the end to accept a bargain struck between white men, North and South, involving their future, and made rather largely at their expense. The price of their powerlessness was obvious enough in the terms of the Compromise of 1877 and the end of Reconstruction.

The relative powerlessness of these participants, in other words, explains much about the relatively nonrevolutionary nature of their resistance. The second thorny problem involved in writing a history of Reconstruction from the black viewpoint here dovetails with the first. Focusing on ultimately powerless participants poses narrative difficulties as troublesome as focusing on ultimately nonrevolutionary revolutionaries. It is difficult enough to keep in focus both ex-slaves' exultant sense that they were living out a revolution and the sober fact that their resistance was short of radical. It challenges the historian's ingenuity no less to make participants who did not dominate the story dominate the frame of reference. This problem of presenting the protagonist in the role of having too often to react to forces beyond his control means, as a practical matter, that one has to talk a great deal about those forces, and that there is some risk of losing sight of the subject. The effect of this powerlessness can be seen in the ease with which the role of the Afro-American is minimized. The whole story could be told quite coherently, in fact has been told, leaving the black man out of it altogether. Any resemblance to the economically deterministic synthesis of the late Charles Beard is purely intentional. It is indeed quite possible to describe the struggle as being between two powerful classes, in the Marxist or the Beardian manner of analysis, with the late slave constituting an incidental tool readier to the hand of the rising bourgeoisie than to that of his temporarily incapacitated late owner. Barrington Moore's *Social Origins of Dictatorship and Democracy* demonstrates how easy it is, by concentrating exclusively on economic forces, to eliminate the Afro-American from the story and have the whole thing hang together.[4]

It is not universally true that economic interpretations leave black participation out. For instance, W. E. B. DuBois's *Black Reconstruction* is an example of an economic interpretation that places the black firmly at the center of Reconstruction. But the very inconsistencies of that brilliant and beautiful book illustrate the complexities of black participation. For instance, DuBois sets out to show how "the will of the mass of black labor . . . dictated the form and methods of government." But further along he as firmly states that "the responsibility of Negroes for the government of South Carolina in Reconstruction was necessarily limited. They helped choose the elected officials and furnished a large number of the members of the legislature. But most of the administrative power was in the hands of the whites." DuBois's second statement on white dominance is no doubt truer than his first statement on black dictation.[5]

Again, DuBois declares that the Civil War ended because arms in a quarter of a million ex-slaves' "hands, and the prospect of arms in a million more black hands, brought peace." Yet the author also seems to agree with William H. Trescot that "when Negroes heard that freedom was coming, there was no impatience, no insubordination, no violence. They remained pretty steadily on the farms of their masters, a very general disposition being manifest to adjust the terms of compensation on a reasonable basis."[6]

Both statements contain elements of exaggeration. But the second implied agreement with Trescot does not sit well with an earlier claim to tell "how the black worker won the war by a general strike."[7] It clearly will not do either to overlook the Afro-American's part in Reconstruction, as Beard did, or become confused with contradictory claims, as DuBois did. In both instances the synthesis cannot accommodate the actual facts of black participation.

In returning the Afro-American to the main cast, DuBois was at least emphasizing a participation in Reconstruction that had always before Beard received considerable attention, albeit attention for the most part unfavorable to blacks. Under the direction of William A. Dunning, the Columbia professor who dominated the conservative historiography of the Reconstruction era when it was first being thoroughly worked out at the turn of the century, the black's part in the play was usually that of lesser among several villains.[8] Nobody tried in any case to deny his significance to the plot. In Dunningite studies, the very best billing the Afro-American got was that of being the Problem or the Issue. The worst was very bad indeed. All Dunningite interpretations reflected to some degree the sense of racial superiority so common among white scholars of the period.

The general conception of Reconstruction that emerged from the Dunning studies was therefore fair to the Afro-American in only one respect, in allotting him a fair amount of space. Nearly every historian who writes today is basically fairer toward the black man. It is recognized that blacks understood they had a stake in the outcome of Reconstruction. Nevertheless, much of the new work rests upon asking new questions about the research and conclusions of an earlier generation of scholars. As a consequence, we have different answers based upon a set of questions posed a generation ago.

Therefore in practice we have a lot of NOTS, an essentially negative view of Reconstruction, if looked at from the black man's point of view. For instance: The Afro-American was NOT, as we are now confident, the largest factor in the corruption of southern legislatures. There were not enough of them in most southern state governments to assure that result even if they had been infinitely more corruptible than whites, an arrogation of virtue that few white people are naive enough to subscribe to these days. The black was NOT the ignorant and unknowing recipient of a freedom thrust upon him by pretended friends; his performance as a free laborer canNOT be blamed for the collapse of the southern economy; friends of the black man were NOT the villains of the piece. These are achievements indeed, considering how well entrenched most of these notions were in the historiography of the period, even as late as twenty-five years ago. But they are negative achievements in that they do not help us conceive positively of what it was like to be a southern black participant.

For most white writers of history, recapturing positive aspects of black participation will require active entry into the mind and spirit of black men and women, and a willingness to think about problems from the point of view of those black people, now long dead, who hoped for so much a hundred years ago, participated vigorously if briefly in the effort to democratize the South, and ultimately failed to secure that goal. They lived all sorts of lives. Some were craftsmen, some were professional people, ministers, and newspaper editors, and so on. Many became politicians. Most were farmers. Their stories will only be found by historians ready to abandon the gleeful negation of findings in the Dunning tradition. We must be ready instead to turn to that inglorious kind of historical effort called local history.

Illiterate for the most part, given few opportunities to express himself, the freedman had few opportunities to leave a trail for the historian to follow. But he did leave an impression; and the historian who is ready to work on local history, too often dealt with contemptuously by "professionals" and dismissed as "antiquarianism," will be surprised to discover that newspapers of the times covered political activities and mass rallies of blacks and that one can learn from such accounts names of local political leaders and also aspirations of the freed black farmer.

From the slave's point of view, freedom was often equated with the Resurrection and the morning of eternal bliss. From the freedman's point of view, this must have seemed at one and the same time both true and false. Few indeed were those who would have gone back (it ought not to surprise anyone that there were some), but the difficulties thrust upon the emancipated father of a family must have been stunning to those who allowed themselves to feel them. Aside from the responsibility of providing for a family, usually without the advantages of owning property or equity of any sort, the freedman often had to determine which of several marriages contracted under slavery he ought to honor. While it is true that much of the traveling about that the Freedmen's Bureau paid for was inspired by the wish to try freedom out, so to speak, a great deal more of it is explained by the laudable urge to find out what had happened to relatives long gone to another part of the world. For the freedman the only way was to go and see, since the magic of writing was denied to him.

One way to grant the proper importance to black participation is simply to understand the major aspirations of these illiterate freedmen. The major aspiration of all aspirations was to own land, and that failing, to rent it. This was how a farmer understood getting a living, and the freedman had learned that much and much more as a slave. He understood the sources of master's economic and social power, and immediately asked for land. When he did not get it, he still proved reluctant to submit to wage labor for his old master, although that was often what the old master preferred when he had the cash. Both former master and former slave understood the extractive potential of, and the kind of supervision that would accompany, the wage system. It was therefore more from the wish of the slave to have a free hand at farming operations than from the old master's foreknowledge of its potential for extracting labor that the sharecropping system first arose. The freedmen may collectively have made a bad choice. But their choices were not very attractive, once the national government abandoned the idea of giving freedmen farms.

Next to desire for land, and second only in importance to it, was the aspiration toward an education. This was as spontaneous and as universal as the wish to own a farm. Black soldiers in every part of the South turned barracks into primary schools. Nobody was welcomed into the South more heartily by blacks in all parts than were northern schoolteachers. It is doubtful if a people ever, in such large numbers, went through such inconveniences to get a little learning. The school became for the freedman almost as symbolic as the church had been.

The historian who wants to see Reconstruction from the point of view of the freedman will therefore follow with special interest the efforts to win land and education through politics. Black leaders were rarely numerous enough in southern legislatures to dictate social changes of the sort many of their constituencies would have desired. Seen from the angle of freedmen, however, black leadership constituted the only chance for improvement in condition.

The smallness of the cadre of black leadership should not be surprising when one considers the rather infrequent opportunities offered by slavery for the emergence of talent. But there were certain opportunities. Slaves who had made the most of them were available after the war to assume responsibilities of leadership. In addition, a considerable number of northern free blacks came South after the war to aid in Reconstruction.

From these materials came the leadership of the freedman during Reconstruction, a leadership that was never independent of white carpetbag influence, but a leadership that nevertheless gave voice to needs and attitudes of newly enfranchised people. It is standard to begin such discussions by analysis of the highest levels of attainment during the epoch. At no time can it be fairly stated that blacks controlled any southern state. With the brief exception of the Louisiana interim governorship of P. B. S. Pinchback, after Henry Clay Warmoth was removed from office, no black leader was Governor of a southern state during the epoch. In South Carolina two blacks became Lieutenant-Governors, however, as did one in Mississippi and three in Louisiana. Blacks became Speakers of the House in several states. In no southern state did black men control legislatures, though they came closest in South Carolina and played a prominent part in Louisiana.

On the national level there were two Senators, Blanche K. Bruce and Hiram Revels, both from Mississippi, both able men. Before the turn of the century there were twenty black Congressmen, eight from South Carolina, four from North Carolina, three from Alabama, and one each from Virginia, Louisiana, Georgia, Mississippi, Florida. Prominent for length of service were J. H. Rainey and Robert Smalls of South Carolina, and John R. Lynch of Mississippi.

Blacks were members in varying strength in each legislature, and were prominent in activities on behalf of civil rights and education. One of the most significant parts of the picture is the presence of blacks in state constitutional conventions that organized Reconstruction governments. In only one state were blacks in the majority. Such was the case in South Carolina, and they assisted in writing one of the most progressive state constitutions, one that served South Carolina well for several decades. It was eventually abandoned at the end of the century for the simple reason that under it there were too many difficulties in driving black men from the polls. In Louisiana black delegates to the Reconstruction Convention were equal in numbers to whites, and in several other states blacks constituted a healthy minority.

Most Afro-American leadership at upper levels of government was provided by northern blacks who came into the South during and after the Civil War. Without any pejorative implication, we may call them black carpetbaggers, though I want to add immediately that many were returning south. Some, like Blanche K. Bruce, had been born in the South as slaves. Bruce escaped during the war, taking his departure from St. Louis. He was a teacher, and an able one. Mississippi was lucky to have his political services during Reconstruction.

Many of these leaders were brilliant and well-educated men. No better-educated man operated during the period than Francis Cardozo, who served as Secretary of State and Treasurer of South Carolina, and before that as a very able supervisor of public education in Charleston. Cardozo had benefited from an education in Glasgow and London. It is ironic that this educator, who rose to office through his expert management of the Charleston city schools, should have had the same last name as T. W. Cardozo of Mississippi, who was charged and convicted of embezzling funds from Tougaloo. Alas, in this respect, as in so many others, black politicians proved neither superior nor inferior to white counterparts. Some Lieutenant-Governors were able, some were not, and from there to the lowest level of organized political activities the same might be said.

Important as it is to know about these leaders, however, it is even more interesting to reflect upon how they gained power. What institutions assisted them, authenticated them, so to speak, to the people? The extremely significant answer is that most black leaders had some connection with newly emerging educational systems of the South, or with churches.

Many teachers were among the elite leaders who came South during and just after the war. Nothing served better to enhance a man's image with the people he represented than association with schools and education. Education represented for most freedmen a means of economic and social advancement, and the people were ready to support men who came under such auspices. Many teachers and agents of the Freedman's Bureau had opportunities to travel widely, and the support they received was consequently greater. As members of active organizations they also secured information they would need later about organizing, financing, and about wringing support from the federal government. Not the least advantage was the occasion to work with white Northerners who would comprise an active and important if relatively small part of the Republican Party in the South. Acquaintance with men whose influence in the federal government was strong was an important asset to black leaders, whether they came themselves from North or South. They were not very rich men for the most part, and often required some kind of appointive office before they could hope for a following at the polls.

Having been a minister at some time was also an important asset in a potential black leader. This is hardly surprising when one considers that the church had been almost the only avenue available to would-be leaders under the slave regime. Cramped and narrow as that avenue had been, it had been there. All students of slavery acknowledged its importance. The slave preacher was the man with the most status on the plantation, was associated with the most important social and emotional outlet of his fellow slaves, and he was heard. It was not without reason that whites suspected preachers when trouble developed, and tended to curtail their activities in times of public fear of insurrection. Therefore the development of a class of native-born leadership came as a very natural thing. Northern ministers who came South during the war contributed to the number of leaders associated with the churches, and sometimes these men did not analyze the problems of the newly enfranchised along precisely the same lines as those who had grown up on the land.

What is unfortunate is that we as yet know so little about local political leaders who took up the essential but undramatic role of organizing at the community level. One supposes they must in fact have arisen from slavery and secured their position as leaders more by means of natural talent than training of any kind. Many were undoubtedly illiterate. Their jobs were infinitely more dangerous than that of major political leaders. One wonders whether these men came from the class called "privileged" bondsmen, or from the field slaves, or from the free men of color. Research at the local level could yield important clues. Some evidence indicates that those who had had special duty or responsibility as slaves emerged as leaders after the war.

The only writer who seems to have attempted to follow these subjects in Mississippi is Vernon Wharton, who concluded that the lower level of political leadership in that state came from persons who in one way or another had enjoyed a privileged position as slaves, or had been free before the war, either in some southern city or in the North.[9] Joel Williamson, in writing about South Carolina, comes to the same generalization by another route: "The one thing that most native Negro leaders were not," he writes, "was fresh from the cotton fields." His analysis of the Constitutional Convention of 1868 is interesting: "Of the seventy-four Negroes who sat in the Constitutional Convention of 1868, fourteen were Northerners. Of the fifty-nine Negroes who had been born and settled in South Carolina before the war, at least eighteen and probably twenty-one had been free. A dozen of these were Charlestonians. Nearly all had been tradesmen. Roughly two-thirds of this group continued to pursue their trades after the war and at least until the time of the convention. The remainder took service as Bureau teachers."[10]

While granting that these assessments are probably correct, one may still wonder about those who worked at the grassroots level, getting out the vote, politicizing plantations, and so on. If the lower counties of South Carolina are examples of a general tendency, I can say with safety that some of these leaders, in fact most, did come straight from the cotton field.

Why is this important? In part it is important because of what it says about slavery. No leaders would have come straight from the fields if slavery had totally victimized all blacks. In fact many men had had opportunities to develop a talent for leading others inside the slave system, which was much more complicated than either defenders or attackers of the Elkins thesis will admit.

I do not mean to suggest here that the uneducated former slave was the typical Reconstruction leader. Most men who rose to prominence seem to have had educational advantages, however limited. I do mean to suggest that then, as now and always, the common touch had advantages.

This is an illustration, I believe, of something most of us accept as being generally true about politics: it is not so much a science as an art, and requires not so much preparation as instinct. Some men had the gift. Others did not. In this respect some contests between black men assume special significance.

One thinks, for instance, of the year 1872 in South Carolina, when a northern black lawyer named W. J. Whipper, a man of greater accomplishments, challenged Robert Smalls, the incumbent state Senator, for the Republican nomination. Smalls, born a slave in Beaufort County, had risen spectacularly during the war by capturing his master's ship and sailing it out of Charleston harbor under Confederate guns. Congress had awarded Smalls prize money for the vessel.

Whipper had, on the face of it, all the advantages of education, support of a newspaper, and such vital campaign issues as the corruption in Columbia. He was recognized as the sharpest lawyer at the county seat by white and black alike. Smalls's popularity, on the other hand, was based to a large degree upon political ability, his Gullah accent, and his intimate knowledge of his people.

At a mass rally of about a thousand people, the two candidates explained their positions. Smalls disclaimed involvement with Columbia frauds and promised to work for reforms. Whipper charged him with having voted for the very measures adjudged now to be so wicked. Damaging charges were then brought forth against Whipper. But the people were persuaded best by the argument, so ironically put, looking backward, that it was best to vote only for southern men. Smalls swept to victory over Whipper.

The ex-slave was subsequently challenged by Reuben Tomlinson, a white carpetbagger who campaigned for Governor in Smalls's backyard. Tomlinson wanted the seat of incumbent F. J. Moses. To win in Beaufort County he would have had to get Smalls's support, and Smalls was an administration supporter. Again the victory was overwhelming, and due in no small measure to Smalls's campaign style. He spoke the people's language, urging them in both elections to vote only for southern men, and their decision was "clear, pointed, and forceful," to use the words of an opposing newspaper.

Behind Smalls's remarkable political success was also a considerable organizing force. Smalls no doubt owed much to less important men whose names appear often in accounts of the election, such local organizers as Pompey Coaxum, Hastings Gantt, and Samuel Green, all former slaves with little or no education. Theirs is an unsung song of Reconstruction.

Such blacks were at a severe disadvantage in competition with white candidates for office once Republican regimes in the South began to crumble. Patterns of violent repression would be worth working out for each state. Often conservative terrorist activities went so far as murder, as in the case of a North Carolina leader named Wyatt Outlaw, the leading man of the Republican Party of Alamance County. Outlaw was but one of several murdered in the county for political activities. And then there was the calculated disruption of meetings, something all black leaders faced at various times during the ten or fifteen years following the war. All told, one gets the distinct impression that, without a certain amount of intestinal fortitude, a black man would have been well advised to steer clear of politics.

Along with moral reserves, a man had to have a little cash, and this brings us to another important aspect of the black man's difficulties as a politician. Some politicians, such as John R. Lynch, were very fortunate in having two black supporters post political bond money. No doubt others were equally fortunate. But when one considers the general poverty of southern freedmen in the morning of their freedom, the problem of financing candidates emerges as a formidable obstacle to political success. It also serves to explain part of the plight of the entire Republican Party in the South, and the relative ease with which petty graft made its appearance. It is in fact difficult to see how the party could have stayed alive without a certain amount of it. The national Republican establishment showed a great deal more interest, spelled cash, in southern Republicans during presidential years than at any other election, and no interest whatever when campaigning was local. The starving times between national elections no doubt occasioned much of the petty graft in which Republicans of both colors were involved to a greater or lesser degree. In fact, the black politician faced very much the same problems others did, aside from the matter of color, and solved them, when he was successful, in much the same way other successful politicians did.

Be that as it may, the question may be asked whether the large proportion of the black leadership coming from the North, or from the urban setting, or the free black environment, properly represented a people new to freedom, poor farmers, illiterate and unskilled. If we are to place the black at the center of Reconstruction, we have to ask if black leaders did the best that was possible, or if they failed to make the most of the few opportunities open to them.

In some respects, black leaders were not so realistic. They sometimes evinced too much faith in the justice and fair-mindedness of the Republican Party and its national and local leadership. One wonders if threats to withdraw support might not have forced greater concessions from the white leadership of the party. Granted that blacks could hardly go to the Democrats. But one sees that they gave support sometimes with great readiness with very little in return.

How did black leaders act to secure their constituents' aspirations? Here we have a most interesting division between leaders from the North and those from the South. All men wanted land, educational opportunities, civil liberties and rights, including the vote. But southern leaders wanted land above everything else, and northern leaders seemed persuaded that the franchise was to be placed first. Few Southerners could see the difficulties of second-class citizenship in a society that withheld legal equality, because they had never even had that advantage. For their part, those of the North could not feel in a profound emotional way what land meant to southern freedmen. Only one southern state witnessed an effort to use the power to tax in such a way as to force large landowners to sell. This radical step proved too radical for most educated northern blacks, who had undoubtedly learned most of their political economy, indirectly or directly, from white economists.

Another matter of contemporary significance is the question of separation versus segregation, a very old pattern of choices in the history of race relations in this country. What did southern black leaders advocate? When Sherman's army came down through Georgia late in 1864, it was followed, as all men know, by throngs of slaves seeking liberation. When Sherman reached Savannah he discussed with some twenty black leaders in the area the problem of settling these freedmen. The question arose whether the island country set aside for their occupation should be reserved exclusively for freedmen. Only one leader objected to this early establishment of a pattern of separation. The others felt that white prejudice would be strong for a long time, and that separation was best. The lone objector was the only formerly free northern black among the number.

One example does not establish a trend. But it does seem reasonable to suppose that blacks who had not lived in the South, but in a segregated northern world, were quicker to recognize the danger lurking in segregation, and that black southern leaders tended to understand instinctively that their leadership would be handicapped if black institutions were submerged in white ones. This same pattern is observable in the churches—important institutions, as we have seen, for black leadership.

Let me recapitulate the difficulties in studying the black as participant during Reconstruction. First, we have the ambiguity of the period when seen on a radical-conservative axis. What was an extremely conservative kind of revolution for the country as a whole was a radical change for the Afro-American. In the second place, because the position of the emancipated slave precluded his exercising critical force upon his own destiny, too often he had to react to actions initiated by others but affecting him at critical points. He thus must ever be seen not just as other men's concern but also as the participant struggling unsuccessfully to control his own problems. And the third difficulty is the absence up to now of much of the research in local history that would remove the negative onus from the Afro-American's role in Reconstruction.

The research is worth doing. Reconstruction gave the silent of slavery a voice at last. A great deal can be learned about that very peculiar institution by the response of its "victims" to freedom. That under such disadvantageous circumstances so many people came forward when they were needed invites some happy speculation. Even under slavery, numbers of persons had learned how to lead and to plan.

Nevertheless, any sympathetic account of the frustrations of blacks during Reconstruction must eventually sadly conclude that never was so much lost for so many, maybe a little because of the mistakes of so few. The Afro-American suffered throughout the period from the disadvantage of his heritage of slavery, his illiteracy, his landlessness, his North-South divisions, and, yes, if we will be quite honest, also from habits and attitudes of deference toward white people born of slavery. No matter what aspect of this subject one considers—no matter whether analysis focuses on the largely nonrevolutionary revolution or the participation of largely powerless participants or the legacy of slavery or the nature of black leadership—there seems, in conclusion, no possibility of escaping an ambivalent treatment of black protagonists during Reconstruction.

III

Slavery and Freedom in American Historical Fiction

7

Four Episodes
in Popular Culture

Doctor Rose presented this Inaugural Lecture as Harms-
worth Professor of American History at Oxford University, Ox-
ford, England, on May 4, 1978. The lecture was printed by the
Clarendon Press, Oxford University, as a pamphlet in 1979. It was
reprinted in J. Morgan Kousser and James M. McPherson, eds.,
Region, Race, and Reconstruction: Essays in Honor of C. Vann
Woodward (*New York and Oxford, 1982*). *Both publications of*
Professor Rose's lecture bore the title "Race and Region in Amer-
ican Historical Fiction: Four Episodes in Popular Culture." Each
contained Rose's full explanatory footnotes.

The Harmsworth Lecture was held out of the hardbook edition
of Slavery and Freedom *so that it could be published first in*
America in the Woodward *Festschrift. The piece is now inserted*
in this paperback edition with the permission of the copyright
holder, the Oxford University Press. The text of the essay and all
citations to the sources are reprinted unchanged. But the title and
the explanatory footnotes have been somewhat shortened, so that
this latest of Professor Rose's essays can slip smoothly into her
book.

Nearly every scholar who has asked himself Crèvecœur's
famous query "What then is the American, this new man?" has
come sooner or later to an explanation that rests on a peculiarly
American view of experience that has little to do with the past,
much to do with the future. The most widely recognized formu-

lation of this idea is R. W. B. Lewis's *The American Adam*, an influential study that regards the authentic American as a "figure of heroic innocence and vast potentialities, poised at the start of a new history."[1] Lewis based his conception on an insightful reading of the great writers of the nineteenth century, particularly those of the first half, and he clearly identified a theme in American letters that has a continuing if diminishing currency. But it surely does no harm to point out that Lewis's concentration on the "articulate thinkers and conscious artists" means that a large area of popular thought was left out of consideration, a matter of some concern to the social historian.

Perhaps this mattered little in the eighteenth century, when what was distinctly American about our experience was still comparatively new, and most expressions of that experience were limited to the "articulate thinker." But by the second quarter of the nineteenth century the level of literacy in American began to rise sharply, along with a wider than ever spread of political participation. The invention of the steam press provided the technology to produce plentiful reading matter for the new popular taste. As a consequence, it would seem that cultural historians may be missing important clues in not studying more carefully the best-seller lists when they attempt to assess that elusive item the "national character."

The historian interested in the influence of popular preferences and political action may find food for thought, for example, in the curious coincidence that four of the most popular reading-viewing events in all American history—they might even be called public celebrations—have been about the great twin problems in American political life. One is the Civil War and its causes. The other, so closely related to it, is slavery and race in that conflict and the Reconstruction period that followed.

For a people uninterested in the past, this coincidence must at least raise some question whether the vast middle reach of American intellectual activity that fills the space between the lower levels of academia and the upper levels of folk culture is very much concerned to discuss our history, to argue points, strike compromises, and justify the past in the enjoyment of historical fiction, in print and in drama. The "authentic" American may be irritatingly prone to assuming a posture of innocence on account of our new start in a new land. But he is not dismissing two aspects of our past: race and region. Few critics have taken seriously even one of the four astonishing publishing successes I have in mind. These works have nevertheless in one form or another (more often both book *and* drama) traveled around the world. They have given a vocabulary to American mythologies and demonologies that is generally understood at home and abroad; and in each case they have been recognized immediately as important statements explaining a point of view in the ongoing discussion of race and region in American history. They endure.

I do not mean to be mysterious. The sequence of reading-viewing events I have in mind begins with Harriet Beecher Stowe's famous book *Uncle Tom's Cabin*, published in 1852.[2] *Uncle Tom* was dramatized promptly by George Aiken and has run almost continuously somewhere in some form ever since. The list continues with the trilogy of works on Southern Reconstruction, especially *The Clansman*, published in 1905, by Thomas Ryan Dixon.[3] *The Clansman*, as a book, is virtually unread today, but it was fabulously successful in its time—and the motion picture by D. W. Griffith from the Dixon text, called *Birth of a Nation*, has brought the lurid story through to our own time. This moving picture may have been seen by more persons than any other ever made. *Birth of a Nation* was the first truly modern feature film, and surely the most controversial ever shown.

More recently, *Gone With the Wind*, written between 1926 and 1929 and published in 1936, was Margaret Mitchell's enduring contribution to the fictionalized Civil War. It has sold over 20 million copies and still (forty years later) sells 40 thousand per year at hardback prices, and perhaps ten times that number in paperback. For the first forty years this makes an average of over 500 thousand copies per year.[4] The classic moving picture made by David O. Selznick is one of the most popular films of all time; CBS television has paid $35,000,000 for the exclusive right to show it once per year for twenty years.[5] This princely payment may have some relationship with the fourth event which set my mind back along the direction described.

Alex Haley's fabulously successful book called *Roots* was published in late 1976; its author refers to it as his bicentennial gift to his countrymen. Some are referring to *Roots* as the black *Gone With the Wind*, in part because it had much the same astonishing and instant recognition, and was quickly turned into a dramatic television marathon that ran for eight successive evenings in the January following the autumn publication. It quickly appeared that this work, which sold a million copies in six months, was viewed by a larger television audience than any previous show, even including *Gone With the Wind*. Perhaps as many as 135 million Americans watched one or more episodes. Surely, if numbers participating count, author Haley provided the most outstanding cultural event of the American bicentennial.[6]

Haley's book purported to trace his family's lineage back to its African origins in a village near the Gambia River in West Africa. He achieved this feat with the aid of linguists expert in the Mansdinka language spoken in contemporary Gambia. Certain "strange" African words, passed down in the Haley family, turned out to be code words for rich African natural phenomena.[7] Further assistance from a griot of the village of Juffure convinced Haley that he had found the very home of his ancestor Kunta Kinte, captured at the age of sixteen in 1767 and transported to Annapolis in Maryland aboard the slaver the *Lord Ligonier*. This griot from Juffure, Kebba Fofana, it turned out, had stored in his memory bank the key story about how the young warrior Kunta Kinte had been out in the woods carving out a drum when he was captured. It was the very story, Haley marveled, that his grandmother Cynthia had told him when he was a boy.

That Kebba Fofana was no true griot, but a song-and-dance man, a popular entertainer, was bound to come out sooner or later. No nonmythical anecdotes concerning individuals are entered in *any* griot's memory bank going back so far as the eighteenth century. Surely none would be there concerning a relatively unimportant personage sixteen years old in a society that values age. Haley had simply let out what he wanted to hear, and Fofana had responded. But the outcry that arose when *Sunday Times* (London) reporter Mark Ottaway opened this information to the general public, along with several other incriminating items, showed that the number of Americans, white as well as black, who had taken Kunta Kinte into their hearts was very large.[8]

The 135 million or so who had seen the television series had willingly suspended disbelief to follow the young hero out of his contrived but beautiful African Garden of Eden into the hell of slavery in North America. His name, along with that of Uncle Tom (whom he did not in any way favor), had entered the vocabulary of race relations. Haley was sitting down to talk things over with the contemporary descendants of his ancestor's first owners, and was on television nearly every other morning to discuss, promote, and defend the authenticity of his research. Following reporter Ottaway's charges, Haley's distant relatives from West Africa were flown over to claim kinship on the air.

All this had something of the style of promotion, something of the style of celebration; it clearly demonstrated that *Roots* had gone down where grass roots are, and on some things the general public does not care for an expert opinion. Haley had insisted on the accuracy of his genealogical researches, but admitted freely that beyond *that* he had improvised at will to give a character and human relationships to Kunta Kinte and his African parents, and to his American connections. Haley called this contact between fact and fiction "faction" and insisted at least on the spiritual accuracy of the *faction*. There is much in the spiritual department that might be challenged about *Roots*, as book and especially as television. The anachronisms on details are so plentiful as to arouse distrust on more important matters in which it is essential to have full faith; the characterizations lack depth, especially those of the white persons in the plot, and the women in general. But since the work was "faction," reviewers of "fiction" could say they supposed the *history* was good enough, and those historians who reviewed it could call it fiction, and applaud its "spiritual truth."[9]

Actually Haley promised to clear up the historical difficulties by producing another book, and was perhaps unaware how neatly he was falling into the pattern already established by his predecessors in the Tom–Klan–Wind–Roots saga. When similarly called to account, Harriet Beecher Stowe produced the famous *Key to Uncle Tom's Cabin* (1853), and when he was challenged on the accuracy of his romantic and exculpatory history of the Ku Klux Klan, T. R. Dixon said he'd get a committee from the American Historical Association to referee and pay $1000 to anyone who could prove an error. Margaret Mitchell simply answered an incredible number of letters, reeling out her citations. Not one of the four authors has yet said it doesn't matter, as a few professional historians did in the wake of the *Roots* phenomenon.[10]

Actually in most instances the writers in this sequence could offer some kind of factual authority for the historical background in their works. However, the common fault of selective omission runs through all of them, accounting for the dramatic story line, the simplicity of the emotional appeal, and the literary accessibility through so wide a range of readers. This may in fact be the historical interface of the division that exists between popular culture and high culture.

Accounting for Haley's success, Haley's comet, as one wit has it, may be hazardous. On the hunch that the appeal of *Roots* touches some of the primary chords that its predecessors played on, it is an observable fact that Haley's story, like all the others, is at bottom a story about the family. It celebrates the strength flowing from the cultural lifeline for blacks.

Although historians of not too many years ago seemed agreed that Afro-American culture owed little or nothing to Africa, most recent scholars who have worked this field have returned a different verdict. *Roots* serves to dramatize this change of view, in keeping with the favor now accorded Swahili, dashikis, and the "natural" hairstyle.

Another aspect of common currency among these spectacular publishing events is that we have in *Roots* a *success* story. The family is victorious over slavery, just as Uncle Tom has a spiritual victory over his oppressors, and as the Southern whites "redeem" their region from the presumed tyranny of carpetbaggers and evil blacks in Dixon's story. Like Scarlett O'Hara, who becomes rich and saves her plantation home, Haley is a Horatio Alger millionaire who has, in celebrating his roots, come right out from the story as its own triumph, an example to all, of a black man who made it, and not in athletics, either. Overnight Haley became a folk hero, and the day the television series ended, more than three thousand persons, mostly teenagers, lined up outside a Los Angeles bookstore to wait for the author to sign their copies of *Roots*. Those who take note of these matters informed the public that newborn babies all over America were being named after Kunta Kinte and his American-born daughter Kizzie.[11]

Haley shared with his predecessors another signal attribute: he had an overt didactic purpose. Haley believed Afro-Americans needed a Garden of Eden and Innocence to look back upon, and so he created a highly romanticized West Africa that owed more to modern anthropology than to history. Here was an African Dixie "before the war." Looking back on the success of the book and the television series, Haley concluded that it was more than his own perseverance that had at last got his book finished, after more than a decade of struggle. "However this sounds," Haley said, "it was one of those things that God in his infinite wisdom and in his time and way decided should happen. I feel that I am a conduit through which this is happening. It was just something that was meant to be. I say this because there were so many things that had to happen over which I had not control."[12]

Leaving Haley in order to slip backward in time, we learn that Harriet Beecher Stowe was equally modest about her part in the writing of *Uncle Tom's Cabin*, once telling an enthusiastic pilgrim who had come to shake the famous hand that wrote it that she had only taken dictation; God had written *Uncle Tom*.[13] In light of President Abraham Lincoln's famous and often quoted remark of her, that here was the little woman who had caused the great American Civil War, Mrs. Stowe may have had a special reason for wishing to share honors with Higher Authority. But it is also true that there is no understanding the phenomenon of Stowe's book without the moral impulse behind it. The work appeared in serial installments in the *National Era* between June 5, 1851, and April of the following year, when the book was published in two volumes and began its spectacular rise. The last episode of the story was actually the one written first, and the real key to the motivation of the plot.[14]

One Sunday during communion at her church in Brunswick, Maine, Stowe's imagination divined a scene set somewhere in faraway Louisiana, where a black man was writhing in anguish under the lashes of two fellow slaves who were beating this black Christian to death at the behest of their cruel owner, the villain who became the infamous Simon Legree.[15] As he lay dying, Uncle Tom, the martyr, brought his black persecutors to a saving knowledge of Christ, and forgave his enemies. When Uncle Tom prayed for victory he was asking for the strength to refrain from betraying others in an escape attempt, and of him his creator writes, "The brave, true heart was firm on the Eternal Rock. Like his Master, he knew that, if he saved others, himself he could not save; nor could utmost extremity wring from him words, save of prayer and holy trust." That Tom's martyrdom is intended as atonement and that he is meant to be the Christ figure is left in no doubt, for in death he calls on God in Jesus' words: "Into thy hands I commend my spirit."[16]

From Mrs. Stowe's decision regarding Tom's character the rest of the action flowed toward this conclusion she had already written. Studying antislavery tracts and narratives of fugitive slaves, and putting these together with a visit she had once made into slaveholding Kentucky some years before, Stowe developed a galaxy of characters and events as alive today as they were a century ago. Her plot has been much criticized, for it is full of extravagant coincidences, surprise endings, and not a little preaching to the dear reader, but it nevertheless served to get Tom to his martyrdom within the year. It drove home Mrs. Stowe's main point relentlessly, with illustration after illustration, from Upper South to Lower South, under all sorts of masters, that slavery could never be ameliorated as a social system so long as slaves were objects of *trade*. The kindness or goodwill of individual owners availed nothing when slaves might be taken for debts. Indeed two of Tom's successive owners are generous to a fault, and Stowe refers to "good-humored indulgence" of masters and mistresses, and "affectionate loyalty" of slaves on some plantations, but it is only to add:

So long as the law considers all these human beings, with beating hearts and living affections, only as so many *things* belonging to a master,—so long as the failure, or misfortune, or imprudence, or death of the kindest owner, may cause them any day to exchange a life of kind protection and indulgence for one of hopeless misery and toil,—so long it is impossible to make anything beautiful or desirable in the best regulated administration of slavery.[17]

Mrs. Stowe's specific target and immediate impulse for writing her novel was the enactment of a new fugitive-slave law as a part of the famous sectional compromise of 1850, a law more stringent and difficult to evade by antislavery men and women who were engaged in aiding fugitive blacks escaping from the South. The enormous and instantaneous success of Stowe's book came in large part because concern about this law was reflected across a far wider spectrum of public opinion than the abolition movement. Stowe's own family had not been in the front of any movement in that direction before this time, and even as she spoke out in the most unequivocal terms against oppression in her novel, she conceded enough to the Southern argument to suggest that she might have hoped to win a few converts there. Of the three successive owners of Uncle Tom, only the last, Simon Legree, is vicious. Mrs. Stowe makes him a pushing, driving Northerner. The other two are Southern-born and easygoing. The failing of the first is that he had let himself get into debt; the second only that he did not live long enough to render his emancipation of Tom effective in the courts. It is in fact through *this* owner of Uncle Tom, the charming, slightly Byronic Augustine St. Clare, that Harriet Beecher Stowe makes a major sectional concession to the South, and a rebuke, if you will, to her fellow Northerners. The slavery question is frequently discussed between St. Clare and his angular New England cousin Miss Ophelia, who has come South to help look after St. Clare's small daughter, the Little Eva of legend. Miss Ophelia is a woman of conscience, who is, says Mrs. Stowe, a bond slave to the word "ought," but St. Clare notices that as trenchant as she is in her observations against slavery and slave-holding, his cousin flinches with displeasure to see Uncle Tom and Little Eva in physical contact with one another. Miss Ophelia shudders. "Confess it, cousin," St. Clare presses her,

> I know the feeling among you Northerners well enough. Not that there is a particle of virtue in our not having it; but custom does with us what Christianity ought to do,—obliterates the feeling of personal prejudice. I have often noticed, in my travels north, how much stronger this was with you than with us. You loathe negroes as you would a snake or toad, yet you are as indignant at their wrongs. You would not have them abused; but you don't want to have anything to do with them yourselves. You would send them to Africa, out of your sight and smell, and then send a missionary

or two to do up all the self-denial of elevating them compendiously. Isn't that it?

And Miss Ophelia admits thoughtfully that "there may be some truth in this."[18]

By conceding racial prejudice to the woman who otherwise speaks the views of the author, Mrs. Stowe was conceding a significant point to the proslavery argument. She did not convert the South, but she did write a book around which all shades of antislavery opinion could rally. One of her favorable reviewers even seemed to believe that her book reopened the hope that some form of gradual emancipation might yet be undertaken, or some amelioration of the system effected by favorable legal reform.[19] There were even reviewers who believed that the great success of the book was rather in spite of its antislavery than because of it, holding that it was the religious faith of Uncle Tom and his small charge, Miss Eva, that swayed the public.[20] The impact of the book surely owes something to religion and family, but Mrs. Stowe placed these in the service of her main theme, which was the terrible suffering caused by the internal slave trade. Few were the young mothers who could not identify with the beautiful mulatto Eliza Harris, who flies from the clutches of the slave-trader with her little boy in her arms, chancing a wintry dash across the frozen Ohio River in her attempt to avoid separation from her child. Few young fathers could help sympathizing with George Harris, the mullatto husband of this brave girl; few could blame him for despairing at the thought of losing Eliza, for choosing life in Liberia over America, for saving his sympathies for his mother's race and not his father's, for saying he wished himself two shades darker rather than two shades lighter.

By playing splendidly on the deepest instincts of her readers, Mrs. Stowe wrote the most effective of all tracts against slavery, so that an English reviewer claimed that *Uncle Tom*, especially after it was put on stage and was being played everywhere in the middle and late fifties, had in effect repealed the Fugitive Slave Act.[21] The same reviewer thought the process was a remarkable transformation that had little to do with rational analysis. Referring to the pandemic racial hostility throughout the North, particularly among working-class people, he pointed out that *Uncle Tom* ran 150 consecutive nights in New York alone, and that George and Eliza Harris had converted "the sovereign people" while audiences cheered them on. The impact of *Uncle Tom* on the coming of the Civil War has never been properly evaluated, but it was great. Surely the fact that Simon Legree could be found cracking his whip in six London theaters at once in the late fifties made it unlikely that the public opinion there would readily yield to Southern desires for recognition once the Emancipation Proclamation had introduced antislavery as a Northern war objective.[22]

Dramatic art is more vulnerable than written literature to the impact of change in popular choice or preference, and the degradation of *Uncle Tom's Cabin* in the late decades of the nineteenth century is a particularly said example of that truth. So long as the idealism of the best aspirations of the Civil War era retained some vigor, the old melodrama retained a certain amount of dignity, however badly played it was in country towns across the land. But soon there was no barrier to making Uncle Tom a poor parody of the brave Christian of the original, and as a traveling road show the play gave rise to the miserable sterotype of shuffling cowardice that has caused Tom's name to become an epithet of derision in the twentieth century. Live bloodhounds to enhance the drama of Eliza's flight, real angels to gather around Little Eva as she died her beautiful death, these all but eclipsed the real meaning of the original book and play.[23]

Fortunately the book, as distinct from the play, with all its flaws, read and imagined, remained an internationally recognized American classic and is now regarded by several highly perceptive critics as being very serious literature indeed.[24] Nobody expressed better the reason this should have happened in time than Henry James did many years ago. As he remembered it,

> We lived and moved . . . with great intensity, in Mrs. Stowe's novel . . . There was, however, I think for that triumphant work no classified condition; it was for no sort of reader as distinct from any other sort, save indeed for Northern as differing from Southern; it knew the large felicity of gathering in alike the small and the simple and the big and the wise, and had above all the extraor-

dinary fortune of finding itself, for an immense number of people, much less a book than a state of vision, of feeling and of consciousness, in which they didn't sit and read and appraise . . . but walked and talked and laughed and cried . . . in a manner of which Mrs. Stowe was the irresistible cause . . .[25]

However ludicrous *Uncle Tom* became at its worst, his was too realistic and compassionate a story to lend itself to the vicious hate-inciting characterizations of blacks that became increasingly common as the nineteenth century neared its close. In time the moving-picture industry would favor blacks and restore much of the original dignity of Uncle Tom, but that development had to wait many years. In fact the most successful movie of the era of silent film was David Wark Griffith's *Birth of a Nation*, a brilliant piece of technology in the development of a new art form, and a drama that gave evidence of the very nadir of race relations and the badly deteriorating images of blacks. The classic picture was released in 1915, and it continues to be seen regularly in spite of its characterizations of blacks as beastly savages, in part because of its historical position in the development of silent film, in part because, at the time it appeared, the National Association for the Advancement of Colored People secured the removal of some of the more shocking scenes. They have been lost, but what remains sums up the clichés for an unhappy epoch in American life and suggests how harsh the excised footage must have been.[26]

The movie was an adaptation of a best-selling novel called *The Clansman*, by Thomas Ryan Dixon, a native of North Carolina, who was brought up in poverty in the shadow of the Civil War and Reconstruction years.[27] Dixon shared some characteristics with his Georgian contemporary Thomas Watson, whose sudden onslaught of racist bigotry at the end of the century is explained by his biographer, C. Vann Woodward, as being born of frustration that reflects a souring of his hopes as a Populist leader working for political cooperation across the color line.[28] Though Dixon was not a Populist, he had been in the decade of the 1890s a highly influential Baptist minister preaching in an unfashionable section of New York, who packed in great crowds to hear his Social Gospel message. He was admirably solicitous of the poor and the immigrants. The words he had for blacks in those days were encouraging and favorable to their progress since emancipation. But, for reasons not entirely clear, the Reverend Mr. Dixon had concluded by 1902 that the Negro was a "menace." Some writers have suggested that America's entry into the scramble for empire combined badly with Dixon's unabashed Darwinism and caused him to turn against blacks; it is true that just at the time this change on race is registered, Dixon began fulminating jingoistic attacks on the Spanish.[29] For his own part Dixon explained that his decision to write a set of novels that would set the Civil War and Reconstruction in a true perspective had come to him when he saw a 1901 revival of *Uncle Tom's Cabin.* In his anger he restrained the impulse to jump up and denounce the play, but decided to "make a merciless record of the facts" instead.[30]

In the first of the triology, *The Leopard's Spots,* Dixon called for complete ·separation of the races, or the expulsion of blacks from the country, claiming, in the words of one of his characters, "in a democracy you cannot build a nation inside a nation of two antagonistic races. . . ."[31] Not so subtly Dixon introduced a few of the characters from *Uncle Tom's Cabin* to make his argument. Now George Harris reappears, still a mulatto, still a well-educated one, but now he is in love with a daughter of a prominent Northern political leader, who instantly sees the error of his ways when Harris asks for her hand. This routine became a cliché in the language of racist argumentation for two generations. Dixon always denied having any but "the friendliest feelings and the profoundest pity" for blacks, and maintained that his book was "the most important moral deed of my life. There is not a bitter or malignant sentence in it." Dixon's brother, A. C. Dixon, who was also a minister, accused him of writing his book for profit, and the aging father once reproached his son for being too hard on the black man, who had too much to bear in any case.[32]

The Clansman followed in 1905 and was used a decade later as the main plot for Griffith's famous film. This novel was openly aimed to redirect sympathies on the main events of the postwar Reconstruction, which it described in lurid detail. There were political aspects surrounding its appearance and reception that indicated the time was ripe for the North to take a more Southern point of view. The central figure of the story is a Southern war hero named Ben Cameron, who has returned home to the Southern Piedmont after convalescing from a serious wound in a Washington, D.C., hospital. He has, of course, fallen madly in love with his attractive nurse, a Northern girl who happens to be the daughter of the United States senator Austin Stoneman. Stoneman is a very, very thinly veiled impersonation of Thaddeus Stevens, whose grim countenance has long graced the American-history textbooks with the appropriate indication beneath identifying him as the chief of the "Vindictives" in Congress, those who wished to impose a severe punishment on the South after the end of the war.

Few scholars today would accord Congressman Stevens that importance, and all would be aware that there was much more at stake in Reconstruction than punishing the South. But in Dixon's story the wicked forces of vengeance in Congress are released by the assassination of Lincoln, for Radical leaders are able to blame the South for this terrible deed, and they employ it to impose a reign of terror on the prostrate Southern states. This is accomplished by the simple expedient of disenfranchising all the white people who have had anything to do with the war, and enfranchising the slaves.

There are significant changes in the film version, but in both book and film black voters are manipulated by wicked Northerners who have come south to humiliate Southern whites, especially the old owners, who suffer many indignities before they resort to violence. Insults were endured by a law-abiding people, but once the safety of pure white womanhood was in danger they did not hesitate, and the hero of the action, Ben Cameron, becomes the leader of the Ku Klux Klan, organized to punish perpetrators of rape. This secret organization, the real centerpiece of Dixon's story, became in his hands the saving instrument of Southern civilization. That it was connected in some way with the rise in the 1920s of the modern Klan is hard to dispute, though Dixon tried to dissociate them altogether, and disapproved of the new Klan.[33] Throughout the story there are many history lessons. One is given by young Ben Cameron when he courts Senator Stoneman's daughter. Elsie Stoneman "began to understand why the war, which had seemed to her a wicked, cruel, and causeless rebellion, was the one inevitable thing in our growth from a loose group of sovereign states to a United Nation. Love had given her his point of view."[34]

Actually the nation itself was having a kind of love feast, celebrating over these years the fiftieth anniversary of the beginning and close of the Civil War. A new, highly symbolic interpretation of the conflict and is close was being worked out, not, of course, by Ben Cameron and Elsie Stoneman alone, but by serious scholars, including Woodrow Wilson, the future president. While ready to pay tribute to the heroism of the Confederate soldiers, and the sacrifices to the lost cause, the South should be glad that the North had won and ended slavery, he said, for its was "enervating our Southern society and exhausting our Southern energies."[35] This new view could arrange a classic historiographical quid pro quo between North and South on the basis of agreement on both sides that the North had been right about the Civil War, that secession had been wrong, and that through the suppression of secession had come the end of slavery, which was a good thing, especially for white people.

On the other hand, the Northern leaders had been much mistaken in their Reconstruction policy—"damnable cruelty and folly," Woodrow Wilson had called it—and their attempt to enforce equal rights for the former slave had been a grave injustice to Southern white people. The sensationalism of Dixon's demonology cast a lurid glare over his fictional history, but many respectable persons, some of them scholars of repute, shared his views if not his style. The images of bestial sexuality and yellow eyes gleaming in the jungle, and the apelike characterizations in the picture seared themselves into the minds of the thousands who saw the film. That these parts were played by whites blacked up with burnt cork completed the irony.[36]

After Dixon's books and the Griffith film the South commanded center court on Reconstruction history for many years. One of the early reviewers of *The Clansman* asked why this should be. There were some questionable matters of historical detail, but more significant was "the apparent ease with which the author makes a decidedly plausible presentation of his defense of the

Southern attitude, and the apparent readiness of the Northern mind to receive that defense in unruffled patience, if not with positive favor." He commented that only a few years earlier such ideas would have been rejected instantly, for American orators were praising political equality as "the immediate jewel of our national soul."[37] The reviewer saw the answer: it was that the idea of political equality was "dangerous and ill-defined," and that "whether it was formerly so or not, the North must now bear with the South its equal share of responsibility for those dangers."[38]

The author might have added that the increased immigration from southern Europe caused many old friends of freedom in the North to wonder if the South hadn't been right in opposing equal franchise. The growth of urban political machines and the power of political bosses over these people whose appearance and languages were strange seemed to threaten the world they had understood. And so the steady march of segregation in the South went largely unopposed. With *Plessy* v. *Ferguson* in 1896 the Supreme Court gave approval to the doctrine of separate but equal. Only one dissenter, the Kentucky-born John Marshall Harlan, reasoned that separate facilities were inherently unequal and designed to fill the excluded with self-contempt; it would be fifty years before a new Supreme Court would see that he was right.

The dominant view of the Civil War epoch popularized at the turn of the century remained powerful down to World War II, when it was at last challenged to its roots by the Nazi holocaust. Then the hypocrisy of maintaining so great a struggle in the name of democracy so badly abused at home smote the consciences of thoughtful citizens. But even before that time the Dixon demonology was much abated, almost directly in proportion to the degree to which the black man was rendered insignificant in the ballot box and invisible at the soda fountains.

After World War I the black image in books and plays is muted and more often assumed than it is explained and illustrated. Dixon's success is registered in this quiet acceptance. The classic example of this tendency was Margaret Mitchell's *Gone With the Wind*, which appeared in 1936, and launched the greatest publishing-viewing extravaganza of all time.[39]

The point to remember about this work was that it had the same power to sweep its readers and audiences into the state Henry James described in the *Uncle Tom* experience. It became a state of mind and as much a part of the late years of the Depression as *Uncle Tom* had been in the 1850s. On June 30, 1936, the day of publication, 100 thousand copies were in print; in three months the figure had nearly quadrupled; and within six months the then unheard-of figure of one million had been sold. The naughty heroine, Scarlett O'Hara, has had the international appeal of Uncle Tom, and as soon as the David O. Selznick movie plans became known, casting the main characters of the story became a favorite parlor game. There were important differences between the book and the play, but together they registered completely the national state of mind about race and region.

Margaret Mitchell had read Dixon's books early in life, and had as a girl-playwright actually adapted one of them for a neighborhood theatrical for her playmates to enact. Miss Mitchell acknowledged this influence in a graceful letter thanking the aging Dixon for writing her a fan letter. She acknowledged Dixon further, and less directly, by using his view of the rise of the Ku Klux Klan to explain the phenomenon in her book.[40] But on the whole the picture of race relations in Margaret Mitchell's work is more paternalistic, and the "good darkies" are highly significant elements of the plot. It is the reverse of the case in *The Clansman*, where the "bad niggers" are important to the action, and the good ones merely background. Mammy is essential to *Gone With the Wind*, and Hattie McDaniel's grand execution of her role in the movie won her an Oscar. She made even more of "Mammy" in the film than Miss Mitchell had in her book, and in doing so disarmed much black criticism that might otherwise have come upon the plantation stereotypes the modern Negro had begun so much to hate.[41]

It was a step forward, if a very small one, to see what a great black actress could make of the stock figure of the plantation mammy. For the most part the rendering of blacks as the happy, carefree plantation darkies was the natural consequence of Mitchell's celebration of the romantic plantation legend. Until the image of black as beast was thrust aside it made no sense to paint a picture of a period of peace and plenty, white columns and peacocks, cotton and serenity back before the war. Dixon had not tried it, and contented himself with some rather simple conclusions about the affectionate, God-fearing life pursued by his Scots-Irish ancestors in the Upcountry of the western Carolinas.

One reason for *Gone With the Wind*'s success was that it became the first fully realized film version of the traditional plantation romance. But it had enough realism, just enough, to make it credible. There is a recognition of economic force in historical explanation totally absent from Dixon. The renegade aristocrat Rhett Butler is Scarlett's supremely realistic romantic foil; he tells the young Southern cavaliers so anxious to get into war that they cannot win. Why not? Not enough munitions plants and woolen mills. What if there should be a blockade, as there surely would be?[42] It was quite as though Miss Mitchell had been reading Charles Beard's economic interpretation of American history. After the heroine returns to the ruined plantation near the end of the war and faces starvation, she becomes frenetic in her pursuit of security. Her trouble has been great, to be sure, and after a dramatic gesture choking on a raw turnip she has devoured to assuage her great hunger, outlined against a red sky, she pledges that she will never be hungry again.

Scarlett solves her problems, essentially by doing what her folks would have called "outyankeeing the Yankees." She goes into trade, and gets for herself a store in booming postwar Atlanta, and then a lumber mill. Her search for security becomes sheer greed, and her shabby dealings in business are meant as a personal characterization of the city of Atlanta itself, and by extension the New South. This is what Margaret Mitchell contributed to the growing legend. Here was a brash young city, burned out in war, rising from its ashes, a country-cousin kind of town when compared with stately, refined places like Charleston and Savannah. By implication these gentle old cities could no more cope with the crude necessities of the postwar world than Scarlett's more aristocratic friends and relatives. "Atlanta," on the other hand, it seemed, "must always be hurrying, no matter what its circumstances might be." Of course, "it was ill-bred and

Yankeefied to hurry. But Atlanta was more ill-bred and Yankeefied (after the war) than it had ever been before or would ever be again." The identification of Scarlett's character and the city is quite explicit: "Atlanta was of her own generation, crude with the crudities of youth and as headstrong and impetuous as herself."[43]

What that city became was what Scarlett herself became, and the cost of success to character in overcoming defeat is Miss Mitchell's second important theme. Atlanta celebrates the vulgarity of new wealth in the accumulation of ugly mansions with massive furniture in the dark, rich, and cloying interiors rendered so faithfully in the Selznick film. In character Scarlett is a match for this crass materialism, fulfilling her pledge that she'll never go hungry again by laying up treasures on earth through the exploitation of convict labor and many other shabby, immoral acts. Her character is meant to illustrate the cost of survival. Gentle people who represent the best of the past fare poorly, and are like Ashley Wilkes, in Rhett Butler's description of him. Such people "have neither cunning nor strength, or having them scruple to use them. And so they go under. . . ."[44] The New South creed was torn between the realism of facing the future with the spirit of Yankee enterprise and comforting its sense of loss with a new devotion to the myth of the lost world of serenity, peace, and plenty.

Therefore Margaret Mitchell was of two minds about the capacity of old aristocrats to endure. For all the Ashley Wilkeses who are going down because they lack some vital force, there are others like his wife, Melanie, who derive strength from the traditional past, who are ready to pay the price in contemporary terms for maintaining the standards of decency and honorable relations that they learned in happier times. They do not go under; but they do not get rich either. The author is almost dividing the personality of the New South between Scarlett and Melanie, for there were both aspects to the face of survival. The value the author assigns to family loyalty and the abiding devotion to land and place and people is important not only in explaining Melanie Wilkes, but also in explaining how Scarlett began her sordid life in commerce. Whatever she is, or is to become, Scarlett holds the family together, forces all to work as hard as she does, and does not scruple to lie or steal, even to sell herself, in order to raise the money that will save her father's plantation from the tax collectors.

Margaret Mitchell's fictional New South of the 1870s was influenced to a considerable degree by the experience of the 1930s' Depression. Themes of hardship and survival had special appeal to the Depression generation, who could understand without prompting how it was to be penniless and confused in the middle of a rich and fallow land. There had to be a little bit of Scarlett and a little bit of Melanie in those who came through that troubled time. Margaret Mitchell had worried ahead of publication that the South would reject the materialism of her work; indeed, Scarlett's survival owes nothing to religion, however much nostalgia she may feel for that lost religion of her good mother. But Miss Mitchell need not have concerned herself. There was the comforting image of what people liked to think their world had once been, in a time of peace and plenty, and any good Southerner could see what a great impression the work was making north of the Mason-Dixon line.

The North was going to adopt the plantation South before the war as its *own* Garden of Eden, and if Atlanta looked and behaved a lot like many New England towns and cities in the Gilded Age and after, then why not regard these qualities at a safe distance? A fully romantic vision of the Old South *and* the New served emotional appeals in both sections. The critics, like Malcolm Cowley and Bernard DeVoto, might rail to their heart's content against the false vision, and they could assail the damaging effects of a belief in the plantation myth as much as they liked, but Miss Mitchell and her friends professed themselves to be amused, and, like Haley later on, could see from the sales that there was a good market for myths, of however recent vintage.[45]

How good are these works? It would not surprise me greatly if *Gone With the Wind* eventually arrives with its strong survival credentials and wins the respect of the more discriminating critics, as *Uncle Tom's Cabin* has now shown signs of doing. *The Clansman* never will, and it is too soon to predict anything about *Roots*. There is good writing and bad in it. But it seems beside the point to assess these works as high culture, as *art*, for they do not need to be. They serve as vehicles for celebration of shared convictions, the public vehicle of new agreements on what to believe, at the growing point of American myth. It doesn't really matter whether some of us like it and some of us do not.

In conclusion may I say that I have seriously searched for other such popular reading-viewing successes that have sustained themselves for so long, and contributed to the shorthand visual images and vocabulary of the American experience in section and race as these have done. I cannot find them. It seems there must therefore be certain characteristics that have marked these books-turned-drama for special favor from the time of their initial appeparance. High inspiration, didactic purpose (in all save *Gone With the Wind*): these, plus the shared theme, pull them together. The major setting of each is the South, except for the African parts of *Roots*. Celebratory effects, mass participation, an *insistence* on sharing the experience, these are the universal style of these events. Each in its own way has positive things to say about family and affirms the force of cultural continuity. Each has appeared at just the moment when a new synthesis was forming concerning the American Civil War and race in America.

This combination of circumstances emboldens me to suppose that somewhere around the year 2000 some such thing may occur again. Whether it will be a good thing or a bad thing I do not feel obliged to guess, but that there are cautionary signals against too free a use of history as national or sectional or ethnic therapy ought to be plain enough. Popular culture, as distinguished from high culture, is widely accessible at some level to a multitude who may or may not be equipped to place what is seen in a perspective. The modern pop culture relies more on pictures than on words, and ambiguities may be lost in the impact of living color and violent action. The advent of television has opened potential problems undreamed-of in Harriet Beecher Stowe's time, when literacy first began to outstrip real education. Reading is in some degree an arranged match between reader and book; if he doesn't understand the words the reader will discard the book.

Thomas Ryan Dixon, in a successful ploy to defuse criticism of his controversial film, invited a very distinguished company of senators, congressmen, and the Supreme Court to a private viewing; and while they watched *Birth of a Nation*, he watched them: "that we had not only discovered a new universal language of man, but that an appeal to the human will through this tongue would be equally resistless [irresistible] to an audience of chauffeurs or a gathering of a thousand college professors."[46] There were few even then who could be at once as appreciative and objective as the poet Vachel Lindsay, who wrote of the film that it was a "picture of crowd splendor" in which the "Ku Klux Klan dashes down the road as powerfully as Niagara pours over the cliff" with "mobs splendidly handled, tossing wildly and rhythmically like the sea." Alas, thought Lindsay, that D. W. Griffith had put this art in service to "the Reverend Thomas Dixon's poisonous hatred of the Negro."[47]

Dixon's father and brother had more detachment than most, when they criticized him for inciting hatred for personal gain. President Woodrow Wilson called it "history written in lightning," and thought it "all too true." He had been a college professor, it is worth remembering, and had picked up some Aryan notions of his own in the same school where Dixon studied briefly.[48] If the college professors of tomorrow are to prove Dixon wrong about their own inability to resist the blandishments of "history written in lightning" they have a very large order; if they are to help others to bring a detached capacity to discern, the order is much larger. It will involve at the very least teaching more history more effectively to more students. The good teacher will be suspicious of the trendy, but sufficiently modest to recognize that what is apparent may also be real. Modesty is the appropriate reading-viewing style.

IV

Reviews of
a Generation's Views

8

An American Family

This review of Alex Haley, Roots (*New York, 1976*), *was first published in the* New York Review of Books, *November 11, 1976. Reprinted with permission from* The New York Review of Books. *Copyright © 1976 Nyrev, Inc.*

Roots is about lineage and blood, history and suffering, and the need to know about these things. The need-to-know is Alex Haley's. Why and how the author of *The Autobiography of Malcolm X* has driven himself for a dozen years to find his own bloodlines, or one strain at least, is almost as intriguing as the saga that has been the result. The costs have been high in time and energy. The author could hardly have guessed twelve years ago that the work would earn him a million dollars and be one of the major publishing events of the year, but he scoured libraries and archives in two continents, consulted university professors of African history and languages, and read widely in history and anthropology. He lectured freely along the way to keep himself going.

All of this he did to connect the stories his grandmother told on the front porch of her Henning, Tennessee, home with the remote African homeland of the most vivid personality in Grandmother Cynthia's tales. Her family originated in America, so it had been told through many generations, with a young African named Kunta Kinte, a man so rebellious that he made four attempts to escape his new owner, received as many vicious beatings, and on the last attempt had half his right foot severed in punishment.

As Haley's story develops (and one cannot tell from the book where Grandmother Cynthia's story leaves off and Haley's research begins), young Kunta was brought in 1767 to Annapolis, Maryland, at the age of seventeen, aboard the slaver *Lord Ligonier*, and soon thereafter taken into Spotsylvania County, Virginia, where he began a long, cruel, and imperfect adjustment to the ways of the white man and his plantation. After monumental effort, and not a little blind luck, Haley found his way back to the African Kunta, alive in the oral tradition of West Africa, stored in the memory of a *griot*, a village storyteller whose memory bank included, among thousands of other matters, the bloodlines of Kinte's people, and the very story Grandmother Cynthia herself had told about how young Kunta had met foul play one day when he had gone to the forest to cut wood for a new drum and was captured by slave traders.

One concrete story. Not much perhaps, but enough to convince Haley that he had brought together two oral traditions separated by two centuries, that he had connected his own American family with an ancient and distinguished tradition of West Africa. Haley promises another volume soon that will explain his search for his roots, that will outline the detective work, and perhaps some of the emotional experience that accompanied his own journey from America to Africa and back again. But for the moment we must assume that something stronger than curiosity, and an urge different in more than degree, separates him from the would-be members of the Daughters of the American Revolution or other likeminded patrons of the census room at the National Archives. Haley's need must have owed not a little to simply knowing the name of the man who made that cruel involuntary journey to America; blood can't be thicker than water until the name is known. But once it is, honor, justice, and loyalty are possible.

Haley's need to know must also be related to the particular pain of *not* knowing shared by most Afro-Americans whose history was so curiously mislaid in America, cast aside as a first sacrifice to survival on the plantations of the New World. Thus Haley's search becomes the vicarious search of many others who hadn't Haley's good fortune in having a Grandmother Cynthia, or for that matter an original Afro-American parent who troubled to

stitch American places and things into the memories of his prog-
eny with African names, leaving clues for the Alex Haley yet-
to-be to follow, as Theseus followed Ariadne's thread out of the
labyrinth.

In pressing backward with his clues, his stories, his tracing of
words like *bolongo* for river (Kamby Bolongo for Gambia
River), *yiro* for tree, *tilo* for sun, Haley at last identified two of
his potential 124 great-great-great-great-great-grandparents, the
mother and father of Kunta Kinte, a pair of high birth and envi-
able social status named Omoro and Binta of the village of Juffure,
not far from the Gambia coast. In Haley's imagining of them, the
pair become almost mythical, with the irreducible qualities of
parenthood ennobled. They are Moslem, and speak the Mandinka
tongue. They provide well for their children, drawing them con-
fidently by proper stages into the rich culture to which they are
born. Nobody could be shamed by the grave and dignified Omoro
or the accomplished Binta. Nor, one should add, think to shame
them either. Their parenting of Kunta reveals more about Haley's
reading in West African anthropology and history than of specific
information about this particular couple, but the imagined specifics of their lives and their natures carry the conviction of all
stories that have been told many many times: what signifies is not
how things were, but how things ought to have been.

If their descendant's book survives either as literature or as
history, which only time will tell, Omoro and Binta Kinte could
possibly become the African proto-parents of millions of Americans who are going to admire their dignity and grace. When
asked whether and how true *Roots* is to life, Haley is reported
to have responded that it is "factional," a strange term that suggests that the primary incidents and historical moments are true,
but that in reconstructing the emotions of his personalities in the
grip of their fates, in supposing their motives, indeed, in filling
their mouths with conversation, he has done the best he could, as
other writers of historical fiction try to do.

Roots is not precisely an historical novel, because the main car-
riers of the story were indeed true people. Although it is clear that
Haley has few specific facts about the three Africans—Omoro,
Binta, and Kunta—even they are more than exclusive construc-

tions of the author's imagination. Nevertheless there is as much fiction as fact in *Roots*, some of it designed to lift the spirit, some to amuse, and all of it to tell the collective story of a people. *Roots* hasn't the plot of a novel but in following the generations it has instead the spirit as well as the form of a saga.

Sagas are usually told in episodes, and for that reason *Roots* is particularly well adapted to television. ABC, as modern minstrel, will not be stingy. A record $6 million is going into a sequence of ten installments. A new Juffure has been created in Georgia for filming the village scenes, and the slave ship is apparently a shocker of realism. Black residents of the Savannah area serving as secondary characters demanded higher wages when they found how horrible playing captives aboard the slave ship will really be. Success for Haley, and for Georgia, on the scale of *Gone With the Wind*'s, seems secure; only time will say more, but the signs are auspicious. The first requirement of a saga is that it must keep going, and *Roots* does. I wouldn't miss the TV movie for the world.

Haley has no trouble beginning his saga, and getting it moving. But the problem of characterizing the individual people of so many generations, of making more than a score of persons come alive in the special circumstances of two vastly different cultures, and over a span of two centuries, challenges Haley the artist, and taxes Haley the historian. There are long sections in the book that will cause the historian to call *Roots* fiction, when literary critics may prefer to call it history rather than judge it as art. For *Roots* is long and ambitious, and all of its parts are not as good as the best parts.

The splendid opening section on African life is beautifully realized. It is an *artistic* success. But that the real Juffure of two hundred years ago was anything like the pastoral village Haley describes is not possible. Whatever bucolic character Juffure may have today, it was in the eighteenth century a busy trading center, inhabited by possibly as many as 3,000 people. It was the chief city of Ndanco Sono, the powerful king of N̄omi who tightly controlled (through customs charges) all comings and goings on the Gambia River. He was ever alert to possible infringements of agreements made with the English and the French that might diminish his appointed part of the profits from the slave "factory" on James Island (within full view of Juffure). The king had only to cut off their food and water to bring them to their knees.

In the year Kunta was captured, a commercial war was brewing between N̄omi and the English because of English reluctance to pay the king's customs for the mere privilege of passing further up the river in pursuit of the slave trade.

Nomi countered by threatening to stop ships from taking on extra crews and interpreters in N̄omi, as they had been doing for decades. The British had the guns of the fort but N̄omi had a fleet of war "canoes," each carrying forty or fifty men armed with muskets. For a time it was a standoff, but quarrels of this kind rarely led to serious fighting or a long stoppage of trade, since neither side profited when trade stopped altogether.[1]

It is inconceivable at any time, but particularly under these circumstances, that two white men should have dared to come ashore in the vicinity of Juffure to capture Kunta Kinte, even in the company of two Africans, as Haley describes it. The capture of Kunta, or indeed of any other subject of the king of N̄omi, owner of an estimated one hundred of those formidable "canoes," would have invited a terrible punishment. It would have been exacted indiscriminately on the crew of the next English ship that Ndanco Sono could lay his hands on.

It could well be that there is an important truth in giving Kunta Kinte a garden of Eden to grow up in that simply outdistances any historical fact. Myth pursues its truth largely outside the realm of reality. But if there were other villages more like the one Haley's hero grew up in, they were at some distance from Juffure. Actually, the section on Kunta's childhood owes more to modern anthropology than to history. In fact history seems entirely suspended in the African section. No external events disturb the peaceful roots of Kunta Kinte's childhood.

Once Haley learned the probable experiences of a Mandinka youth up to the age of seventeen, he simply handed those experiences to Kunta. This works, and Haley has only to relate the passage of time to the idealized life of a lad who learns fast. The scenes in the forest as Kunta travels with his father are memorable for their serenity; when Kunta goes to his training for manhood we share his fear and pride; we understand his complex relations with his brother, and with his mother, who is, like Juno, occasionally jealous. All of this is clearly Haley's creation, and not a product of Grandmother Cynthia's remembering, but these moments are convincing in ways that some of the New World scenes are not.

Conveying the passage of time becomes a serious problem, both aesthetically and historically, after Kunta Kinte reaches America. Haley writes with power, and often with lyrical effect, but his feeling for the probable talk of slaves is often marred by a too-exposed mechanical purpose. He puts these conversations up to little lessons in history that are more distracting than informative. He has difficulty showing how the information picked up at the white man's dinner table, or from the driver's seat of the massa's buggy, or from a surreptitiously read newspaper, is relayed in the kitchen and the quarters. In one scene, for example, the subject is the United States' undeclared naval war with France of 1798, and Toussaint L'Ouverture's struggle for an independent black Haiti. The Big-House cook has the floor:

> "You 'members few months back when one dem tradin' boats got raided somewhere on de big water by dat France?".
> Kunta nodded. "Fiddler say he heard dat Pres'dent Adams so mad he sent de whole Newnited States Navy to whup 'em."
> "Well, dey sho' did. Louvina [the waitress just back from the dining room] jes' now tol' me dat man in dere from Richmon' say dey done took away eighty boats b'longin' to dat France. She say de white folks in dere act like dey nigh 'bout ready to start singin' an' dancin' 'bout teachin' dat France a lesson."

What follows is about "dat Haiti," where "dat Toussaint" is struggling against a revolt led by a "*mulatto*" and how "Massa Waller" thinks Toussaint too dumb to run a country, and that "all dem slaves dat done got free in dat Haiti gwine wind up whole lot wuss off dan dey was under dey ol' massas." The too frequent "dat" spoils the cadence, which is otherwise not unreasonable, even when it is staged.

Kunta Kinte's own life poses no such problems about time for Haley, for the process of assimilation is one of the strongest and subtlest themes in *Roots*. For the miseries of Kunta in the land of "*toubob*" (white man), the reader will not only feel a vivid sympathy; he may even laugh a little at the incomprehensible ways of Kunta's captors. There was a word, for instance, that bothered Kunta from the beginning. He heard it often, "What," he wondered, "was a nigger?" Kunta, the devout Moslem, was daily offended by the smell and sight of pork, which he never knowingly tasted. (These people "even fed the filthy things.") Especially effective is the inner contempt the African hero (for that is his role) feels for those of his color who shuffle and scrape when they say "Yassuh, Massa." Those who had learned this manner of dealing with power returned Kunta's contempt with a predictable suspicion, for they saw in the African's wild ways the courage of desperation, and its dangers.

It is all convincing, for we are made to feel that inevitably this is how things happened. We know as well that Kunta must at last bow a little or die, and we know that he will live. We recognize that he will marry Bell because she is kind to him, and looks like a woman of his people. He will marry her in spite of her noisy Christianity and her generous vision of their massa, whom she regards as being a human being, to Kunta an amazing idea. We know that Kunta and Bell must have a child, as they do, so that Grandmother Cynthia may be eventually informed about all that happened to the African while he was discovering so painfully what "nigger" means.

But the account of the external conditions in which Kunta lives in Virginia before, during, and after the American Revolution is disconcerting. The reader of any basic book on southern history will be startled to learn that Kunta was put to work picking cotton in northern Virginia before the Revolution (or ever, really), under the whip of an overseer, in fields loaded with the white stuff "as far as Kunta could see." Surely this is Alabama in 1850, and not Spotsylvania County, Virginia, in 1767. Haley next employs Kunta at wire fencing, nearly a century ahead of its general use. Okra is a food little known, even now, in the Old Dominion, and the expletive "cracker" has never had much currency there either. This reviewer has not seen the word "redneck" in antebellum writings, and only rarely afterward until it achieved political and pejorative connotations in the twentieth century. "Po' white" was the word in Virginia straight along.

These anachronisms are petty only in that they are details. They are too numerous, and chip away at the verisimilitude of central matters in which it is important to have full faith. Are the attitudes ascribed here to whites realistic for the different periods in which they are said to occur? Attitudes toward slaves being taught to read or write? Toward possible insurrection? On the private right of emancipation? In conflating several generations of the institutional history of slavery Haley has only done what most modern historians of slavery tend to do. But the cost of such conflation for a book pursuing a narrative line is naturally higher, and every small confusion of fact, time, or place becomes more exposed.

Haley's sense of historical setting becomes more sure-footed in the pre–Civil War decades, and after Reconstruction, when the whole family moves under the guidance of the steady blacksmith Tom to Henning, Tennessee. The appearance of such memorable characters as "Chicken George" in a more crowded field of relatives and ancestors enlivens the close of *Roots*. Chicken George, by reputation the greatest gamecocker in North Carolina, is too fantastic not to be real. His services were won from George's hapless owner by an English lord in a game at high stakes, and George was carried off to England to train the nobleman's cockerels. He stayed there more years than his devout wife Matilda cared to recall, but reappeared in his classic style, on horseback, "wearing a flowing green scarf and a black derby with a curving rooster tail feather jutting up from the hatband." He died in 1890 at the age of eighty-three.

Sagas must have many persons and many stories, many deeds. But there should be one dominant soul, and in *Roots* it is Kunta Kinte, whose gloomy intelligence inspires the action through three-fifths of the work. Kunta's final departure from the book (and not by death) is its most poignant moment, and the subtlest statement on the finality of slavery that this reviewer has read. Kunta has counted the months and years of his bondage by putting a small stone in a gourd every full moon, so that he may eventually determine how many rains (or years) he has lived. Kunta had been twenty rains in toubob's land before he married Bell, and his beloved daughter Kizzy had soon blessed their love.

It was through Kizzy, and only through her, that the African's stories were passed to her son, Chicken George, and from him to the somber blacksmith, his son Tom, and on at last to Grandmother Cynthia. Kizzy was not yet twenty herself when the unthinkable (for Kunta and Bell at least) happened on one dreadful morning. With lightning swiftness Kizzy was torn from her parents and turned over to the sheriff, who sold her into another state. Her parents' high position in "Massa Waller's" favor could not save her from his wrath when he learned that Kizzy had aided her sweetheart in attempting an escape.

Kunta, felled by a blow from the departing sheriff's pistol butt, recovered only to recall in a dazed way what was done in Africa to assure the safe return of traveling loved ones. He limped to his cabin door and scooped up in his hands the clearest print of Kizzy's foot he could find in the dust. Bursting into his cabin, his eye fell upon his gourd as a place to put his dust, but the finality of what had happened then came upon him, and he knew that Kizzy was gone forever.

His face contorting, Kunta flung his dust toward the cabin's roof. Tears bursting from his eyes, snatching his heavy gourd up high over his head, his mouth wide in a soundless scream, he hurled the gourd down with all his strength, and it shattered against the packed-earth floor, his 662 pebbles representing each month of his 55 rains flying out, ricocheting wildly in all directions.

Halfway into the next page, the reader knows that Kunta too is gone forever, that only through Kizzy could more be learned of her father; only through her could Grandmother Cynthia learn. Only in death or a fairy tale could Kizzy hope to return to Virginia. In its perfect finality, slavery was no fairy tale.

9

Killing for Freedom

Biographers of men who lived in violent times have the special problem of dealing with the abstractions about means and ends that clutter the rhetoric of political systems in a state of polarization. When do men mean what they say? How a biographer's subject responds to a call to action may come as near as anything else to exposing the inner quality of the man, the elusive combination of impulse, emotion, practicality, and reason that we call character. The recent publication in paperback of the two standard biographies of Frederick Douglass, the first written in 1948 by Benjamin Quarles,[1] and the second in 1950 by Philip Foner,[2] who edited Douglass's writings at the same time,[3] invites a reconsideration of this dynamic editor and orator, America's most important black abolitionist, who lived in violent times.

Two of Douglass's three autobiographical works have also been reissued recently. The first of these is *My Bondage and My Freedom*, written in 1855, and the second is an illustrated edition of Douglass's final autobiography, written shortly before his death in 1895.[4] It appears now in a much edited and reduced version by Genevieve S. Gray, intended for young readers.[5] The handsome drawings by Scott Duncan add much to the charm of the volume, although they have in some instances a very tenuous relation to the text. Benjamin Quarles's *Black Abolitionists*,[6] the first general study, contributes much to our understanding of Douglass by considering him in the company of his fellow black militants as they grappled with the question of means and ends in the anti-slavery cause.

A few years before the Civil War, Douglass faced the choice between the rhetorical justification of force in the emancipation of slaves, and the use of physical violence to that end. Stephen Oates's exciting new biography of John Brown,[7] together with a new edition of Louis Ruchames's collected letters and eulogies of Brown, *The Making of a Revolutionary*,[8] provides a fresh view of the man who brought Douglass to that choice.

The only book among the seven under review failing to mention the last meeting of those two famous abolitionists is the only one that was written before the meeting took place. When Douglass wrote *My Bondage and My Freedom*, he was thirty-eight years old, and had been well acquainted with John Brown for approximately seven years. John Brown had already caused Douglass to rethink his earlier commitment to the pacifism of the Garrisonian abolitionists, but the relationship between the two men had not reached its dramatic culmination. This took place on August 19, 1859, two months before Brown's attack on the federal arsenal at Harper's Ferry, when Douglass met Brown secretly in an abandoned stone quarry near Chambersburg, Pennsylvania. For three days the old guerilla captain discussed with the young orator the uses of violence in the pursuit of justice.

The question was specific. Would Douglass join John Brown and his small band of raiders in their attack on the arsenal, and provide, as Brown planned that they would, a signal for a mass rising of the slaves? Only Douglass, who had enormous influence among all blacks, free as well as slave, would perfectly serve Brown's purpose. "When I strike," he urged, "the bees will begin to swarm, and I shall need you to help hive them."

Douglass would not. He saw that Brown's plan, since they had last discussed it together, had undergone a fatal expansion of purpose. Opening a front of guerilla activity in the Virginia mountains, offering slaves an escape route to the North and ultimately to Canada, would have been risky, but it was conceivable.

To a raid on a United States arsenal in a slave state, with the purpose of inciting servile insurrection, there could be only one outcome. To argue with John Brown was always futile, as his old friend surely knew, and Douglass left him at last to his own disastrous vision of justice and glory. Douglass next had positive news of Brown after the assault had failed and Brown's men were scattered or killed. The survivors awaited trial for treason in the jail at Charlestown, in company of their wounded captain.

Douglass's biographers have tended to accept Douglass's own explanation that his refusal to join John Brown was based on expediency, an unwillingness to undertake a hopeless cause. Douglass said at the time, and never altered the story, that in the Harper's Ferry test he was "most miserably deficient in courage," and that he had been smarter than to promise John Brown his presence in the action. Nevertheless one wonders if in fact Douglass was not deterred by a fundamental aversion to real violence. The haunting question that the biographers of all Brown's allies and co-conspirators somehow miss asking is how well did Brown's eastern men know the man whom they supported with every encouragement that money could buy until he was captured, and whom they joined ranks to canonize after the execution?

Although Douglass was not one of the famous "Secret Six" who joined the Brown conspiracy, he probably knew more about John Brown than any of them. No more than they, however, was he in a position to tell all he knew. To ask, that he sacrifice the legendary John Brown, whom he had helped to create, to the historical John Brown was asking too much.

America's national saint, her martyr on the altar of freedom, was a man of blood and violence, who died at the wrong time, in the wrong place, for the wrong crime, if crime it was. The main facts of the life and death of John Brown have long been available to anyone interested in gaining access to them, but unfortunately for the credibility of history, few historians, not to speak of the dramatists and propagandists, have had the courage to assemble those facts and consider them dispassionately for their historical meaning.

This is a pity, because the lesson to be learned from such an exercise ought not to be lost on an age much in need of instruction on the relationship of intellectuals to revolutionaries, and of rhetoric to violence. Most of the unresolved questions about John Brown concern those who accepted him at his own evaluation of himself, for the simple reason that in their opinion he found the best cause in the world to die for.

On December 2, 1859, Brown, a grizzled man of fifty-nine, old beyond those years, died on the gallows for having organized an attack on a federal arsenal. He made the gallows glorious as the cross, Emerson and Thoreau said, and there were hundreds of other favorable comparisons made to the Holy Founder of Christianity, comparisons that appeared at the time to be at least partially authenticated by the dignity with which the martyr met his death. The praise of John Brown has been continuous from that time to this, but never has it been unanimous.

On only one point are the John Brown writers in reasonable agreement: the Governor of Virginia made a primary mistake in allowing the execution. For those who looked only upon Brown's last year, upon his revolutionary attempt to expand the liberty promised by this republic to its people, Brown had paid the supreme price exacted by a slaveholding state which, by its very existence, denied that promise. For other writers, the governor's mistake was tactical. He missed the opportunity to excuse Brown on grounds of insanity, which would have had the contemporary effect of voiding Brown's own wish (in which most of his erstwhile supporters concurred) to make himself a symbolic martyr to the cause of freedom, and the historical effect of obliging scholars to ask whether John Brown was in fact mentally responsible for his acts. It would also have had the effect of forcing scholars undertaking this question to explore the whole of John Brown's life as carefully and thoroughly as the end of it.

Stephen Oates has done this, and has given us the most objective and absorbing biography of John Brown ever written. Its title, *To Purge This Land with Blood*, captures perfectly Brown's own conception of his role in the antislavery crusade. Oates describes with subtlety and detail John Brown's early career, his struggles with poverty, illness, and death, the desperate straits the man was put to in support of his large family of twenty children. He tells us that Brown came to the armed phase of his abolitionist career at the end of many business ventures and as many failures, unsuccessful speculations, lawsuits, and bankruptcies, even misappropriation of funds. Brown dealt with his family as a stern Calvinist, fearful that his neglect in punishment of even the smallest faults would advance the work of the devil. Only rarely did his tenderness find expression, but Oates shows that it was there.

In John Brown's career in the Kansas territory, as leader of a small guerilla band of Free State men, Oates finds the occasion to explain the messianic streak that compelled Brown to become first a criminal and then a saint. To Oates's credit, he describes John Brown's crime as unflinchingly as he describes his hardships, endured under what Brown took to be the chastisement of God.

Lawrence, the main town of the Free State government in the territory, had been attacked and burned by proslavery forces bent on driving the Free State men out of Kansas. Brown undertook to become God's instrument of vengeance. On a moonless night in May, 1856, he took four of his sons, a son-in-law, and two other followers and separated himself from the main body of armed settlers. This band descended upon the sleeping community of Pottawatomie Creek, where Brown called forth from their homes five men and had his band hack them to death with swords he had sharpened especially for the purpose. After washing the murder weapons in the waters of the creek, Brown went into hiding with his men, and began the career of outlawry in the cause of freedom that certain newspapers at the time, and many historians since, have found heroic.

Oates shows plainly that these murders, which Brown's defenders have preferred to call "reprisals," instead of helping the cause of freedom in Kansas, began the worst phase of the undeclared war on the frontier. What Brown had to contribute after Pottawatomie as a guerilla captain was insignificant, for he could take orders from no one, nor could he cooperate with other leaders to any common purpose.

The astonishing thing about Brown's contemporaries and historians since, who have built and protected the legendary Brown, is the indifference they have shown to Brown's victims. Who has asked the names and ages of the slain men, or whether they were guilty of anything, or if they were in fact a threat to other settlers in the region? Louis Ruchames, for example, describes them simply with the opprobrious word "proslavery."

There were no slaveholders among Brown's victims, two of the men were hardly men at all, being twenty-two and twenty respectively, and there would have been a fourteen-year-old boy among the dead if his mother had not interceded for his life. The one thing the adults had in common was an association with a court that was shortly to hear a case in which Brown would be a defendant. So great is the investment of presumably "liberal" scholars in the legendary Brown that they often stoop to intellectual blackmail of other scholars who explore the pre–Harper's Ferry Brown carefully. Ruchames, for instance, in his Introduction to the Brown letters singles out James Malin's older work,[9] where for the first time Brown's Kansas career was fully described, and refers to the author as one

> . . . who seems unable to forgive the North for having used force against Southern secession, or the Abolitionists for having taught that the abolition of slavery would be a step forward for American society, or the Negro for having believed that his welfare would be furthered by a forceful elimination of slavery.

Whatever Mr. Malin's failures in scholarship or objectivity may have been, Mr. Ruchames does not answer any of the charges Malin brought against Brown. Nor will his charges against Malin be convincing so long as Ruchames identifies Brown with that group of antislavery men and women who were "devoted to the highest ideals of equality and democracy, influenced by the best in the Judaeo-Christian tradition and all that was good and noble in the thoughts and actions of the Founding Fathers."

Presumably Ruchames feels that Brown was justified at Pottawatomie Creek by the "historical context." In support of that view he cites expressions made some twenty years after the event by Brown's neighbors, who by that time had a considerable moral investment in the legend. Oates, however, makes it clear enough that, although many acts of violence had been perpetrated upon the Free States settlers, and certainly many threats had been uttered, nothing that preceded Pottawatomie justified Brown's cold-blooded act, and that the event marked the beginning of the most vicious period of an undeclared guerilla war. John Brown's own neighbors were unanimous and unequivocal in their condemnation of the massacre at the time it took place.

One by one Oates strips away the excuses Brown's contemporaries and later historians have used to shield Brown's memory from the responsibility for his act, even to an exposure of that most unbecoming trait in martyrs, mendacity. To those who *knew* his guilt, Brown declared, "God is my judge," and to those who did not, he simply denied it. Sometimes this denial was accomplished with stunning craftiness. Mr. Ruchames's volume includes a letter that Brown wrote to his wife shortly after the killings. He reported that he had left the main body of armed Free Staters with his "little company" and

> . . . encountered quite a number of pro-slavery men, and took quite a number of prisoners. Our prisoners we let go; but we kept some four or five horses. We were immediately after this accused of murdering five men at Pottawatomie, and great efforts have since been made to capture us.

He asked his wife to send a copy of this letter to Gerrit Smith, the rich philanthropist of Petersboro, New York, who was Brown's chief financial supporter, because he knew "of no other way to get these facts . . . before the world. . . ." Such an elliptical and technical view of the truth, advanced with glittering sincerity, goes far to explain the influence of Brown upon the eastern antislavery intellectuals who subsequently joined the conspiracy that led to Harper's Ferry, and supplied the money for the insurrection Brown planned. C. Vann Woodward pointed out nearly twenty years ago that John Brown understood these sophisticates very well and that he "could have told them much that they did not know about the psychology of fellow travelers."[10] But their gullibility is still hard to explain.

Unlike Ruchames, Oates sees clearly in the crime at Pottawatomie certain unheroic elements that sit poorly with the saint of Harper's Ferry and the Charlestown jail. In the shadow of the gallows Brown engineered his legend as he wanted it to endure, and made the fullest use of the platform afforded by his trial. His words in those last weeks were patient, brave, forgiving, and entirely convincing. But he did not stick to the truth. He denied having planned an insurrection, and insisted that he had merely planned to provide a haven for refugees in the mountains. Frederick Douglass knew better, for that had been the substance of their dispute at Chambersburg. Apparently it was never subsequently in Douglass's interest to expose the "inaccuracies and falsehoods"—to use Oates's phrase—of Brown's testimony at his trial.

Making a sensible connection between the John Brown of Kansas and the John Brown of Harper's Ferry has been the great challenge for Brown's biographers. James Malin and the other anti-Brown writers do so by interpreting Brown as a wicked person of completely ruthless expediency who welcomed the opportunity to carry on a life of brigandage; others have taken at face value the nineteen affidavits of insanity in Brown's immediate family offered at the time of his trial. Oates accepts neither pattern of explanation. He is not convinced by the affidavits, and he points to Brown's brilliant exploitation of his position at his trial to obtain the maximum benefit for the antislavery cause as a sign of complete sanity.

Both Ruchames and Oates point out that calling a man insane for hating slavery enough to make a war on it is misguided, to say the least. In such times those who hate slavery less may also be called a little mad. It is only fair to point out, however, that it is not his hatred of slavery that has caused historians to call Brown mad; it is also right to say that there is nothing in either book that will resolve the question of John Brown's mental health. One's mode of behavior delineates madness, not one's convictions. At this point, of course, no clinical proof or conclusive answer is possible, because aside from Brown's acts, about which one may believe what one will, the main evidence rests with the affidavits, which were gathered for the purpose of saving Brown's life.

Both Ruchames and Oates avoid the explanation of insanity, but beyond that point the similarity in interpretation ends abruptly. Ruchames manages some forty pages of introduction without mentioning the religious aspects of Brown's nonconforming abolitionism, or the man's curious identification with the bloody heroes of the Old Testament who served Jehovah with the sword.

For Oates, Brown's Calvinist view of the world, and of man's time of trial in that world, is central to understanding him. He sees this as the essential matter that set Brown apart from the other abolitionists of his time, Douglass included.

Brown's was the sword of Gideon, which did not discriminate or make fine distinctions among its victims in the service of the Lord. For Ruchames, Brown is explained, even justified, by his pure hatred of slavery and slaveholders. Brown's concentration on their extirpation, though "intense and unusual for his day," was, in Ruchames's opinion, "not unusual" when compared to that of William Lloyd Garrison, Wendell Phillips, Theodore Parker, and the other great abolitionists. Of course it was unusual. Brown was ready to employ violence, even to murder, and none of the rest was ready to do so. Theodore Parker did enter Brown's conspiracy and supported him with money, but he asked to be kept in ignorance about the specific plans.

It is likely that this distinction between word and deed was exactly what prevented Douglass from going further with John Brown than Theodore Parker did. But Brown seems to have held the black man more responsible. It appears that in his last days John Brown reserved his only bitter words for Frederick Douglass. A visitor in the Charlestown jail recalled that Brown told her husband of a "great opportunity lost" that was owing "to the famous Mr. Frederick Douglass." Brown's family also in later years was under the illusion that Douglass had somehow let John Brown down, and Douglass himself often felt compelled to explain his curious relations with the old man who had become a martyr to that freedom Douglass had himself struggled so hard for.

What Douglass had done was exactly what other close associates and financial supporters, with a solitary exception, had done. He had placed himself beyond the reach of federal authority and, after the hanging, had joined other intellectuals in the canonization of a man who may have been a saint, but who was also, by any definition accepted by civilized nations in peace or war, a cold-blooded killer.

It is clear that Douglass's supposed defection had nothing to do with the fate of John Brown, which would have been the same either way. But there are many questions as yet unanswered concerning the relations of the two men. Did Douglass know about

Pottawatomie before Harper's Ferry? Did he ever know? A Congressional report of July 11, 1856, had directly connected Brown with the slaying, and there had been widespread publicity about the troubles in Kansas; but then Brown had always denied responsibility for the killings. Did Douglass and Brown's other supporters believe him innocent as he claimed to be? Or did they simply condone his acts on the basis of their "historical context" as some historians have since done?

From Douglass's final *Life and Times* comes the line that Brown was "then [at Chambersburg] under the ban of government and heavy rewards were offered for his arrest, for offenses said to have been committed in Kansas." *Said* to have been committed? Did Douglass then, so near the end of his own life, believe that there was no truth in the charges? It is doubtful. In his eulogy of Brown at Storer College in 1881, it is amazing how much more closely Douglass's verbal imagery applies to what happened out on the Kansas prairies on that May night in 1856 than to what happened in Virginia. The people were "roused from their slumbers" and they "felt the keen-edged sword of war at their throats"; and then Douglass added that "the knife is to feeling always an offense."

Douglass believed that Harper's Ferry could not be "viewed apart and alone," where it would "rank with the most cold-blooded and atrocious wrongs ever perpetrated . . . ," but had to be seen as a "nemesis," as "the judgment of God" or "retributive justice" for the evils of slavery and the horrors of the slave trade. John Brown would have accepted that interpretation of his role in history.

Neither Foner nor Quarles has asked whether Douglass knew about the Pottawatomie slayings. The question may not be answerable. We do know that the two men were "confidential" with each other, and that Brown spent much time in Douglass's home. We can therefore only guess that the sight of the 950 Bowie knives Brown had welded to the tips of iron pikes and brought to Chambersburg roused in Douglass insurmountable conflict. He was not emotionally prepared even then for that kind of fighting. For the intellectual the resort to violence is a confession of the failure of words, his chosen instruments.

Although Douglass's final confrontation with the idea of armed insurrection is not fully explored for all its implications in his two major biographies, the road toward Chambersburg necessarily constitutes an important theme for each book. Foner's biography was originally written in sections to introduce the writings of Douglass, and it therefore has a more public character than Quarles's volume, which examines personal motivation with more care. However, there is plainly evident in each treatment a stress on Douglass's intensely pragmatic approach to emancipation. It was Douglass's sense of what was most likely to bring about abolition that led him from pacifism, through a commitment to political action, to militancy, and back again to political action.

It was largely a matter of chance that brought Douglass so soon after his escape from slavery to the attention of the Garrisonian abolitionists of New England. His commanding presence, evident in his earliest appearances on the antislavery platform, describing his experiences as a slave in Maryland, was living testimony to the false claims of black inferiority spread by the proslavery apologists. As an antislavery lecturer Douglass developed rapidly, and soon an astonishing fact emerged: he was too good to be true. Audiences doubted that so good an orator could ever have been a slave, and the doubts multiplied as Douglass departed more and more from the simple recital of wrongs to a more philosophical denunciation of slavery itself. In vain did his sponsors urge him to put a little more of the plantation manner into his discourse. Douglass was simply outgrowing the role for which he seemed so perfectly cast, and it was then merely a matter of time before he would cut the leading strings.

In 1847 Douglass left Massachusetts for Rochester, New York, to begin publication of the *North Star*, a black newspaper that would illustrate clearly the views and capabilities of black abolitionists. It was a cherished project that admirably suited Douglass's literary gifts, and it was made possible by the support of English contributions. But it meant that Douglass moved into an entirely different realm of abolitionist thought, and that he was open to new influences. He began to question the basic tenets of the Garrisonian faith. His pragmatism was undoubtedly important in the change in Douglass's view of the Constitution, which was to Garrisonians a proslavery document, "a compact with hell." It logically followed from this view that abolitionists should not participate in conventional political action, hoping to influence legislatures and elections, but should rather hope and work for disunion from the slaveholding states.

The abolitionists Douglass met in the western New York region, however, had maintained faith in party politics, and they reasoned that the Constitution, properly construed, was an antislavery document. Douglass began to accept these views as his own, but his defection from the faith of the Garrisonians brought him into a bitter conflict that was marked by ugly charges that hurt him deeply. Unable to see that Douglass was thinking for himself, the Garrisonians assumed that he had changed his views because he stood to gain financial support for his paper from Gerrit Smith, and worse yet, that he had come too much under the influence of Julia Griffiths, an Englishwoman who assisted Douglass in his editorial duties and in the financial management of the newspaper. In *My Bondage and My Freedom* Douglass explained his position as it stood after this break with simplicity and restraint.

Although he would return to a belief in the political system in time, during the 1850s Douglass's faith came under increasing pressure. The Fugitive Slave Act of 1850 was especially threatening to northern blacks. Frightening also were the shrill demands of the slaveholding states for protection of slavery in the territories, and Presidents in seeming collusion with southern leadership. With the cause of the slave apparently more hopeless than ever, Douglass became increasingly despondent about the prospects of successful political organization against slavery.

From their first meeting in 1847 Douglass began to adopt one of Brown's justifications of armed revolt: slavery was in itself a warfare of the slaveholders against the enslaved. By 1856 Douglass was ready to say of slavery that "its peaceful annihilation is almost hopeless. . . ." Although he did not expand his views on violence in *My Bondage and My Freedom*, he had by that time begun to make speeches recommending the violent overthrow of the slave oligarchy. This explains Douglass's readiness to pass over Pottawatomie in silence, if he knew about it, but it does not explain his last flinching from the random shedding of blood that the 950 iron pikes symbolized. That was written in his character.

In comparing his own career to Brown's, Douglass once wrote, "I could live for the slave, but he could die for him." Douglass's future vindicated his choice at Chambersburg, for half a useful life lay ahead of Harper's Ferry. When the long fuse lighted in Kansas exploded into civil war, Douglass regained his faith in politics. He agitated until black troops were recruited and emancipation became a part of the Civil War effort; he agitated for the suffrage amendments and the Civil Rights Act until these legal advantages were secured during the Reconstruction; then he agitated to see that these should come to have more than abstract meaning for his black fellow citizens. He was a consistent and continual foe of segregation in all forms, and the breadth of his interests was matched by few of his contemporary reformers. His last speech was delivered in 1895, on the day of his death, in behalf of woman suffrage.

In his fine chapter in *Black Abolitionists*, "Shock Therapy and Crisis," Quarles shows how Douglass and other black leaders who had been unwilling to stand with John Brown at Harper's Ferry *were* ready when war broke out to join battle for freedom. "Our national sin has found us out," wrote Douglass in 1861, and in many respects the Civil War became the expiation of that sin, certainly in historical imagery, if not in fact. Lacking Marx, most thoughtful men of the nineteenth century fell back on God to explain the role of violence in history.

By 1865 there was another martyr to rank with John Brown in the symbolism of the age. In 1861, however, Abraham Lincoln had not been possessed of John Brown's conviction that God commanded him to raise the sword. Rather, God's peace came like a blessing after years of struggle. Thus he was able to say, in the great Second Inaugural, that if it was God's will that the war should continue "until every drop of blood drawn with the lash, shall be paid by another drawn with the sword, as was said three thousand years ago, so still it must be said, 'the judgments of the Lord, are true and righteous altogether.'" John Brown received his authorization from Jehovah at the moment he acted; Lincoln received an indemnity from God for past actions. The difference in timing was important.

10

Off the Plantation

This review of books on non-slaves who experienced slavery's coerciveness was first published in the New York Review of Books, *September 18, 1975. Reprinted with permission from* The New York Review of Books. *Copyright © 1975 Nyrev, Inc.*

As the crisp outline left when a cooky-cutter has finished its business serves to remind us, it is occasionally possible to see the shape of things as well from the outside as from within. That plantation slavery was much more than a labor system most readers of American history understand well enough: how much more is being slowly absorbed as the studies of those who lived just outside the system accumulate. In the last year several distinguished works have appeared on slavery as slaves and their owners experienced it. But it is a measure of the increasing sophistication of this field of scholarship that we also have several important new works of historians who have gone off the plantation, so to speak, to explore the social meaning of slavery for abolitionists and the free black victims of society, those who were in a technical sense the chattel property of nobody.

Even for these "outsiders" slavery was a dominating and coercive condition of life, dictating personal choices and public action. This was true for Angelina Grimké, the well-born daughter of a Charleston slaveholding family, who experienced the challenge of slavery very personally; the challenge became, in the view of Katherine DuPre Lumpkin, the spur that led in time, almost too late in time, to her self-liberation from the psychological and social limitations of nineteenth-century women.[1] Angelina came through at last, and so did many of the free blacks and black leaders in the antislavery movement, whose difficulties "just outside" slavery have been described in new works by Ira Berlin[2] and Jane and William Pease.[3]

But the *collective* story of each group is on the whole depressing, filled with more frustration than triumph. The defeats are a register of the solid entrenchment of the peculiar institution in the social and political fabric of the nation, even as the economic position of slavery in the Upper South was deteriorating. The victories were usually personal; the defeats the result of fragmentation as organizations fell apart over what the Peases call "rightlessness" and "powerlessness."

The struggles of the South's free black caste and black antislavery spokesmen in the North are all the more chilling when read in conjunction with certain of the more recent works on slavery itself, which tend, on the whole, to sound the upbeat, to stress how even in the jaws of chattel bondage the enslaved were able, in the words of Eugene D. Genovese in *Roll, Jordan, Roll*, to lay "the foundations for a separate black national culture while enormously enriching American culture as a whole."[4] If slaves were able to do that, how is it that free blacks, northern and southern, met with so much frustration and despair?

Though Ira Berlin's main concern is to give an authoritative account of how things were, rather than why they were not different, this question is implicit in his very important, detailed study of the South's free black population. His answer is at once simple and complex. The slave had at least whatever practical protection the master's economic interest afforded him, and sometimes he had as well the personal concern afforded by a lifetime of close association. But as a category, with some exceptions, the free blacks were exposed and vulnerable at every turn, the slaves of society. The majority were pushed into the lowest-paying and least dignified jobs, visited with many social and legal restrictions, and they were ready-made scapegoats for rising internal tensions in a slaveholding society out of touch with its century. Those who fared better were able to do so only by subordinating themselves to the economic and psychosocial needs of the dominant whites in their world.

Whenever fears of a slave revolt swept the countryside, the free blacks, with their greater mobility, came under immediate suspicion, even though they were very seldom identified with insurrections or plots. They lived on the outer perimeter of a system under siege and engaged in justifying itself with a theory that slavery itself was a "positive good" for blacks and whites alike. If black people could survive as free men, and some obviously *throve* on freedom, the unwelcome suggestion that masters were perhaps unnecessary was bound to arise.

Berlin has written a more comprehensive study of the status and condition of free blacks in the South than any other we have yet seen, but his findings on the civil oppression of black freemen will not surprise students of southern history. Their story has been told in part many times: how their testimony in courts was restricted, how they were denied the right to serve on juries, how they had to present "free papers" on demand, could be harassed by patrols with impunity, how barriers against their entry into one state after another were raised, and how they faced a stony white hostility that wanted almost from the beginning to pack them off to Africa. But Berlin's account is far more than a recital of grievances. The originality and signal contribution of *Slaves without Masters* derive from the author's choice to treat his subjects in the stream of time, to see them as poised precariously in a fluid and dangerous state reflecting the dynamics of changing political and social currents in the white world. By this evolutionary approach he also provides a better understanding of how the free blacks came to be free, and under what impulses, drawing significant distinctions between their social positions in the Upper South and in the Lower South.

The foundations of the relatively large free black population of the Upper South were laid in the wake of the American Revolution, for there were very few slaves emancipated in the first part of the eighteenth century. Afterward many owners emancipated their human property en masse, and numbers of slaves emancipated themselves by absconding. This was easier after a large number of free blacks existed to provide cover. Both kinds of emancipation owed much to the ideals of the Revolution and the spread of evangelical Christianity, not a little to the declining price of tobacco, and nothing at all to the complexion, light or dark, of the emancipated. The newly emancipated were as likely to be full-blooded Africans as the slaves were.

Berlin shows that the free black caste of the Lower South origi-nated in entirely different historical circumstances and grew under different impulses. In Louisiana a large free black creole population of mulattoes had evolved under Spanish and French rule, and their numbers rapidly increased with the arrival in the port cities of the Lower South of thousands of light-colored and socially elite refugees from the black revolt in Saint-Domingue. Later the slaveowners of the Lower South pursued a highly selec-tive policy in emancipating slaves, freeing those who stood in some particular relationship of blood or friendship to themselves. Often that relationship was that of father or lover.

Tracing the demographic consequences of these contrasting circumstances in the origins of the free black caste, Berlin shows that the Lower South freemen were lighter in color, higher in socioeconomic status, and more likely to be city dwellers. Some became wealthy slaveowners themselves, and they drew further and further away from the mass of slaves. This elite caste was less feared by whites, and was never so closely circumscribed as more northerly free blacks were. The Lower South free blacks became an effective buffer between the whites and the slaves, and not sur-prisingly many of them rushed to the defense of the Confederacy when the conflict came. "Nowhere else in the South," Berlin writes, "did whites treat free Negro liberty with such respect."

In the Upper South free blacks were far more numerous, more identified with the general slave population in economic condition and color, and they tended to be more freely scattered among the slave population. Nervous whites placed them in an increasingly disadvantageous legal position. The paradoxical result was that in the Upper South, where the notion of slavery as a "positive good" gained ground more slowly, and where the ideals of the Revolu-tion died very late, if ever, free blacks suffered a harder lot than the Lower South, where the positive view of slavery caught on much faster. These were the polar positions of a spectrum that tended in general to restrict the owner's right to liberate his slaves privately, to prevent the build-up of free blacks, and to frustrate their upward economic and social mobility. By the 1850s the free blacks were in a crisis: although many were better off economically than they had ever been, slavery was under heavier attack from the North, and those states with a high free black population began seriously to agitate the question whether they should not be deported.

Although Berlin's thesis explains many of his findings, and should be considered very seriously by scholars more particularly interested in the laws codifying "slave" status, some confusion results from his heavy emphasis on the differences between the free black castes in the two regions. The division does not explain all the phenomena, and the emphasis on laws may assume too much. Questions arise in the middle chapters devoted to the free black community and the mechanics of white dominance. The African church was the cultural focus of the black community, and the seat of many accomplishments of long-lasting value. Berlin assumes, without developing the point extensively, that free blacks were the leaders in the establishment of separate churches. He is probably right. But one would then suppose that separate churches would have been more hotly resisted in the Upper South, when in fact at first they were resisted everywhere, and the opposition apparently slackened earlier in the cities of the Upper South than elsewhere.

One learns that Charleston (a Lower South city?) was especially forward, first in abolishing the power of blacks within the "integrated" churches, and subsequently in closing down the separate church founded there under the auspices of the American Methodist Episcopalians. But blacks, getting indirect help from whites who wanted blacks out of their churches, did found their own institutions, and one learns that throughout the 1840s, and even during the 1850s, when white hostility and fear peaked again (especially in the Upper South), these institutions increased dramatically in number.

When we read that such Upper South cities as Baltimore and Richmond were the special scene of such development, the question naturally arises whether the unique character of New Orleans has not caused Berlin to generalize too widely about the distinctive character of the Lower South. If that city were omitted from calculation, then perhaps a more effective dichotomy might be made between urban and rural communities, between more complex economies and those resting primarily on plantation agriculture. If we use either of these explanations, we could relate hostile state legislation to the legislative strength or weakness of municipalities, and to the particular notion of a particular municipality of how best to deal with the free black "problem." Certainly hostility was endemic, and petitions against free blacks came from urban and rural areas, throughout the South.

It is also worth noting that in spite of legislation hostile to private manumissions, Upper South owners continued to find ways of manumitting slaves, and slaves found ways of manumitting themselves. Slavery was deteriorating in economic importance in the Upper South, as Berlin writes, in one of the bravest and most challenging sections of his very important work. In suggesting that economic forces may have been equal to or even more significant than demographic ones in distinguishing between patterns of treatment in different parts of the South I do not mean to suggest that Berlin overlooks these factors. It is merely a matter of emphasis.

So much has now been written about disagreements among abolitionists over the best means to ring down the curtain on slavery that there would seem to be little to add. But there is. Jane and William Pease, who have been for some years the closest students of race relations in the abolition movement, have shown in their new work, *They Who Would Be Free: Blacks' Search For Freedom, 1830–1861,* that it was not only the question of the best means to end slavery that divided the antislavery forces. They also show that between the black abolitionists and the white there were widely differing perceptions of freedom itself. "Whites," they write, "conceiving of their own freedom as absolute and never having experienced its opposite extreme, embraced a simple duality. For blacks the alternative was not between slavery or freedom but between more or less freedom and more or less slavery."

This "basic dualism" is central to understanding the problems black leaders had with their white colleagues, and it is the unifying theme of the Peases' sensitive exploration of the quality of leadership provided by those who suffered the economic and social consequences of second-class status while simultaneously working to liberate southern slaves. White abolitionists were simply less interested in the problems of northern blacks than they were in the struggle against slavery. The more sophisticated conception of freedom and bondage as a continuum was the only possible position for those who daily struggled with what one black abolitionist called "semi-emancipation." Until northern "free" blacks had equal civil rights, he maintained, the North could not possibly "concentrate its moral and intellectual power. . . ."

Excluded from the franchise, forced into the lowest-paying jobs, denied equal access to education, the larger part of the northern free black population was relegated to pauperism, many unable even in their own living to illustrate that emancipation was a practicable course. Or unable to do so to their own satisfaction, or to stop the mouths of those who quoted morbidity and mortality statistics to "prove" black maladjustment to "freedom." From this point of view the struggle for equal rights in a "free" society was an indispensable corollary, or precondition, for emancipation in the South. The consquence for organized abolition was that blacks had a more pragmatic and flexible attitude to issues, and less and less sympathy for the more abstract perfectionism of their white colleagues. Some of their time, in short, was given to advocacy of race pride, self-help, and to an insistence that blacks be allowed to take more dominant positions in the antislavery societies.

These conflicts have a curiously contemporary ring. Blacks resented being kept in "the short frocks of childhood," as one put it, excluded from decision-making roles, and patronized. Samuel Ringgold Ward, speaking to an English audience, charged that whites "assume the right to dictate to us about all matters," that "they dislike to see us assume or maintain manly and independent positions; they prefer that we should be a second-rate set of folks, in intellectual matters."

There was ample ground for these charges. After Frederick Douglass defied the advice of the Garrisonian abolitionists with whom he had worked so closely for so long, to found the *North Star,* a paper dedicated specifically to black aims, Garrison's anger fell upon him, his paper, his supporters, and his character. Douglass was "thoroughly base and selfish," "destitute of every principal of honor, ungrateful to the last degree, and malevolent in spirit." When James McCune Smith accused the Garrisonians of excluding black speakers from their lecture series in 1854, the *National Anti-Slavery Standard* denied the intention, pointing to William Wells Brown's participation and charging Smith with thinking that no man was "really 'colored' who [had] not by faithlessness to old friends proved his heart to be as black as his skin."

Whites rang the changes on the ingratitude theme. It would be agreeable to add that the vicious infighting stopped at the color line, but it did not. There were the historic disputes over nomenclature, and whether to organize separately for specific black aims. Some black leaders deplored the attention the majority gave to economic and civil advancement of the black community, and held that separate black movements and organizations were diversionary, racism in reverse.

After the passage of the Fugitive Slave Act in 1850 this position became harder to defend. Abolitionists, white and black alike, could only view this law as a giant step backward in a seemingly fruitless twenty-year struggle. But for blacks the measures for the recapture of escaped slaves, and the legal hurdles the government placed in the way of a fair trial for those *accused* of being runaway slaves, jeopardized the freedom of all blacks, not merely that of bona fide fugitives.

This was the northern counterpart of the problem Ira Berlin's free southern blacks faced in the same decade. In three fine closing chapters the Peases trace the response of northern leaders who now gave themselves to the rhetoric of violence in the face of a new dilemma. Separation and nationalism gained ground, and there were curious shiftings of position among the advocates of accommodation and resistance. Even a militant leader like Martin Delany organized an emigration project, saying that there was no hope for black equality in the United States, and Frederick Douglass gave up the pacifism of the Garrisonians, announcing firmly that he was finished with nonresistance. Blacks were in the vanguard of those who resisted the Fugitive Slave Act, forcibly releasing black captives, often in the teeth of the courts. Blacks who did not advocate insurrection came very close to doing so when they applauded the prospect. Neither extreme, of course, emigration or insurrection, carried the day. Aiding the escape of fugitives from the South was the outer boundary of violence, because it was the outer boundary of common sense. The Peases explain: "Nowhere in the North was there a population density of Negroes sufficient to sustain race war—even had the inarticulate been ready to respond to rhetoric." The rhetoric, they observe, "offered no viable solutions," and was only a gauge of banked frustration. The talk of emigration was headed off by leaders who recognized these schemes as colonization in reverse, who declared the equal right of blacks to remain in their own country.

One reasonable test of a work of history is whether the facts are delivered, and have been made to say enough and not too much. The Peases have written an authentic account of what was a failed effort. If it sometimes lacks focus, the reason is that the movement they record was hardly a movement at all, but an accumulation of individual performances responding to events beyond individuals' control, but not beyond their criticism. In that respect their literary problem is much the same as Berlin's, to synthesize the actions of a minority within a minority. The Peases honestly and reluctantly concede that neither black nor white abolitionism had achieved much by 1860, if "partisan victories and visible changes" in social institutions are "the only measures of success."

But they are not the only measures, and the authors believe the antislavery movement stiffened popular resistance to the encroachments of the slave power. Most Northerners rated the Fugitive Slave Act an outrageous encroachment, and when white antislavery leaders organized for the specific purpose of flouting this law (even to the point of violence if necessary), they were building an antislavery public opinion. They were also for the first time following the leadership of the black antislavery spokesmen, who had been organized for fugitive slave rescues for several decades when the act of 1850 was passed.

Other "very real achievements" for the black leaders were the blocking of colonization and emigration plans, the black convention movement, and the creation of new organizations for specific aims of the black community. And yet it is only fair to say that some historians have seen in the evidence more positive achievement than the Peases do, and that others have been less critical than the Peases are of the white abolitionists in their dealings with the blacks in their organizations. Among honest historians there will always be such differences of emphasis, and they require no referee. If some scholars have celebrated victories, the Peases explain why they were so limited.

The women's rights movement was related to the antislavery cause in much the same ways blacks' struggle for civil equality in the North was: women and blacks alike were frustrated in their advocacy of abolition by legal and social restrictions on their activities. If blacks were mobbed, and even denied passports when traveling abroad as antislavery lecturers, a woman's presence lecturing before a "promiscuous" audience was enough to announce her as a promiscuous woman. Conservatives in abolitionism were always nervous that too prominent a role for either group would discredit the entire movement before a general public that disliked seeing either far from their customary "places." But opposition notwithstanding, it was through involvement in antislavery that a number of American women had their first taste of independent action and personal recognition. Angelina and Sarah Grimké threw antislavery circles into a general furor when they toured New England in 1837 telling audiences what they knew about American slavery from personal experience.

The Grimké sisters were the most improbable recruits in the entire roster of antislavery, two young aristocrats from a large, brilliant, and affluent slaveholding Charleston family, whose complex relationships with one another and the two causes they served are Katherine DuPre Lumpkin's subject. The emancipation of Angelina Grimké is on one plane the translation of a vivacious antebellum belle into an electrifying orator, a translation which was an essential step, if not the first or the last, in Angelina's private road to personal autonomy.

The first lap of Angelina's long journey was her conversion from the formalism of her wealthy family's Episcopalian creed to a pious and devout Presbyterianism preached by a young evangelical minister with whom Angelina soon fell in love. "Life had taken a glorious turn," writes her biographer, for Angelina's vigorous involvement in church affairs brought her knowledge of her abilities, and "a conviction of high purpose," though she did not know what her mission was to be. The second lap was more costly. Under the influence of her older sister Sarah, who had become a Quaker during an extended visit to Philadelphia, Angelina began unloading the trappings of her girlish and worldly life. "My dear Angelina proposes destroying Scott's novels," wrote sister Sarah, "which she had purchased before she was serious. Perhaps I strengthened her a little." The sisters cut up the novels; Angelina's personal finery, the laces, veils, and flounces, all "superfluities of naughtiness," came next. The Reverend William MacDowell and his church cost Angelina more, but she made the sacrifice, went to Philadelphia, and joined her sister's faith.

The two were never parted in all the years that followed; from Quakerism to antislavery to women's rights, through a curious period of marriage, child-bearing, and semiretirement for Angelina, they lived together. Few public figures have left so intimate a record of their restless combings of conscience, or so full an account of the failings of the dearly beloveds in their lives as Sarah, Angelina, and Angelina's husband Theodore Dwight Weld.

The psychological dynamics of this trio are Ms. Lumpkin's special fascination. Until Angelina became an avowed abolitionist, ready to write and expose herself publicly in the cause (something Sarah's conservative sect of Quakers disapproved of), Sarah maintained a personal ascendancy that she obtained at the age of twelve, when she stormed successfully to be named the godmother of baby "Nina." Until the girls were grown Angelina often addressed Sarah as "Mother." Only when Angelina determined that it was God's purpose that she should become an antislavery lecturer were the tables turned. Over Sarah's objections she held to her plan, and then Sarah too defied the Quakers, saying, "Whither Thou goest I will go . . ."

Angelina's stunning successes on the platform owed much to her firsthand remembrances of slavery, much to her phenomenal speaking voice, and even more to her brains and ambition. The ambition was worrisome, for Angelina feared that the acclaim she received gave her too much personal gratification. Her husband, Weld, worried about it too, and so did sister Sarah. They told her so, from time to time, for these God-driven people took the state of their souls seriously indeed. That there could be furtive self-serving motives on Weld's part (he excelled in oratory too) for parking Angelina's ambition and her career (along with his own), and on Sarah's as well, for similar reasons, seems not to have occurred to any of this curious *maison à trois*, though Ms. Lumpkin is clearly on to the pattern of their conscientious criticism. One can't avoid sympathy for those who exposed themselves so thoroughly in their diaries and letters to each other, which were read by all parties, often more than once.

Maybe there should be a rule protecting the psychological naiveté of the last century from the analytic pryings of our own, but biographers would be out of business, and the public would be deprived of some good books, of which this is among the number. Although Ms. Lumpkin is occasionally heavy-handed, especially with Sarah and Weld, the lapses are rare, and the general sensitivity of her explanations is enough to redeem psychohistory from some of its extraordinary contemporary malpractice.

Much to the author's credit she does not attribute the "calling" of Weld and the Grimkés to psychological maladjustments, but to a sincere religious conviction. This is refreshing and convincing, for we see that we are not dealing with hypocrites. If in their innocence they hamstrung one another, they did so in ways we have come to see are endemic with the human condition.

In antislavery work the Grimké sisters were far more free from the latent (and sometimes not so latent) racism the Peases see as dividing the movement than most of their fellows. Angelina found occasion to beg black women to participate in antislavery meetings and to speak of their injuries arising from racial prejudice, and to do so even if they suffered social slights. The mortifications "will tend to your growth in grace and will help your paler sisters more than anything else to overcome their own sinful feelings. . . ." The sisters easily made Francis and Archibald Grimké, who were the natural sons of their brother Henry by his household slave, members of their own family. Angelina's conversion to women's rights came quite naturally, because her own *human* rights were "invaded" when she worked for the slave. Both causes were "a part of the great doctrine of Human Rights" and thus "the rights of the slave and women blend like colors of the rainbow."

But theory is not action, and Angelina remained long under the subtle dictation of her duties as wife and mother. The final step in her self-manumission was her recognition that for twelve years following her marriage she had seen her duty in life more through the eyes of her husband and her sister than through her own. Thus ended Angelina's withdrawal from active participation in her causes, a period in which she bore three children and nursed the home fires after her fashion, restlessly and without much talent. In this period she had again deferred to sister Sarah, who had the knack (and the drive) to mother Angelina's children.

By 1854 Angelina again put her foot into the water, hesitantly at first, and then more firmly, as an advocate of women's rights. The day of her great fame had passed, and younger feminists were leading the charge, but one supposes that Angelina in bloomer costume had found a kind of peace. *The Emancipation of Angelina Grimké* is, simply, an interesting book. Although it deals with a significant epoch in the history of freedom, it says less that is new about antislavery and feminism than it does about human interaction in a high cause and the difficulties of self-liberation from the toils of custom.

11

What We Didn't Know about Slavery

This review was first published in the New York Review *of Books,* October 17, 1974. *Reprinted with permission from* The New York Review of Books. *Copyright* © *1974 Nyrev, Inc.*

For six or eight generations writers have been pegging slavery up and down on a moral scale that buckles alarmingly with the temperature of the social issue that slavery entailed. So long as the peculiar institution was a contemporary reality the question was absolute. Was slavery a moral institution, or was it not? Abolitionists saw in it "the sum of all villainies" because it encouraged every other sin. But defenders of slavery pointed to Holy Writ, where they found ample precedent but no condemnation, and widely advertised their conclusion that God had His purposes: slavery was a positive good.

But once slavery became history, the question attained a degree of sophistication. The question of the morality of slavery, being settled in the negative, gave way to another: how repressive was slavery *in practice* in the United States? The ramifications of the question in this form were intensely political and contemporary. A suitably negative answer could be used to explain the quality of contemporary family life in the black community (judged to be bad) and the survival of racial hostility (judged to be unchanging), and as a check on our progress (or lack thereof) in approaching a healthy biracial society. In this form the question automatically introduced a comparative dimension. Slavery in the United States was more or less repressive, more or less benign, in comparison to what?

Brazil has been, for twenty-five years, the main target of reference. Since the simultaneous appearance in 1946 of an English translation of Gilberto Freyre's powerful work *The Masters and the Slaves*[1] and a short book by Frank Tannenbaum entitled *Slave and Citizen*,[2] slavery in this country has been contrasted, usually to its disadvantage, with Latin American slavery in general, and Brazilian slavery in particular.

The Tannenbaum-Freyre argument, simply put, is that the institutions of the Portuguese settlers, especially the Roman Catholic Church and Roman civil law, were favorable to the recognition of the basic humanity of the slave. The English colonists, on the other hand, built their slavery out of whole cloth, there being no legal precedents in English common law, pro or con, to hamper them, and they built it to suit a young, bustling, and extractive capitalist economy. Because of the separation of church and state, the Protestants, of however good will, could do little to hinder the inevitable pressures to debase the slave and his family and to strip them of every human right. The idea was persuasive, because it seemed to explain so much about contemporary differences in the two worlds: there was Brazil with a fluid racial pattern based as much on economic status as on color, while the United States retained well into the twentieth century a rigid caste system based on race.

The Tannenbaum-Freyre thesis has had its advocates and attackers on both sides of the border from the start, and Carl Degler's *Neither Black Nor White* is but the latest recruit. It is likely to be the last for some time, however, because it deals so objectively and comprehensively with all the questions raised by this particular comparison. The work is good history and good sociology in that it explores the contemporary facts and ambiguities of Brazilian race relations more thoroughly than others have done.

For a number of years scholars in this country and in Brazil, especially those of the São Paulo school, have been chipping away at the Tannenbaum-Freyre thesis, the assumption that institutions alone could have affected the course of history on two raw and malleable frontiers so drastically. What did laws mean if they had to be passed over and over? And what could priests do when they were so few and the friendly dependents of the master class to boot? Like others before him Degler quickly disposes of the role of the Church and law as defenders of the slave and outriders of freedom: "Insofar as physical treatment was concerned," he writes, "it would seem that Brazilian slavery was less likely than United States slavery to give either the master or the slave an awareness of the Negro's humanity." Mortality was high in Brazil, and suicide a serious problem. Averring that he never saw illustrations in the literature of slavery in the United States of slaves wearing masks, he pointedly suggests that to put a mask on a slave, as was done in Brazil, is very like muzzling a dog.

But the Tannenbaum-Freyre assumption was easier to dispose of than the stubborn fact that had inspired Tannenbaum's original investigation. Why had life *after* slavery assumed such different aspects in the two countries? Brazil never developed a system of rigid segregation of the sort that replaced slavery in this country, and blacks of Latin countries retained much more of their African culture. Degler's explanation hinges on a single important circumstance of great significance for the future of blacks in freedom. In Brazil manumission was easier, because of demographical and economic circumstances, while in the United States it was hedged about with discouragement and difficulties, especially in the nineteenth century, after most avenues to freedom were systematically closed.

The consequence was the development in Brazil of a large class of free mulattoes, who stood waiting, in effect, as a community for freed slaves to join at the lower end of the economic scale after manumission became general. Degler nurses no illusion that Brazil is, or ever was, a color-blind society. Indeed Brazilians appear to be very aware of the significance of *degrees* of blackness or whiteness. But that is just the point. The gradations from one color to the other were so thickly populated that moving a notch or two up the social scale, by means of economic or intellectual achievement or a "good" marriage, was by no means impossible. "The strict and sharp line between the races so characteristic of the United States is absent there; always there are the individual exceptions, the mulatto escape hatch, or the 'bleaching' power of class."

But why did no mulatto "escape hatch" develop in the United

States? Degler's explanation owes little to religion, law, or ideology, but much to contrasting historical experiences and the demographical divisions between races and sexes at significant periods in the histories of the two countries. Mulattoes quickly appeared in both countries, but in mainland North America they were promptly defined "out" of the white world, and into the black, as Negroes. This happened not only because of excessive fear (and consequent hatred) of blacks, but because blacks were in the minority, and it was feasible to handle them thus. In Brazil it was not. The Portuguese also began with legal restrictions on intermarriage, but such laws "were not enforced or rendered unenforceable by local conditions."

The law simply could not keep pace with miscegenation in a land where slaves were being imported at the rate they were in Brazil, and where whites, mostly male, were in a small minority in an overwhelmingly black and mulatto population, constituting only 19 percent in 1790, and nearer to 10 percent most of the time. With the possible exception of New Orleans, no "place" developed here for the mulatto as a social class; therefore every pressure of society worked to foreclose for him anything approximating the economic, legal, and social position available in Brazil.

In only a few particulars does Degler move away from his steady emphasis on demographic causation. In answering why Englishmen were more shamefaced about their unions with black women, and less ready to grant their mulatto offspring legal and social standing, Degler reminds us not only of the relatively small numbers of Brazilian white women at the formative stage of the slave system, but of their legal and social inferiority when compared with Englishwomen. These last were, as Degler says, "a quite different breed," accustomed to approximately equal rule within the home, freer to speak their piece on all subjects, and even to engage in some trades. It amazed a German visitor to North America to see what "great liberties and privileges" women had, and he was plainly shocked that in a Pennsylvania court a mere serving girl had won a suit against her master for getting her pregnant.

These pushy Englishwomen were largely successful in getting their husbands' adultery out of the house or, failing that, under the rug. They often named a black competitor in divorce suits, and they looked sourly on mulatto offspring. They wanted the result of miscegenation called bastardy, and had their way. In Brazil the woman's position was so low, even in the home, that one observer said she "acquired a character of sullenness and timidity that disfigured her like a slave; in the midst of every repression and prohibition." It was improbable that Brazilian women could exercise an effective brake to the demographic forces creating the "mulatto escape hatch" in a freewheeling, miscegenating society.

Two further cultural factors are introduced by Degler as supporting the population trends outlined so forcefully as originally creating the status of those who were "neither black nor white." The Portuguese heritage lacked the "work ethic" English Protestants were bringing to the New World. The Portuguese gained no social status for the performance of physical labor, and were not attracted to a whole range of trades and skilled crafts the English eagerly sought. Since Brazil no less than other societies required these services, the mulattoes stood ready to push the unresisting whites aside. The training and skills they required then lifted them into an economic position that paralleled their social life between the worlds of white and black.

English artisans had considerable success in restricting slave labor to plantation agriculture. The implications for the transit of blacks to free status are clear. In Brazil mulattoes had entered dozens of trades and crafts in force, and before the general emancipation, while in the United States this entry was largely blocked by whites sufficiently numerous to man the posts. Their effective political strength in protecting their interests suggests the further consideration that the working-class English, as colonists and later as citizens of the young republic, exercised more influence on the polity than their fellows in Brazil were able to do. An open competitive society therefore permitted and encouraged a popular expression of racial hostility based on economic interest.

But even after accounting for the social role of women and the more democratic political institutions of the English, it is clear that Degler regards these factors as supportive of and not as equal to demographic factors and the timing of events. The total historical experience of the two countries was more important than institutions or ideology in the widely contrasting racial patterns that have emerged in Brazil and the United States.

What Degler has said about Brazil may not be entirely new to students of Latin American history, and some scholars of slavery in the United States may feel some restlessness about the author's consistent minimization of ideology, culture, and psychology at the expense of demography. Though economic forces are clearly at the bottom of several of Degler's postulations, he does not develop them chronologically in his argument. And yet it is not along these lines that the ultimate assessment of *Neither Black Nor White* must rest. Degler's argument encompasses the entire route from slavery to freedom in the two largest slaveholding countries of the West, and some major trends of necessity had to give way to his delineation of the central role of the mulatto in the contrast he depicts. A discussion of evolutionary factors along the time line in the two countries might have been desirable, but Degler succeeds admirably in bringing logic and common sense to the main question that has dominated historians for twenty-five years. His synthesis of the Latin scholarship with what is now known about slavery in this country is lucid, and stands up to several close readings.

Several distinguished works on slavery in the English colonies have also exploited demographic and geographical factors in explaining contrasts between the slave systems that developed in the Caribbean and on the mainland. Among the best is Richard Dunn's *Sugar and Slaves*, a remarkable account of the rise of the planter class in the West Indies.[8] Struck by the rapidity with which the English planters of the islands developed an altogether different way of life from their brothers who headed for the Chesapeake and Massachusetts bays, Dunn, in explaining it, cannot call on the influence of prior ideas on religion, politics, or common law, for they were shared ideas. But because of economic and geographic circumstances the islanders quickly became "far richer than their cousins in the North American wilderness. They lived fast, spent recklessly, played desperately, and died young."

By 1700 the planters of the islands had become as different from their fellows on the mainland as the English were from the Portuguese. They owed both their financial success and their social disaster to the early discovery that instead of growing mediocre tobacco they could raise sugar cane, a product Europe sought more eagerly than even first-rate tobacco. By 1640, within fifteen years of settlement, the planters of tiny Barbados had already begun to switch to cane, and within another twenty they had evolved a master class bent on riding the sugar boom to wealth and power. There were disastrous social costs.

Today's holiday visitors to the islands in the sun may find it hard to conceive the physical hardships endured there in the seventeenth and eighteenth centuries: insect pests, extremes of heat and cold, and ferocious storms defined life as a chancy affair. White indentured servants with a choice in the matter were not tempted to leave England for a place that was called "hell on earth," and those who came found conditions of labor outrageous by home standards. They became restless, unmanageable, and finally undesirable laborers.

Slavery filled the void like a flood, and on slaves and sugar the Barbadians rode to their fortunes. "Virginia might be the Old Dominion and Massachusetts the Bible Commonwealth, but Barbados was something more tangible: the richest colony in North America." From Dunn's skillful use of a 1680 census and lists of persons permitted to leave Barbados, a much clearer picture emerges than we have had before of an island crowded to the gunnels with 40,000 slaves, 2,300 white servants, a negligible number of "householders" and freemen, and dominated from the top by 175 great planters who held all the important offices and had no trouble keeping one thousand smaller planters in line. Dunn's is rich social history, based on factual data brought to life by his use of contemporary narrative accounts, which describe life in a tropical paradise becoming uninhabitable through overcrowding.

The sugar-slave formula took easily to export, first to the Leeward Islands, and then to Jamaica, fast becoming the buccaneering capital for the English. It was, according to one explicit visitor, the very "dunghill of the Universe," swarming with prostitutes, drunks, convicts, and pirates. But soon its matchless agricultural possibilities drew from Barbados and the Leewards the less affluent whites who fought, first with the Spanish, then with the fugitive slaves who had established themselves in maroon colonies in the hills, and then with the buccaneers, for the chance to accomplish in Jamaica what the Barbadians had achieved a generation earlier. By 1713 the "sugar and slave" system had developed in classical proportions, and could be seen "in its starkest and most exploitative form." By the close of the seventeenth century the English planters of the West Indies had brought to six small islands a quarter of a million slaves, "and branded them as perpetual bondsmen."

Dunn deals mercilessly with the emergent planters, their *"nouveau riche"* vulgarity, and their slave system, "One of the harshest systems of servitude in Western history." The slaves reacted, when it was possible and intelligent to do so, with the fury of desperation. Their revolts coincided practically with the possibilities of success. Few occurred in Barbados, which was thickly settled, with few places for slaves to gather and hide, but in Jamaica, with its hills and woods, there were frequent revolts between 1650 and 1700. There were six major uprisings in the last quarter of the century, and several lesser ones thereafter.

But if real revolts matched opportunities, plots and rumors coincided neatly with white fear. Barbados had plenty of that, and of courage the blacks had enough. "If you Roast me today," cried the slave Tony, about to be burned for his part in a Barbadian plot uncovered in 1675, "you cannot Roast me tomorrow." As others before him have observed, Dunn sees a correlation between the tendency to revolt and the numbers of native Africans in the population, which would be one way to explain the high incidence of slave revolt in Jamaica. But he thinks this factor was less significant than the superior opportunities Jamaica afforded for success.

The islands became "a demographic disaster area," writes Dunn, because the slaves were

overdisciplined and underfed, while their masters were underdisciplined and overfed. The blacks, male blacks in particular, were shocked into early death by captivity, forced labor, and neglect. The whites, the male whites in particular, catapulted themselves into early death by their strident, showy mode of behavior. The specter of death helps to explain the frenetic tempo and mirage-like quality of West Indian life—gorgeously opulent today, gone tomorrow. No wonder the blacks looked forward longingly to their afterlife in the pleasant mountains of West Africa. No wonder the whites looked forward longingly to an early retirement in England.

Dunn writes well. For all his severity in handling the planters of the West Indies, he seems clear in attributing their greed and cruelty to economic factors when he writes that "the initial difference in the two sectors of English America is that the island colonists plunged into the slave business and the mainland colonies inched into it." To the extent the West Indian planters wanted to build homes as well as get rich, Dunn's criticisms are justified; to the extent their collective aim was only to get rich, they could only be criticized for wanting the wrong things.

A traveler coming from the West Indies to Virginia at the close of the seventeenth century would have encountered striking contrasts. As Wesley Frank Craven informs us in *White, Red, and Black*, the plantation system was just forming there, and the racial distribution reflected that fact emphatically.[4] By 1713 there were four blacks for every white in the English islands, but on the mainland there were six whites for every slave. Life in Virginia was still raw, even the rich were not "opulent," and white indentured servants were still doing most of the hard labor for the larger landowners. Whites of the "middling sort" were doing their own. But Craven's fine study of the Virginia population reveals that the Virginians were inching along just as little faster by 1700, and that the slave population more than doubled in the last two decades of the century. Craven's figures are somewhat lower than those of several of his predecessors, but they result from a careful study of the assignment of head-rights in land to those who imported labor, black or white, into the colony.

By studying the names of the imported slaves Craven concludes that two-thirds of the slaves were men, that they were imported in small lots, that they were still a minority among the more than 60,000 whites. Although the disparity between the sexes was even greater among the whites, Craven believes "there were enough Englishwomen present to determine social conventions," and public policy discouraged miscegenation. The slave population did not expand rapidly in the seventeenth century, not because of an excessive mortality, but because of the scattered arrangement of the farm settlements in the back quarters and sexual imbalance. Masters did not encourage childbearing because women in the field were more immediately useful than a woman in confinement or nursing a baby. It does the work of Craven a disservice to summarize thus briefly his findings concerning the slave population. Verifiable evidence on seventeenth-century Virginia is discouragingly small, and the careful attention this distinguished scholar has given to the fragmentary record has produced in one concise essay as much as we are likely to know about the seventeenth-century black population.

Our imaginary colony-hopper in train from the West Indies via Virginia to South Carolina in the year 1700 would have found himself at his last stop in a society halfway between the maturity of the plantation economy of Barbados or Jamaica and the raw beginnings in Virginia. South Carolina had by then a population composed in nearly equal proportions of blacks and whites, in the characteristic frontier distribution of more numerous males than females of each color. In 1700 the settlement at Charles Town was only thirty years old, and showed the unmistakable imprint of Barbadian immigrants on its foundation. Their baggage included not only their West Indian chattels but the Barbadian slave code as well.

Like the Jamaicans, the Carolinians had been a part of the general movement out of the tiny island after the best lands had been taken up; and like the Jamaicans they too emigrated in the hope of establishing prosperous plantations. Thus, writes Peter Wood in *Black Majority*, South Carolina was "a colony of a colony."[5] As the Barbadians had found sugar after some experimentations, the Carolinians in 1695 found rice. Within two decades the culture took firm hold, and the demographic pattern shifted to accord with the increased demand for labor. Blacks drew abreast of whites and then surpassed them in numbers, producing early in the eighteenth century a "black majority," and with it the racial tensions that had already become acute in the islands. Wood, in tracing this development in rich detail down to the year 1739, the year of the Stono revolt, accomplishes as fine a piece of social history as the study of slavery has yet produced.

The two most striking aspects of *Black Majority* are Wood's care to illustrate the active role of blacks from the first settlement, and his steady and fruitful concentration on change itself. He rightly rebukes American historians for their tendency to deal with slavery thematically rather than chronologically, which has left an inaccurate impression that this institution, unlike all others, remained static throughout its 250-year history. By reading backward, the unwary could assume that slavery was always what it became in the last two decades of its existence. Wood writes that in the period between 1690 and 1720, the approximately 15,000-strong black majority "to a degree unique in American history—participated in—and in some ways dominated—the evolution of that particular social and geographical frontier."

The blacks were able herdsmen of cattle, the first enterprise of the colony, and they were especially important, if Wood's informed guess is true, in conquering the mysteries of rice cultivation, a crop with which the English had no experience. There is evidence from slave advertisements that Africans from the rice-growing areas of Africa were especially prized for their expertise. The blacks also brought with them from their African homeland a greater resistance to malaria, and Wood's careful summary of what we know about sickle-cell anemia and its relationship to malaria resistance is an impressive piece of medical history.

The Africans appear here as carriers of their own culture, which they had a better opportunity to preserve in South Carolina than anywhere else on the mainland, because of the speedy rise in their numbers once the colony turned to rice, and the regular reinforcement of new arrivals from Africa. Exploiting such a versatile population under the kind of caste system that evolved later in the eighteenth century was impossible, and in any case entirely unsuitable. Take, for instance, the grandfather of the Revolutionary general Peter Horry, who founded the famous Huguenot family line in this country. He reports that he "worked many days with a Negro man at the Whip saw," presumably clearing the lands that became the seat of his estate. The evolution of a caste system based on color, with its "brutal enforcements," had to await a safer time; until then the "crude and egalitarian intimacies of the frontier" prevailed.

But the steady increase in the slave population introduced the inevitable tensions. From 1717, when the first law prohibiting miscegenation was passed, the status of blacks, free and slave, was steadily depressed. After the bloody Stono revolt of 1739 the legislature enacted a general "Negro Act" lumping free blacks and slaves into one category, and prescribing speedy second-class justice for both. Private manumissions were now forbidden, and South Carolina was on the way to an unenviable reputation as the mainland colony with the harshest slave code.

Wood's work on South Carolina is an excellent demonstration of how sociology and anthropology as well as demography can come to the aid of history. His emphasis on the importance of the kind of work people do, in spite of their status, in shaping their view of their world and their style of accommodation or resistance to their condition, is most illuminating. Fortunately Gerald Mullin's *Flight and Rebellion: Slave Resistance in Eighteenth-Century Virginia* exhibits these virtues too. Mullin's work is especially remarkable for its psychological insight into the stresses of the acculturation process for the slaves. Employing the advertisements for runaway slaves as a means of separating "New Negroes" from the acculturated ones, he discovers distinct styles of resistance, that of the former being inward-directed and sometimes self-destructive, and that of the acculturated slave being more successfully directed toward the specific goal of freedom. Africans planned their running away in groups, the acculturated slave ran off alone.

Although the legal status of slavery in Virginia had been fixed firmly as early as 1600, the conversion of the institution into a rigid color-based caste system required longer than it did in South Carolina. Even though Mullin's eighteenth-century Virginia had moved rapidly away from the world Craven describes, and could now sport numerous tidewater aristocrats in their Georgian mansions, slavery remained throughout the century, he maintains, "remarkably flexible and unstructured in part because society itself was unstructured, rapidly growing and insecure." Tobacco had not yet become the intensive monoculture sugar had become and rice was becoming, and the Virginia colonists were engaged in a variety of enterprises, agricultural and mercantile. For the slaves the important consequence was that they were still scattered about on small farms and upland "quarters" and in small units. Those who learned English and English ways were set to every sort of occupation, trained to crafts, and often assigned responsibilities that involved geographic mobility. They traveled about, learned about the country and the people, and some improved their lot by escaping.

Actually, as Mullin discovered, the Virginian colonists, though not getting rich in the Barbadian style, were striving for what William Byrd of Westover called a "kind of Independence on Everyone but Providence," making clothes at home for everybody but the lord and lady, tools for the farm, furniture, food for all, and building their houses with bricks made on the plantation. Ironically, as Mullin discovered, everything that was done to achieve this independence depended on creating among the slaves themselves a class of resourceful and mobile artisans, poorly suited to accept slavery, restless, and far more capable of resisting the coercions of the master. Their description reminds the reader of Degler's mulattoes, with the important difference that these acculturating slaves were a part of a minority, and defined "out" of the white world.

What Stono was to South Carolina, the Gabriel plot became for Virginia. In the generation after the American Revolution, some of Virginia's sons of the Enlightenment deluded themselves for a time in the hope that slavery could be ended peacefully, but the hope was doomed by the tensions that inevitably mounted with the numbers of the black population and especially of free blacks. If Gabriel's revolt had materialized it would have been more sanguinary than any that ever came off in this country, and it did not pass unnoticed that among the prominent leaders the slave artisans, particularly those with geographic mobility, figured largely. Taking alarm, Virginia settled down with slavery, attempted by law to fix slaves as firmly as possible to agriculture, and to hinder liberal-minded masters in any private effort to emancipate their slaves.

In stressing the paternalism of the eighteenth-century slaveowners Mullin may be generalizing too much from men like Landon Carter, fusty and neurotic, concerned about everybody's health, including that of his slaves, and attentive to small details. Paternalism does not, of course, have to be benevolent, for all "fathers" are not kind. Yet one expects of it some faint resemblance to relations the masters had with their children, and the eighteenth-century record is speckled (far more than the nineteenth) with accounts of outrageous punishments, indifference to housing and clothing and proper nourishment. Few seem to have had any concern about the religious instruction of their chattels. Improvement in these respects in the nineteenth century undoubtedly owes something to the suppression of the slave trade and the general gentling of life in an older slaveholding region. But Mullin's work is nevertheless an insightful study of the interpersonal relations of slavery, informed, lively, and judicious, the best book yet on slavery in Virginia when the institution was on the eve of an important transition.

The most noticeable shift the newer works signalize is a reluctance to make moral judgments apart from the geographical and demographic pressures experienced by the total slaveholding society. Even Dunn, in excoriating the world the planters of the West Indies created for themselves, informs the reader completely about those pressures. Even so, geography and demography cannot alone explain the divergences in the post-emancipation patterns in the Western Hemisphere. Degler's understanding of the "mulatto escape hatch" fits comfortably with what we know about Brazil and the United States, but not quite so well with what Dunn saw in the British Caribbean, where the demographic proportions (blacks to whites, men to women) were more like those of Brazil than in the British mainland, but did not produce the same result.

But in emphasizing the interplay of those forces over the passage of time the authors are showing how sociology can best serve historical explanation. Degler, Wood, and Mullin are to be congratulated particularly in their success at that most elusive task of extracting from an unwilling record the part blacks themselves played in our total history. In all this there is hope that eventually moral judgments, the inescapable ultimate task of the social historian, may be made with more accuracy, grace, and compassion.

12

The New Slave Studies:
An Old Reaction or a New Maturity?

Mrs. Rose presented this essay-length review of her generation's work on slavery to a Princeton University seminar during the academic year 1974–75. The lecture, never before published, well indicates her position as part of a wave of scholarship—and poised to make her own waves too.

It is now a banality among scholars that historians of all nationalities are influenced by their times, and that their work reflects, if not prevailing views of their people and their age, at least a reaction to problems and questions that permeate their world. The student of North American slavery will see no cause to disagree with that proposition, and may even conclude that historians of the southern United States have a severe case of "presentism." There has been a disturbingly close relationship between the presumed best wisdom of scholars on slavery and the dominant attitudes of the dominant white culture. This was true certainly so long as white culture dominated the public view. During the 1960s, for a brief time, one could detect a slight exception to this pattern. But even that exception went in the direction of accommodating to a particular phase of the so-called black revolution dominating certain academic circles. Alas, when historians have disagreed with the "dominant" view, they have either been ignored, or have been forced, too often, to defend not only their opinions but their characters.

Few have escaped being placed on the defensive at one time or another (and I include both black and white scholars) regarding the purity of their racial attitudes, defined always in twentieth-century terms. Veterans of many stormy sessions at Southern Historical Association, American Historical Association, and Organization of American Historians conventions will understand immediately what I mean. They may also share my uneasiness about the sudden quiet that has fallen on academic conclaves in the seventies, and wonder, as I do, just what this means.

Peace is good, of course, and the return of courteous discourse can hardly hurt scholarship. Yet one must reflect uneasily that there *was* a connection between the long hot summers of the violent sixties, those dreadful academic quarrels, and the publication of some good and very many bad books on slavery. It seemed to many of us who participated in slavery debates six or eight years ago that peace and honesty all around would be impossible until racial problems had been more equitably settled, for contemporary issues kept muddying the water.

American society has since found some partial solutions to its social conflicts. But nobody would argue that contemporary social problems are really adjusted. And yet now, in this academic year of 1974–75, several works have been published that may be taken in one sense as presenting a far more conservative view of the peculiar institution than anything written in the preceding decade. They carry important implications, potentially conservative implications, for contemporary American life. All the same, the roar of the sixties has subsided to a murmur. Indeed, we find much quiet acceptance of the premises and findings of the new works.

These circumstances raise the question I want to explore: namely whether the contemporary crop of slavery studies reflects and represents a new maturity soundly based on scholarship in its best sense? Or is the new work but the old familiar reaction to what many took to be the political excesses of the sixties? In a time when the voices of Shockley and Jensen are heard in the land, speaking the old language of innate inequality in intelligence, are historians of slavery precursors (witting or unwitting) of reaction?[1]

Before considering the new works, I must, at the risk of annoying some of you who already know all about it, explore the dominant wisdom of the preceding decade. For more than half of that period the most widely read general work was Kenneth M. Stampp's *The Peculiar Institution*, published in 1956. That work had emphatically driven from the field the conclusions of Ulrich Bonnell Phillips's *American Negro Slavery*. Phillips had taken a view of slavery comfortable to white conservatives, and his view had been widely accepted throughout the Progressive Era and down to the mid-fifties. Slavery Phillips saw as being a part of an organic world of give and take. The system he viewed as less harsh and exploitative than southern slave codes would lead one to believe. Slavery was not profitable. It survived because it served to maintain white control in a biracial society where blacks were presumed innately unequal.

Kenneth Stampp was the first scholar to match Phillips's monumental research, and his conclusions were striking departures from those of his predecessor. Working in a time when sociological investigations began to give us a clearer and more appreciative view of Africa, and in an era when Americans began to see that environment affected attitude and performance, and in a period when Americans horrified by Nazi anti-Semitism began to blush at blatant racism here, and in a decade when court decisions began to attack segregated school systems, Stampp took a far more critical view of that organic agrarian society Phillips had seen as serving the common good.

Stampp saw slavery as having been based primarily on force. Slaveholders' primary purpose, he urged, was to extract labor from an unwilling people. The system lasted because it was profitable, and it continued to be profitable until it was overthrown. Blacks were NOT happy in their bondage but given to many forms of resistance, from slowdowns and feigning illness to outright rebellion.

In 1959, Stanley Elkins produced a work that concentrated more exclusively on the plantation system's effect on its "victim's" personality. Banking on supposed differences between North American and South American slave systems, Elkins stressed what he believed to be the important distinguishing characteristic of bondage in the United States: In Anglo-America, as opposed to Latin America, slavery evolved in a capitalistic world lacking countervailing church or state institutions to check despotism from proceeding directly to its most extreme form. Elkins described North American bondage as uniquely a closed society in which the slave had only one "significant other," his master.

The consequence was, in Elkins's view, an adoption, uniquely by the North American slave, of the very view of himself that the master had. This extreme self-devaluation meant that the slave became incapable of organized and serious rebellion. The bondsman was rather an accommodating servile who is best remembered as "Sambo." Elkins also saw the slave family as all but destroyed, a conception not very different from the one implied by Stampp, but nevertheless stressed to the degree that made the work a ready reference for social scientists concerned with fragmentation of the black family in the contemporary ghetto. Elkins's own position on fragmentation and dehumanization in slavery times extended to the point of comparing North American bondage with that most victimizing of twentieth-century totalitarian systems, the Nazi concentration camp.

Not surprisingly, Elkins's famous concentration camp analogy brought out enemies from the right. How could slavery be compared to that horror? they asked. The master's own interest, humanity aside, would have prevented a Gestapo mentality.

Liberal scholars, black and white, were no happier. They were unwilling to accept the notion that blacks had ever made the accommodation Elkins outlined, or that family feeling had ever been so obliterated by the slave system, or that the personality of Sambo had any real validity beyond Elkins's abstractions. But liberals were in a worse corner than conservatives. They usually agreed with Elkins's postulations about the severity of the closed system. But they could not accept Elkins's commonsensical notion that severe systems have severe effects.

As we shall see, subsequent scholarship has proved Elkins wrong in some respects. Nevertheless he raised issues that have been dominant concerns for the past fifteen years. Elkins wrote, in the truest sense of the word, a "seminal" work, in that it refocused issues, opened new fields of investigation, and released historians from many tired moralistic conceptions.

If Stampp and Elkins represented the first wave of revisionist scholarship on slavery, they wrote their works at a fortunate time, on the eve of the militant phase of the black revolution. The timing explains much about the reception of the books. Both works were identified with the idealistic or "Tennis Court Oath" phase of the coming revolution, a period in which ideals of equal rights and opportunities (defined in twentieth-century terms) were coming to prevail. It could hardly have occurred to anyone then, in an era that hoped for full integration on an equal footing, to question the relevance of Stampp's famous statement that black men were, "innately . . . only white men with black skins, nothing more, nothing less."

For more than ten years, nobody thought to criticize this statement, not until the whole ideal of integration began to be questioned, not until black separatists began to be heard late in the 1960s. For during the earlier phase of the militant civil rights movement, in the times of the March on Washington, and the bus boycotts, and the Birmingham riots, and the Selma March, the ideal of innate equality, however unfortunately phrased, served well enough.

During the early 1960s, many found it perfectly credible that the grave problems we faced were almost exclusively owing to the heritage of bondage. This was a sufficiently remote institution to become an acceptable scapegoat for contemporary whites and blacks alike. The notion was especially appealing to whites, perhaps secretly a little uneasy that blacks had not produced four and one-half million Horatio Algers in 1865. Slavery and its protracted blighting effects were also simpler for many whites to accept than the role of such contemporary institutions as Social Security and racially exclusive labor unions. Failure to understand these and other social institutions caused many to look ever further into the past to explain the contemporary problem. Slavery became a least common denominator for persons of good will of both races when they sought to explain contemporary difficulties.

But the civil rights movement's mounting frustrations, delays, and small gains soon gave influence to those who instinctively spotted the subtle patronizing in Stampp's statement that blacks were nothing more or less than white men with black skins. Black separatists and cultural nationalists gained sudden influence with those who began to be persuaded, on the evidence, that blacks were indeed something more, if nothing less, than white men with black skins.

For many discouraged and angry blacks, the old concept of equality and the old goal of integration began to be less attractive than a new idealization of indigenous black culture and the African heritage, worn unimaginably thin perhaps, in some areas, but yet with some reality left to dignify its meaning. African dance forms and new hair styles raised the consciousness of blacks to a distinct cultural heritage. Characteristically this movement found more adherents among those who saw opportunities to consolidate political support on racial lines than among those who saw no such opportunity. It was more often an urban than a rural phenomenon, and its headquarters in academia were more often in the sociology and anthropology departments than in history. And yet historians also strongly reflected currents of this period.

There was, for instance, an almost unbelievable fracas over a novel, of all things. William Styron's *The Confessions of Nat Turner* appeared in 1966.[2] Whatever its literary merits, the book was at rock bottom a sympathetic fictional exploration of the complex mind and heart of a revolutionary, a white novelist's interpretation of what he knew about our most sanguinary slave insurrection. It was attacked in forum after forum, by historians as well as political activists, for a hundred faults, some real, some not, but all coming down in one way or another to the novelist's choice of religious, psychological, and sexual explanations of motive rather than purely political, black power motivations. To my knowledge no worthy work came out of this cheap quarrel. But it seemed to serve, symbolically, as a point of departure, to set off a new phase of black historiography that witnessed an examination of whatever might make black different and distinct and beautiful.

We cannot know whether this tendency would have pleased Melville Herskovits, the anthropologist whose *Myth of the Negro*

Past, celebrating similar ideas about the African past, had been not so well received in 1941. I doubt that Herskovits would have approved of the style of the arguments now becoming, quite suddenly, all the rage in the late sixties. In any case we heard a great deal about black English and soul food, and we saw new hair styles.

The discovery that "black was beautiful" was not so much a discovery as it was a way of raising the consciousness of blacks and whites alike. For a time academe considered such consciousness-raising "education." Out of such education came much nonsense, some of it published, most unfortunately.

Of course the hothouse atmosphere of the late sixties witnessed publication of several excellent works: one thinks especially of Winthrop Jordan's *White over Black* and David Brion Davis's *The Problem of Slavery in Western Culture.* Both volumes were history grand in conception and rich in execution. But both works were begun well before excitements of the decade swept reason before passion; their initial inspiration owed more to the 1950s. Much of what was conceived and written on the subject in the late 1960s, on the other hand, was done in haste, for a political market, and would not bear a second washing.

It is not my plan to give a bibliographical rundown of all that happened on the slavery front in those years. Rather, I wish to point out the parallel course between the scholarship of the period and contemporary racial issues, and to expose the resulting question concerning the most recent works that is, I dare to say, secretly troubling many Americans who read them. This brings me back, somewhat indirectly I grant, to the ominously quiet reaction of the mid-seventies to such works as Robert Fogel and Stanley Engerman's *Time on the Cross,* a quantified approach to plantation slavery, and Eugene D. Genovese's *Roll, Jordan, Roll.* Fogel and Engerman have marshaled computers to find that the plantation slave received in-service, cradle-to-the-grave Social Security, if you will. Blacks received back, in necessities and even in a few luxuries, a full 90 percent of their productivity, much higher than the take of the free industrial worker of the same period. Fogel and Engerman also urge that the domestic slave trade did not often break up the slave family. Servile living conditions were, to be short about it, not so bad. U. B. Phillips was, to be still shorter, rather right.

What would have been said of this work if it had appeared six or eight years ago is not hard to imagine. As things now are, the reviews have been mixed. Some have in fact accepted the work as "absolutely stunning," "exciting and provocative"; and the *Times Literary Supplement* reviewer believes the authors are justified in their claim "to have produced 'a more accurate and complete portrayal of slavery than was previously available.' "[3]

Others have leveled serious criticisms at the authors' figures as well as conclusions drawn from evidence that many consider to be inconclusive of anything.[4] And yet, on the whole, historians appear to be willing to sit back and digest the implications of the work and to match it critically against conclusions and research of others, in the good old way. It is too soon to say what the eventual scholarly reaction will be. But the caution in the more popular reviewing media with respect to some conservative implications of Fogel and Engerman suggests a possible connection with the slowdown on school integration, particularly in northern cities, conservative court decisions on busing, and the general letdown mood of the 1970s.

Another giant among studies published this year is Eugene D. Genovese's *Roll, Jordan, Roll*, hailed as a masterwork and, quite accurately in my opinion, as being as rich and deep a study of the world the slaves made as anything yet to appear. The reviews have so far been very favorable. The book explores sympathetically human aspects of the slave system, humane and inhumane. It views the plantation system as an organic whole, in ways U. B. Phillips once did.

David Brion Davis has raised the question of whether Genovese's radical reputation in politics will spare him from criticism for being too close to Phillips. Genovese's "professed Marxism," Davis noted, could "provide protective coloration against the charge of sentimentalizing or romanticizing slavery." Along the same lines Davis points to the undeniable fact that *Roll, Jordan, Roll* "is saturated with defenses against racial bias." Genovese himself seems to display nervousness about whether the public will react to his scholarship on its objective merits.[5]

Although it is far too early to predict the public reaction, I will hazard one anyway: *Roll, Jordan, Roll* will become the general work most read by students in the coming ten or twenty years. This will not be the result of Genovese's reputation for radical politics, though it will owe much to his general sympathy for the personalities and types of both races that he describes so well. It will be largely because the book arrives at an excellent time. The reading public has begun to understand that most of our intractable contemporary problems must be met by contemporary solutions—that it gets nowhere, and could quite possibly be dishonest, to lay at the door of several thousand long-dead slaveholders the massive social dislocations we experience today.

This freeing, as it were, of the past from blame for everything in the present liberates the historian of slavery from grinding contemporary axes. Historians can feel freer, and readers can feel freer, to seek an objective picture of what a lost world was really like. And what has made this new attitude so effective is that it has come accompanied with powerful new tools of conceptualization and analysis. I am thus ready to believe that the more peaceful reception of books that would have caused a great disturbance a decade ago reflects not so much a return to the good old days of U. B. Phillips as a new maturity based on the substructure of solid scholarly achievement.

I see this new maturity as resulting from several identifiable and wholesome tendencies. First has been a greater comprehension of the positive role blacks have played in the development of the country, economically, socially, and culturally. The figure of black-as-victim that dominated the 1950s has given way to the more positive image of black as cultural and economic contributor, so reminiscent of the "black is beautiful" ideology of the hothouse 1960s. I truly believe that the spirit of that phase of the movement has had a constructive impact on more sober works now appearing in the 1970s. The inspiration transcended its first not entirely admirable fruits. One thinks particularly of Peter Wood's *Black Majority*, stressing Africans' contributions during the first decades of settlement of South Carolina. One thinks also of blacks possessing a surprisingly strong sense of family (as Herbert Gutman and John Blassingame[6] tell us), of blacks as the real farmers or foremen on many plantations (as Fogel and Engerman assure us), of the bondsman as preacher, doctor of herbs and magic, and so forth.

Genovese makes perfect use of this new and positive image, and from what he has done a careful reader can see that to develop this aspect necessarily required a severe modification of the prevailing conception of a slave system sometimes described, in Elkins's terms, as the worst the world had ever known. Rather than total power all on one side, Genovese sees slaves' clever manipulation meeting and frequently overmatching masters' crushing paternalism. A richer understanding of the interpersonal relations of bond and free, love and hate, accommodation and resistance are the reward—a reward only going to those so "conservative" as to concede the system was not that of the Gestapo.

I am not really persuaded that the positive image of blacks in taking up the Protestant work ethic, projected by Fogel and Engerman, can be altogether accepted. Nor am I really persuaded that the servile consequences for slaves of taking up the role of fawning dependency, projected by Elkins, can be altogether rejected. We must learn to balance the slave's power against the slave's dependency. But every historical reaction has elements of exaggeration. This "black power" reaction, I am persuaded, has moved us closer to the unexaggerated truth.

A second major tendency of the scholarship of the seventies that suggests to me that books now coming out are not simply a conservative political reaction is the heightened concern to see North American slavery in a general New World setting. Many scholars are now devoting themselves to comparative studies of the Caribbean and Latin America. Such studies have, generally speaking, served to destroy Elkins's idea that the Catholic Church, the Roman civil law, or any other Latin American countervailing institution so effectively checked the Latin American slaveholder as to make North American regimes more total.

The most important comparative study, Philip Curtin's *The Atlantic Slave Trade: A Census*,[7] has instead demonstrated, in hard, unanswerable, statistical terms, that in some ways North American slavery was rather softer than the Latin American variety, whether that conclusion is "conservative" or not. In cool and dispassionate language, Curtin advances his findings that only 4.5 percent of all slaves brought to the New World were brought to British North America, and that the rate of natural increase among blacks kept pace with that of whites, thus accounting between them for one of the most stupendous population explosions in human history. Coming after this work, Genovese's arguments, modifying the physical hardships of slavery in North America stressed by Stampp and Elkins, will seem more plausible. For one may certainly ask, if comparative conditions of life were so much more favorable in the Caribbean than in North America, why it was that everywhere in the New World (exception: North America) the slave population could only be maintained even at a steady level by new importations. If Curtin's statistics mean anything, they mean that day-to-day life was rather more difficult than less for slaves in the Caribbean, whether their owners came from England or Spain. Richard Dunn's fine recent study, showing that Englishmen who built Barbados quickly created there a demographic disaster area compared to the English planting domain on the Chesapeake, adds further credence to Curtin's "conservative" implications.

In addition to fresh emphases on blacks as participants and on slavery in comparative perspective, a new interest in the temporal dimension of bondage indicates the maturity of the new scholarship. But the element of change over time has yet to be expanded and developed into a full synthesis of North American slavery. Since U. B. Phillips was driven from the field by Stampp's work, scholars have most generally neglected the evolutionary aspects of slavery as a social institution; they have also neglected regional variations within the South. The system is treated and described in its parts as though it were a fly under glass, or frozen in amber, unchanging over the 250 years of its existence, unaffected by currents of economic, social, religious, and/or cultural life, always the same in whatever time or space. This is as true of Genovese's new work as of the books of Stampp and Elkins, which are both organized sociologically.

But there are signs that this evolutionary approach too will soon be forthcoming. The appearance of several excellent studies of eighteenth-century slavery promises to provide that sense of the passage of years so vital to the historian's task. Until we know more about the early period, it will be hard to explain fully the role slavery has played in our general social history, not to speak of our national political life. Gerald Mullins's work on eighteenth-century slavery in Virginia and Peter Woods's even better work on South Carolina promise that the general study going from 1620 to 1860 may not be impossibly far away.

Certainly Ira Berlin's book on the free blacks, entitled appropriately *Slaves without Masters*, illustrates very well the advantages of treating his subject (which is just on the periphery of slavery) from an evolutionary point of view. The condition of free blacks is shown in its relationship to slavery and to white fears of servile insurrection. Fluctuating demographic patterns are also shown to be important in determining the position of free blacks, as are regional variations. The distinction, for instance, that Berlin draws between the position of free blacks in the Upper and Lower South suggests that slavery itself might be profitably studied with a view to regional and chronological variations. For the fascinating conclusion Berlin reaches is the reverse of what might be expected. The free black's position in the Lower South, where slavery was regarded as a positive good, was in many respects superior to the free black position in the Upper South, where slavery was regarded as a necessary evil. The reasons for this phenomenon are complex, and they are demographical and historical (which is to say they relate to what happened *where* and *when*). One can hope that Mr. Berlin's example will be followed by a historian who will look to slavery in regional terms and as changing over time.

The fourth healthy sign concerning tendencies of recent scholarship seems to me to be the employment of a greater variety of source materials, with superior methods of analysis. Sources giving the slave's-eye view of life were once rejected as biased; now they are studied to see if and how they are biased, and used if they pass the test. Historians now use songs, stories, oral traditions to resurrect the very feeling of life on the underside.

As for the methodology of the computer-Cliometricians, for some things they are unchallengeable, and we have to welcome them to the ranks of the traditional craftsmen. But we must not be intimidated by their machinery. Fogel and Engerman are apparently as often right as they are wrong, and an army of graduate students with punch cards to count the happinesses and unhappinesses of slaves should not prevent fellow scholars from pointing out when the wrong information has been punched in. I am happy to observe that literary types have rallied and are doing their job.

Everywhere historians of slavery seem to be doing their jobs with a salutory new maturity. Because of new awareness of black power and of comparative history and of temporal dimensions and of nontraditional sources, they seem better able to recreate the past as it was. Furthermore, because of new confidence that what long ago happened need not determine what will occur tomorrow, historians seem better able to let the chips fall where they may.

Thus I feel somewhat relieved, having thought this through, about the future of scholarship in slavery studies. Even though Genovese has empathetic words for the plantation Mammy, sympathetic ones for the slave driver, and comprehending ones at least for old mistress and master; even though Fogel and Engerman describe the slave's take-home goods as rising to 90 percent of what he produced, I am ready to see this not in the light of a political reaction, or identify it with white mulishness on busing, or other contemporary slowdowns, but rather as the product of real work in the archives and a more complete absorption of the realities of human nature at work even in a slave society. Perhaps we may also have developed a little more courage. U. B. Phillips has not arisen from the grave. We have survived the realization that even he may have done some things right.

If we are lucky, these findings will not afford ammunition for a reaction, or give comfort to enemies of racial harmony and justice, but rather contribute to our general understanding of how things really were. But our luck would appear to depend to a great extent on continued progress in the social arena: on solid gains in civil rights, jobs, and educational opportunities. If these are not forthcoming, there is still cause for alarm that history may again be employed in the service of political and social reaction.

V

Views on the Sources

13

An Analytical View
of the Documentary Sources

In 1976, Oxford University Press published Mrs. Rose's
A Documentary History of Slavery in North America, *her only
previous book-length study of slavery and freedom. Mrs. Rose's
introduction to that documentary volume is no less a commentary
on the drafting of this book. For she here explains what evidence
she was finding most valuable, how she was using the documents,
and what conclusions she was aspiring to drive home.*

*The essay is here reprinted with only those few slight verbal
changes needed to remove the piece from the front of a book of
documents and to place it near the end of a book of essays. Quota-
tions already in this book have also been shortened or deleted.
From* A Documentary History of Slavery in North America *by
Willie Lee Rose. Copyright © 1976 by Oxford University Press,
Inc. Reprinted by permission.*

There is an inherent frustration in assembling documents. Like
the child who has arranged his building blocks several ways, the
historian may reach the conclusion at last, if he is a resolute real-
ist, that he hasn't got a house. The documents will not speak for
themselves, and the historian hasn't unlimited license to do it for
them. To build a house, one needs mortar, a little paint, a builder's
permit, and responsibility. Therefore this particular builder must
ruefully confess that a collection of documentary materials cannot
be a history of slavery, but rather an aid to *thinking* about the
history of slavery, which is just what has been done in putting the
documents together.

The effort began with the modest ambition to print a few significant documents that came to my attention in the course of research on a related topic. But as the collection grew, the idea evolved to make the documents illustrate the historical development of slavery in this country, to fit the pieces into a loose chronology that would suggest some of the paradoxes of our dark experience with bondage and mastership in a democratic republic. How slavery grew in the English colonies of North America in a particularly severe legal form at a time when free workers were among the freest and best-paid in the world raises questions as yet unanswered. How the Founding Fathers contented themselves with words against slavery and took no action, at the very time when opposition to what Judge St. George Tucker called *political* slavery grew strong enough to raise a revolution against England, is not, even after close attention by brilliant scholars, entirely clear. How slavery itself became milder in practice and harsher in statute and more restrictive of personal liberty during that very period when democratic and humanitarian influences were expanding poses a question that would in the answering, no doubt, resolve many another thorny question.

I have ventured to indicate the remarkable variety of sources available to the study of the "peculiar institution": travelers' accounts, fugitive slave narratives, songs and riddles, newspaper advertisements, legal cases, criminal trials, statutes, petitions, planters' diaries and inventories, letters of slaves themselves (that most elusive kind of evidence), and finally those tiny snippets of large documents which represent some unique aspect of slavery, or some crucial moment in the development of the institution. Such documents primarily demonstrate the value of the uncalculated offhand observation for the close scholar who distrusts set-piece adversary performances as mirrors of truth.

But beyond suggesting historical paradoxes, and demonstrating the variety that exists among the sources, a collection of documents can illuminate some of the problems created for the historian by the shortcomings of the sources. Many readers will require no prompting to recognize the problems associated with the interpretation of documents. The most intractable questions connected with American Negro slavery are still intractable because of the nature of the sources. For the early colonial period, especially the seventeenth century, the record is fragmentary, and limited—more than the historian would like it to be—to court records and statutes. Understanding these is often complicated by ambiguities of language, the change in the meaning of certain words over time, and further by the age-old difficulty of determining whether a given law reflects majority opinion and practice as it existed at some remote and particular moment in time, or an effort to change common habits of the common people. For instance, we may ask whether colonial statutes punishing miscegenation indicate that this practice was regarded by the lawmakers with special aversion, or that it was so common as to appear menacing to white society. The implications about race prejudice in practice among the colonists would be exactly opposite. All we can say with perfect safety and confidence is that some citizens practiced miscegenation, and that others, for some reason, either economic, social, or religious, did not approve.

A slightly different problem is posed by the barbarous punishments meted out to slaves in the seventeenth and eighteenth centuries. How, in a period when free white offenders were for some crimes punished by branding and mutilation, when the heads of victims of the law rotted in full view of the public at the Tower of London, can we determine how much of the brutality experienced by slaves in the colonies was owing to their legal condition, built on racial slavery, and how much to the pervasive callousness and indifference of the society at large to human suffering? One thing is certain: historians should be most careful to pick their illustrations from the particular period they are studying, for the meaning of these punishments as an indication of social attitudes was much changed over time. What would have been shocking in the mid-nineteenth century would have been little more than a vague disturbance in ruder, cruder times, even though the victim's pain and humiliation were certainly as great.

With the advance of the eighteenth century, evidence of all kinds increases in volume, but it only reaches satisfactory proportions in the nineteenth century, when slavery began to be recognized as anachronistic, and as an acute moral and political dilemma. From the third decade of the nineteenth century the problem is no longer a problem of skimpiness—for reams were written about slavery—but one of credibility.

In one of his finer ironies, Jacob Burckhardt once wrote that "ill deeds should, as far as possible, be committed naively, for the aesthetic effect of legal justifications and recriminations on both sides is deplorable."[1] Burckhardt, the great Swiss historian of the Italian Renaissance, had international exploitation and shabby conquests in mind, but the reader of many abolitionist attacks and certainly of the larger portion of the proslavery defense will understand the application. Slavery was not "committed" naively. Americans north and south, defenders and attackers in both sections, recognized that slavery was at variance with the principles of the Declaration of Independence, and the particular aesthetic effects of defending the institution in those circumstances were indeed deplorable.

Aside from the problem of aesthetics, however, the historian is left with the disagreeable fact that much of what he must regard as "primary evidence," and patiently consult as "the record," is in fact either polemical or defensive, and directly or indirectly influenced by the slavery debate. Because few thoughtful men of the nineteenth century were indifferent to the moral question—for which we must be grateful—few of our sources are morally indifferent. The historian is much in the position of a conscientious juror in a difficult murder trial. He must anticipate that the truthfulness of all important witnesses will sooner or later come under attack; yet in the end he must make up his own mind. He will be fortunate if his own integrity is not assailed by fellow jurors who have been persuaded to a different view.

It is fortunate that documents do not have to be truthful or accurate in every detail in order to be useful to scholars. With regard to the sources for slavery studies this becomes increasingly the case, because the questions that now interest the historian and the modern reader are no longer quite the same as those of the century-old slavery debate. At least they certainly ought not to be the same. There is no longer the need to demonstrate that slavery was a destructive, immoral, and unjust social institution, but rather to discover in what ways it was destructive, the degree to which it was recognized as immoral, and the effects of its injustices on both the enslaved and the enslavers. Thus it is possible to find collateral uses for evidence that might once have been laughed out of court.

The utility of the source depends upon what sort of question has been raised. Even if the historian dismisses altogether the writings of abolitionists and the arguments of the proslavery writers—and this would in each case be an unnecessary handicap—he still has such unintentional evidence as plantation manuals and account books. He has also planters' letters, travelers' accounts, and narratives of fugitive slaves, and other self-conscious evidence that may be of great value if used with close attention to motive and interest —economic and ideological, overt and covert. But however much the historian may question some of the evidence he must use, he has to be glad that there is so much of it, because he has to sift it so carefully, and check it against other pieces of verifiable data. Too often the author must depend upon his own instinct to tell him when he has struck an important clue, and trust that the instinct is soundly based on a good understanding of his particular traveler, his particular fugitive slave, the circumstances of the slave's revelation, or his particular planter, and the circumstances of *his* revelations. It is, if anything, more dangerous to quote outside an understood context in the study of slavery than it is in almost any other topic in our history.

It is significant to know, for instance, of Austin Steward, who recounts an almost unbelievable instance of slave resistance in the late eighteenth century, that he was a responsible citizen who wrote his own book, who had held important offices in a community of organized fugitives in Canada, and that his autobiography is concerned with many subjects beyond the slavery debate.[2] Of John Hartwell Cocke's report on the morals and morale of his Alabama estate, it helps to know that he put private funds into the colonization of his own freed slaves in Liberia. About George Featherstonhaugh's report of the Creole father counting his children, one recalls that it is, after all, hearsay, however charming and witty in the telling. Of the slave Rose, recalling in her old age a mating forced upon her in her youth, further pros and cons must be borne in mind. One must be distrustful of a story told long after the event, to someone else, who took it down.

That person could possibly have influenced the form of the story. But would Rose have told a story so sensationally unpleasant to a person who seemed unsympathetic? And if Rose had been aiming at sensationalism herself, would she have dealt so charitably with her former master, his grotesque requirement of her notwithstanding? Alas, the story bears the evidence of truth. It is good to know that Lucy McKim Garrison, who had a large part in gathering slave music, was a very well-trained musician for her day. Even Nat Turner's account of the Southampton insurrection has to be read with the fact in mind that it was taken down by Dr. Thomas R. Gray, who was white, and not free of the passionate feelings then raging in his country.

The historian must sketch in enough of the context of documents chosen to permit the reader to make his own discount for the prejudice of the author, and to judge the value of the "evidence." I have not attempted to snatch that obligation from the reader. I must assume responsibility for the choices, however, and to the extent that these reflect my own ideas of what is interesting about slavery as it existed in the United States, there is a built-in bias. The reader has a right to know about that.

My chosen documents reveal a preference for what might be called the "interior" aspects of the "peculiar institution," for the bits of evidence, sometimes most casually and indirectly offered, about the personal and psychological consequences of slavery for the persons of both colors who lived in its thrall, a taste for the human response that glimmers just beyond the tangible facts of work in the field, tedium, and hard discipline. Such evidence is elusive. Much of the best of it is unselfconsciously rendered, often buried as a casual aside in something wordy on some altogether different subject.

With a few exceptions, writings specifically identifiable as contributions to the antislavery or proslavery arguments are to be avoided. But certain aspects of the slavery debate are so thoroughly woven into the internal workings of slavery as to be indispensable. A slaveowning planter's defensiveness may be of the kind that protests too much, that searches Scripture too feverishly for holy sanction, that always prefers the word "servant" to the word "slave," or even "Negro." Such passages can speak loudly about the man as master. Sometimes one is able to make a calculated guess about whether the planter had suppressed feelings of guilt, and if he had, whether those surfaced as aggression against his slaves, or a private life of personal torment, or some further complicated form of masochism. The witness of a slave master who criticizes others of his class for bad treatment of slaves is about the most persuasive condemnation of slavery readily available. It also reveals some sense of the fitness of things as understood in the planter's community, and is therefore valuable because it does so.

Fugitive slave narratives are in a number of instances valuable, even when the author was a prominent abolitionist, as was Frederick Douglass. Douglass's narration seems relevant to the interior theme: it seems to explain some difficult psychological points for the comprehension of moderns living relatively free lives in the mid-twentieth century. Certain things only a slave could know, and only a fugitive had an opportunity to describe. Aside from the songs and stories, the riddles, and other cultural survivals from slavery, there is no other way to resurrect the underside of slavery than through the recollections of survivors themselves.

But to say that the emphasis is on what might be called the "interior" aspects of slavery is to do no more than fix an angle of vision. Actually many of the most lively and tightly argued controversies in the scholarship of this subject hinge upon still unresolved enigmas of this interior view. A number of questions would yield to analysis more readily if we had a clearer idea of what life was like from day to day on certain given kinds of plantations, in certain given periods of time, in definable regions. We would then know better how to interpret actions of masters and slaves, and would be better able to determine whether some actions of slaves are called more properly accommodation or resistance. What *is* resistance in a slave society? Were some slave groups more militant in their resistance than others because of the tradition they came from, or the life they entered in the New World? And can we distinguish between a consciously adopted role of servile obedience and the role as it was internalized in "Sambo"?

So much for the first general area of debate. A second that would profit also from a closer view of the inner workings of slavery has to do with the role of law in the evolution of slavery as an institution in this country, and the significance of the statutory law as governor and indicator of personal relations under the slave regime. Was race prejudice, or the need for labor in good supply, the stronger force in the seventeenth-century beginnings of slavery? To what extent did religion and nineteenth-century "sensibility" soften the harsh face of the law? What role did racial fears and tensions play in the retention of slavery?

Above all, it must be recognized that only through an "interior" view is it possible to reach a sensible conclusion concerning the nearly exhausted subject of the personality of slaves, the degree to which slaves were able to maintain a sense of individuality in the face of a regime designed to obliterate individual urgings. The same may be said of the other face of the "personality" question: what were the effects of owning slaves on the slaveowning class? Like the opposite poles of a magnetic field, slave and master held one another in suspension. They were what they were because of each other, and each, in no fanciful sense, created the role of the other.

The master's power was so nearly absolute that his effectiveness in this process is easier to recognize than the slave's. This was not because the statutes failed to define the wanton killing of a slave as murder, for they did; or because cruel and unusual punishments were not forbidden, for they were; but because the slave himself had no procedural means of redress worthy of the name. His testimony could not be accepted in court against his master, even if his case got that far. Whipping was not regarded in any case as being out of the ordinary unless conducted with great viciousness, and calculated to kill, which was a very difficult matter to prove. Given this situation, the slave's role as an exploited agricultural laborer was laid out for him by every sanction of society, and society expected the master to keep his slaves from offending other white people by word or deed, if not by thought.

But when we observe families discussing what to do about child abuse, when we come upon "Box" Brown relating his own condition as a slave to the Christian religion professed by himself as well as his owner, when we find slaves making decisions for themselves and for their owners, we know that this is no easy question to answer, and that it is necessary to look behind the laws to discover the practice of slavery in individual communities and on individual plantations. Only then can a satisfactory generalization arise, one that covers the full variety of response on the part of the master and the slave.

Because men are not animals, even slaves were dealt with best by the provision of some human incentives; and so we discover, in the case of a master whose slaves are about to be hired for work in an iron foundry, a certain reservation about sending them where they do not want to go. They could run away, and it is therefore the task of the employer to outwit the slaves, if he can, and somehow show the owner that he will not suffer a disadvantage. The diverse occupations slaves were put to indicates more than specialized training for special tasks; it often indicates as well the necessity of the slave's assuming responsibility for choices. To a much larger degree than has been supposed, slave "drivers" made decisions about farming operations as well as the morale of the workers. They were often "broken" by their masters for failure in the second responsibility, and being "driver" was in that way not altogether unlike appointment to political office.

It must also be said, however, that not every master regarded force as a failure of diplomacy, but rather took force as a first recourse. Triumphant manifestations of the human personality had difficulty surviving on plantations owned by such men. The master made the difference, and some there were too avaricious to care for the feelings of their slaves or their neighbors, too sick of mind to notice either, or too stupid to consult their own best interests.

Such questions as those suggested above do not yield to statistical analysis. Even if one chose some arbitrary indicator that could be counted—for instance, the numbers of uprisings, the numbers of runnings-away, or the numbers of slaves who had their own economic enterprises apart from their masters—the incidents themselves could not be read correctly without a close study of the context of each incident. Unlike housing and mortality statistics, or rates of morbidity, psychological attitudes yield to individual analysis only. Only one measure comes to mind as a partial aid.

The numbers of freedmen who took the initiative for their own fate in 1865 indicate that the majority of slaves had gained a respect for education and understood the value of independently owned farm property for a man who must make his living on farming. And of course others were for some time bewildered by the challenges of freedom appearing so suddenly. At the other end of the spectrum were those who offered violent resistance to the slave system, but when resistance was undertaken impulsively and individually, the action was usually self-destructive. Most slaves learned how to channel their opposition more effectively.

The survival of individuality among slaves is owing not exclusively to the master's perception of the wiser course in dealing with his chattels, but as much to the slave's knowledge of the psychological needs of his master, and the slave's competence in deploying subtly his tenuous advantages as a "dependent." By this means the slave had a hand in creating the master's role. By working assiduously for his master's interests, by strictly subordinating his own will (or appearing to do so), the slave could win for himself some room for maneuver. By excessive gratefulness, by flattery, by praising his master to others (who might tell the master), a certain kind of slave could, in a manner of speaking, put a certain kind of master on his best behavior. Conversely, a foresighted slave might add to his quiver of rewards a few poison arrows: the tendency to break, lose, or destroy equipment, extreme puzzlement over simple instructions, or abuse of livestock. These were, of course, very dangerous weapons if not judiciously employed, and could easily backfire. Whether they are properly called "resistance" is a matter of controversy, one that depends on how much political organization and intent a given historian requires for a definition of "resistance." But surely psychological manipulation gained the slave the opportunity to score occasionally in the battle of wills.

There is a certain kind of strength that goes with weakness, and a certain weakness that goes with strength, as the diaries of courtesans will demonstrate, and as children have always known. This is because power likes approval, and there are means that power dislikes to employ. The slave who learned to exploit these techniques for survival on the precarious raft of another man's good will has been called "Sambo," an inglorious sobriquet indeed, with cowardly connotations. But it is presumptuous in posterity to dismiss contemptuously the methods that enabled generations of slaves to endure their harsh lot in life, and to snatch from it a few human satisfactions.

From masters with elegant manners to those with the worst, all shared a common attribution of uncommon power. Slavery, under these circumstances, did not have to be the most profitable institution available for investment, but merely a viable one. There were so many other gratifications. "Besides the advantage of a pure Air," William Byrd wrote the Earl of Orrery early in the eighteenth century, "we abound in all kinds of Provisions without expence. . . . Like one of the Patriarchs," declared Byrd, "I have my Flocks and my Herds, my Bond-men and Bond-women, and every Soart of Trade amongst my own Servants, so that I live in a kind of Independence on every one but Providence."[3]

"Independence" is the key word, for Byrd and for those who followed him. Studying their behavior, and the behavior of those who lived under, with, around, behind, and beyond the little autocracies the planters built, has provided me with many hours of reflection about the nature of freedom and bondage. In the slave era these conditions were nearly absolute, though those who lived in the two respective conditions lived in close proximity. In more recent times the conditions have lost much of their sharpness, and there are few who would say that they are absolutely free, but rather under some bonds to a distant and intangible economic force, a political authority, a human failing of their own, or even a tyrannical idea. The bonds are various and harder to identify. If fragments from the record of human slavery reflect some incidental light on the significance of freedom, and the art of living a free life, the historian can be well satisfied.

14

A Bibliographical Introduction to the Sources

This bibliographical introduction, first published as the last chapter of Mrs. Rose's Documentary History, *serves equally well as a final chapter here. It will be seen that the essay was intended as an* introduction *to the bibliographical process rather than as an up-to-date bibliography. Thus attempts to update the material seem inappropriate; any updating would, at any rate, quickly become dated. Some of the most important books on bondage published since Professor Rose wrote her bibliographical introduction are discussed instead in the editorial introduction to this book.*

Mrs. Rose's bibliographical chapter is here republished with only the slight changes necessary to sever it from a documentary volume published six years ago. This essay, along with her Princeton lecture on the secondary sources, published above as Chapter Ten, and her introduction to the primary sources, published above as Chapter Eleven, illuminates her overall viewpoint on the range of material available about slavery and freedom. From A Documentary History of Slavery in North America *by Willie Lee Rose. Copyright © 1976 by Oxford University Press, Inc. Reprinted by permission.*

A complete bibliography of slavery in the United States would require far more space than is available. The following pages attempt much less, aspiring only to provide practical suggestions to the student engaged in building a bibliography on a topic in this field for the first time. The suggestions will, I hope, afford constructive leads to more specific items in other books, and in the libraries.

The largest single body of manuscript material originating with those who were once slaves is the collection of narratives made by the Federal Writers Project in the 1930s, based on interviews with aging survivors of the slave system. The originals are in the Library of Congress; fortunately, however, these recollections have been reprinted in their entirety, without editorial corrections or changes of any sort, as volumes 2–17 of *The American Slave: A Composite Autobiography* (Westport, Conn., 1972); volume 1 of the series is *From Sundown to Sunup: The Making of the Black Community*, by George P. Rawick, a work that makes extensive, though not exclusive, use of the slave narratives to recreate the cultural life of the slaves beyond the field. Volumes 18 and 19 include similar matter drawn up at Fisk University. Many of the most fascinating of the WPA narratives were collected and edited in B. A. Botkin, ed., *Lay My Burden Down: A Folk History of Slavery* (Chicago, 1945).

The best evaluation of the advantages and limitations of these narratives, which were taken down in response to questions of interviewers of varied abilities, perceptions, and prejudices, is found in C. Vann Woodward, "History from Slave Sources," *American Historical Review* (1974). Norman Yetman's *Voices from Slavery* (New York, 1970) includes a hundred of these narratives, edited heavily, and providing an analysis of their utility to the scholar. A much shorter collection of autobiographical material based on similar interviews is John B. Cade's "Out of the Mouths of Slaves," in *The Journal of Negro History* (1935).

A second general category of primary source material revealing the slave's view of his condition consists of narratives of fugitives and those survivors of slavery who bought their freedom, or were manumitted by act of their masters, or by the Civil War. These works, somewhat inadequately categorized as "fugitive narratives," found their way into print before, during, and after the Civil War, and were sometimes written by blacks directly involved, and sometimes by friendly amanuenses—usually white abolitionists though not exclusively so. While the accuracy of these narratives has been freely challenged by historians of slavery, the tendency in recent years has been to employ them, exercising caution and common sense, subjecting them to the same standards of credibility a thoughtful historian would apply to other sources. John W. Blassingame, in *The Slave Community: Plantation Life in the Ante-Bellum South* (New York, 1972), pp. 227–38, offers a very useful appraisal of this material, listing (on p. 235) those narratives he believes to be the most informative and accurate. His bibliography includes most of the best works in this category. The most extensive single listing of this large literature—which became very popular reading matter in the antebellum North and in England—is found in the bibliography of Charles H. Nichols's *Many Thousand Gone* (Leiden, 1963). This listing is not annotated, and the reader must be discriminating in using the titles.

A third category of primary material arising from the slaves themselves reflects indirectly the emotions and attitudes of slaves to their condition. These are the songs, riddles, and stories that survived long enough after slavery to be recorded. Most of this material was published after the Civil War, but it is nonetheless valid for that circumstance. The publications of the American Folklore Society reveal clearly that stories taken down late in the nineteenth century and early in the twentieth century are really stories originating in slavery; and these provide a significant insight into the interpersonal relations of the slave system as perceived and sublimated by slaves themselves. The most complete and valuable collection of slave songs was made during the Civil War by a group of young people involved in the education of the freedmen: William F. Allen, Charles P. Ware, and Lucy McKim Garrison, eds., *Slave Songs of the United States* (New York, 1867).

The legal specifics of the southern slave codes may be followed in their development over time in the two-volume treatise of a Northerner, James Codman Hurd, *The Law of Freedom and Bondage in the United States* (Boston, 1858). Another important work on the state laws and their interpretation by southern jurists is Thomas R. R. Cobb's *An Inquiry into the Law of Negro Slavery* (Philadelphia, 1858). These learned works are not only valuable in themselves but also provide the best approach to the state reports, which reveal specifically and by example how the laws were interpreted in individual instances in the high courts of the southern states. Because the background of the cases is included in the report of a case on appeal, these state reports provide vivid, if often clinical, views of the day-to-day activities of slaves and masters, overseers, and others involved in the system and its enforcement. By learning just what becomes a judiciable point, we can often determine what was usual or unusual in a given jurisdiction. The thousands of cases included in brief summary in Helen Tunnicliff Catterall's *Judicial Cases Concerning American Slavery and the Negro*, published in five volumes by the Carnegie Institution (Washington, D.C., 1926–27) are indispensable as leads into the legal aspects of slavery.

The records of lower courts are not so complete, or so well preserved, as those of the high courts of appeal, especially before the nineteenth century. The Virginia State Library is exceptional in having numerous local court records and legislative petitions for the eighteenth and nineteenth centuries. In other states many local records are now available, or are shortly to become so, on microfilm. The Church of Christ of the Latter-Day Saints has microfilmed many such records, and exchanged for cooperation from the localities copies of the records for each state. A short bibliography of published works on the law of slavery, based on legal compilations, is to be found in Stanley Elkins's *Slavery: A Problem in American Institutional and Intellectual Life* (Chicago, 1959), in an extended footnote on page 3.

Travelers' accounts are of mixed value for slavery studies, some being very useful, and others impressionistic and biased. A listing of the most reliable and best-known of this category may be found in Elkins, *Slavery*, in an extended footnote on pages 3 and 4. By general consent, scholars denominate the works of Frederick Law Olmsted outstanding in this genre for their readability, balance, and comprehensiveness: *A Journey in the Seaboard Slave States* (New York, 1856), *A Journey through Texas* (New York, 1857), and *A Journey in the Back Country* (New York, 1860). In *The Cotton Kingdom* (New York, 1861), Olmsted made his culminating contribution to the subject. While no other traveler left so extensive and valuable a record, one so free of bias, even

Olmsted's work must be evaluated with a view to his orientation as a classical liberal in economics, and some of his views on the productivity of slave labor may well have been affected by these convictions.

The memoirs, letters, and autobiographies of the slaveholding class also contribute to the historian's understanding of the slave system. The inquiring historian will find listings of the most valuable of these in Blassingame, *The Slave Community*, pp. 242–44. Although no more concerned with slavery than with other dominant aspects of southern life, the published letters of the Charles Colcock Jones family, because of their sheer volume, contribute much to our knowledge of the relations between slaves and masters in the best educated and most humane circles of southern society. These letters were edited by Robert M. Myers as *The Children of Pride* (New Haven, 1972).

Among the most illuminating half-dozen or so similar works are Susan Dabney Smedes, *Memorials of a Southern Planter* (Baltimore, 1887), and Mary Boykin Chesnut's *A Diary from Dixie*, edited by Ben Ames Williams (Boston, 1949). Sharply critical of the entire slave system. Frances Anne Kemble, then the wife of the large slaveholder Pierce Butler, also left an important record of her impressions of life on her husband's Georgia estate in her *Journal of a Residence on a Georgia Plantation in 1838–39* (London, 1863). For eighteenth-century slavery *The Diary of Colonel Landon Carter of Sabine Hall, 1752–1778*, edited by Jack P. Greene in two volumes (Charlottesville, 1965), is the best single printed source deriving from the planter class in its period.

Newspapers are very important for the study of slavery, not only for what they reveal about prices and markets and the general economy of the plantation South, but also because runaways were often advertised. Gerald W. Mullin, in his *Flight and Rebellion: Slave Resistance in Eighteenth-Century Virginia* (New York, 1972), makes good use of such advertisements to determine the characteristics of eighteenth-century fugitives. Important publications available for this kind of work in the colonial era are the *Maryland Gazette*, the *South Carolina Gazette*, the (Williamsburg) *Virginia Gazette*, and the (Richmond) *Virginia Argus*. For the nineteenth century the indispensable source is the New Orleans publication *DeBow's Review*, edited by James B. Dunwoody DeBow, which carried many articles relating to the management of slave labor, the health of slaves, their nutrition and housing. *Niles' Weekly Register* also reported on topics relating to slavery—often very critically. Agricultural journals concentrate on the same subjects. General information on the newspapers and agricultural magazines most useful for the various regions of the South may be found in the bibliographies of the state monographs named in the final section of this bibliographical note.

The United States Census Reports for 1820, 1830, 1840, 1850, and 1860 offer a wealth of demographic and social data, showing changes over time in the concentration of slave population, conditions of life, and the plantation economy. Easy access to some of these statistics is afforded by *Historical Statistics of the United States, Colonial Times to 1957*, prepared by the Bureau of the Census and the Social Science Research Council, and published by the U.S. Government Printing Office in 1960.

The larger manuscript libraries, especially in the southern states, offer vast treasures of letters, documents, and rare books bearing on the slave system. The most famous of such resources are the Southern Historical Collection at the University of North Carolina in Chapel Hill and the Library of Congress in Washington, D.C.; other less thoroughly worked libraries are equally significant for the researcher, especially if he has a particular aspect of slavery in mind. The Alderman Library at the University of Virginia is richly endowed with materials from the eighteenth century, and in the industrial use of slaves. The South Caroliniana Collection in the University of South Carolina (Columbia, S.C.), the Department of Archives at Louisiana State University (Baton Rouge, La.), and the Duke University Library (Durham, N.C.) are notable collections. To name all would be futile, and the inquiring student could hardly do better at the beginning than to consult the list of libraries visited by Kenneth M. Stampp in *The Peculiar Institution* (New York, 1956), pages 431–36. But he should consult also the best index to manuscript collections, the *National Union Catalogue of Manuscript Collections* (Ann Arbor, Mich., 1962–), remembering always that, in manuscript work, patience pays. Many libraries have vaster holdings than their economic substance permits them to catalogue thoroughly, and in most instances the librarians and archivists are able, and more than willing, to assist the scholar who can describe with some accuracy the kind of material he wants to see. Archives present a problem for students accustomed to manuscript libraries, for in manuscript libraries, materials are organized under the names of persons who wrote, received, made, or donated the letters, whereas in archives materials and documents are usually organized under the institution, department, bureau, or branch of government that accumulated the materials in the course of business. Many materials are overlooked because the researcher fails to trace clues through their probable course into some archival repository. These repositories are often rich in the substance of social history; thus, in studying slavery the state and federal archives should be consulted, as well as the historical society collections and university libraries.

Several manuscript and document collections have been assembled, edited, and published, and for students unable to travel extensively on a research project, these are especially important. All of Ulrich B. Phillips's *Plantation and Frontier, 1649–1863* (Cleveland, 1909), and volumes 1 and 2 of John R. Commons, and others, ed., *A Documentary History of American Industrial Society*, 11 vols. (Cleveland, 1910), contain rich and varied slavery materials. James M. McPherson and others, eds., *Blacks in America: Bibliographical Essays* (Garden City, N.Y., 1972), on pages 12–13 offers a listing of original documents reproduced in collected anthologies, and William K. Scarborough in the bibliography of his *The Overseer: Plantation Management in the Old South* (Baton Rouge, 1966) pp. 236–37, offers an excellent list specifically relating to the slave system.

The natural way to begin the serious study of slavery is through the outstanding general works and monographs on individual states, localities, or specific aspects of the slave system. Not only does the reader discover in such books the areas of scholarly contention; he also finds the footnotes and bibliographical matter valuable leads to sources that could be of even greater value to a researcher who checks them again for a use other than that of the original researcher. Success would depend on the question asked of the material, and the intervening progress of scholarship. For instance, in Albert Bushnell Hart's *Slavery and Abolition, 1831–1841* (New York, 1906), will be found an excellent basic bibliography. Hart's work reflected a New England and anti-slavery background, a view quickly challenged by the Georgian Ulrich B. Phillips, in his monumental *American Negro Slavery: A Survey of the Supply, Employment and Control of Negro Labor* . . . (New York, 1918). His *Life and Labor in the Old South* (Boston, 1929) represented a considerable modification of views expressed or implicit in the earlier work, and suggests that if Phillips had lived longer he might well have eliminated the flaw that has opened his work to so much criticism in recent years.

Although Phillips's work was flawed by his assumption of black racial inferiority—a prejudice shared by most white writers of the period—he is nevertheless essential reading because of the broad knowledge of southern agriculture he displays, the developmental and evolutionary framework of the special topics covered, and his footnote references to a wide range of sources. In time Kenneth M. Stampp wrote a work of transcendent importance on a scale comparable to Phillip's *American Negro Slavery*, but free of Phillips's racial assumptions. *The Peculiar Institution* contains in its footnotes numerous helpful leads, and in its bibliography a listing of the important manuscript collections in southern libraries.

Also basic as an introduction to the study of slavery is Stanley Elkins's *Slavery*. The bibliographical footnotes cover a great variety of topics, and the evaluation of the importance of the works he mentions is not the smallest part of their value to the inquiring scholar. Although Elkins's view that blacks were to a large extent shattered by their experience in bondage (with serious and per-during effects on personality and family life) has been challenged by many scholars, his work opened many fruitful areas of investigation, and remains a most important book for the study of slavery. A more recent and comprehensive study of slavery is Eugene D. Genovese's *Roll, Jordan, Roll* (New York, 1974), especially important for its coverage of the slave's ideas about time, religion, his life. Another newer work providing interesting contrasts is Stanley Engerman and Robert Fogel, *Time on the Cross*, in two volumes (Boston, 1974), a work that relies on a computerized analysis of available statistical data to reach favorable conclusions about the physical care of slave property at variance with much that has been written since Phillips's volumes appeared. Their conclusions about the profitability of slavery, on the other hand, would have surprised Phillips, while most subsequent writers would question only the extent of the profitability and efficiency Fogel and Engerman have described.

Since the appearance in 1959 of Elkins's *Slavery*, scholars have become increasingly involved in the comparison of slavery in North America with slavery in other parts of the Western Hemisphere. In a general collection of essays on this topic, edited by Laura Foner and Eugene D. Genovese as *Slavery in the New World* (Englewood Cliffs, N.J., 1969), reference is made to most of the best work done before its publication. The towering work of David Brion Davis, *The Problem of Slavery in Western Culture* (Ithaca, 1966), deserves special mention in this category for its breadth and erudition. The author's concern with the response of institutions to the problem of slavery is carried forward in the more recent work *The Problem of Slavery in the Age of Revolution, 1770-1823* (Ithaca, 1974).

Many important general books on slavery have been omitted from the preceding paragraphs, but those noted seem essential, and useful especially for the initial development of a working bibilography. Further aid will be found on special topics in James M. McPherson and others, *Blacks in America*, mentioned above. On pages 4–7 are listed dozens of further bibliographical books and articles. A work not listed in that section of *Blacks in America* but of special value in the bibliography of slavery is Bennett H. Wall's "African Slavery" in Arthur S. Link and Rembert W. Patrick, eds., *Writing Southern History: Essays in Historiography in Honor of Fletcher M. Green* (Baton Rouge, 1965), pp. 175–97.

For the convenience of the general reader, or the purposes of a person working up a bibliography for a particular period, state, region, or topic, the following titles are suggested as being interesting in themselves, and suggestive in their bibliographical references. For the seventeenth and eighteenth centuries see Winthrop D. Jordan, *White over Black: American Attitudes toward the Negro, 1550–1812* (Chapel Hill, 1968), with its superb "Essay on

Sources"; the above-mentioned Gerald W. Mullin, *Flight and Rebellion: Slave Resistance in Eighteenth-Century Virginia;* Wesley Frank Craven, *White, Red, and Black; The Seventeenth-Century Virginian* (Charlottesville, 1971); Thad W. Tate, Jr., *The Negro in Eighteenth-Century Williamsburg* (Charlottesville, 1965); Edmund P. Morgan, "Slavery and Freedom," in *Journal of American History* (1973). For comparable work on South Carolina consult Peter H. Wood, *Black Majority: Negroes in Colonial South Carolina from 1670 through the Stono Rebellion* (New York, 1974), and Eugene Sirmans, "The Legal Status of Slaves in South Carolina, 1670–1740," in *Journal of Southern History* (1962). Other works in the area are John Spencer Bassett, *Slavery and Servitude in the Colony of North Carolina* (Baltimore, 1896), and Lorenzo Greene, *The Negro in Colonial New England* (New York, 1942).

The following state studies are valuable for differing reasons: some because they are the only books readily available for their states, some because of their intrinsic merits or readability, some because they have good footnotes and bibliography. James C. Ballagh's *History of Slavery in Virginia* (Baltimore, 1902), though quite old, is the only effort to date to comprehend the entire slave period in Virginia. Jeffrey C. Brackett's *The Negro in Maryland: A Study of the Institution of Slavery* (Baltimore, 1889) belongs to the same period. Howell M. Henry's *Police Control of the Slave in South Carolina* (Emory, Va., 1914) is similar to the other two works in time of writing, in its emphasis on the entire period of slaveholding, and on the legal aspects of its development. Harrison A. Trexler's *Slavery in Missouri* (Baltimore, 1914) is another book from the same era of writing, with a political emphasis.

Ralph B. Flanders's *Plantation Slavery in Georgia* (Chapel Hill, 1933) and J. Winston Coleman, Jr., *Slave Times in Kentucky* (Chapel Hill, 1940), are from a more recent period, and standard for their states. More recent studies include Chase C. Mooney, *Slavery in Tennessee* (Bloomington, 1957); Charles Sackett Sydnor, *Slavery in Mississippi* (New York, 1933); Joe Gray Taylor, *Negro Slavery in Louisiana* (Baton Rouge, 1963); James B. Sellers, *Slavery in Alabama* (University, Ala., 1950), and Orville W. Taylor, *Negro Slavery in Arkansas* (Durham, N.C., 1958).

The standard work on the internal slave trade is Frederic Bancroft's *Slave-Trading in the Old South* (Baltimore, 1931), but Wendell H. Stephenson's *Isaac Franklin: Slave Trader and Planter of the Old South* (University, Ala., 1938) provides a fascinating account of an individual trader. The footnotes and bibliographies of both books afford numerous leads into the original sources of this subject. For further suggestions consult McPherson and others, *Blacks in America,* pp. 58–59. Lewis C. Gray, *History of Agriculture in the Southern United States to 1860,* 2 vols. (Washington, D. C., 1933), has long been the standard reference for its topic, but a recent book affording more up-to-date references to sources and other books is Harold D. Woodman's *Slavery and the Southern Economy: Sources and Readings* (New York, 1966).

Slavery in the Cities: The South, 1820–1860, by Richard C. Wade (New York, 1964), includes no bibliography, but the explicit and valuable footnotes, which may be reached through imaginative use of the index, will lead the reader directly to the sources. Robert Starobin's *Industrial Slavery in the Old South* (New York, 1970) includes useful footnotes and a bibliographical essay. For further suggestions on this area of investigation consult the essays of Charles B. Dew, especially "Disciplining Slave Iron Workers in the Antebellum South: Coercion, Conciliation, and Accommodation," in *American Historical Review* (1974). Finally, a listing of bibliographies on slavery may be found in McPherson and others, pp. 4–7. In the revised *Harvard Guide to American History* in two volumes (Cambridge, Mass., 1974), drawn up under the direction of Frank Freidel, all the better bibliographies will be found under subject entries.

Notes

Preface

1. Willie Lee Rose, *Rehearsal for Reconstruction: The Port Royal Experiment* (Indianapolis, 1964). The editor would like to thank Professors Eugene Genovese and Steven Hahn for illuminating criticism of this preface.
2. Kenneth M. Stampp, *The Peculiar Institution: Slavery in the Ante-Bellum South* (New York, 1956); Stanley M. Elkins, *Slavery: A Problem in American Institutional and Intellectual Life* (Chicago, 1959). All references to Elkins, except note 7 to this introduction, are to the 1959 original edition.
3. This argument appears on p. 4 of that untitled draft which comprises one of the three essays synthesized below into Ch. 6, "Blacks without Masters."
4. Eugene D. Genovese, *Roll, Jordan, Roll* (New York, 1974); James Roark, *Masters without Slaves* (New York, 1977); Leon F. Litwack, *Been in the Storm So Long: The Aftermath of Slavery* (New York, 1979).
5. Lawrence W. Levine, *Black Culture and Black Consciousness: Afro-American Folk Thought from Slavery to Freedom* (New York, 1977); Herbert G. Gutman, *The Black Family in Slavery and Freedom, 1750–1925* (New York, 1976).
6. Ira Berlin, "Time, Space, and the Evolution of Afro-American Society in British Mainland North America," *American Historical Review* (February, 1980), pp. 44–78.
7. Stanley Elkins, *Slavery: A Problem in American Institutional and Intellectual Life*, 3rd ed (Chicago, 1976), part VI.
8. Kenneth M. Stampp, *The Imperiled Union: Essays on the Background of the Civil War* (New York, 1980), ch. 2.

Remarks on Editorial Procedure

1. Don E. Fehrenbacher, ed., *History and American Society: Essays of David M. Potter* (New York, 1973), p. vi.

1. The Impact of the American Revolution on the Black Population

1. "Oration, delivered at Corinthian Hall, Rochester, by Frederick Douglass, July 5, 1852," as reprinted in Benjamin Quarles, ed., *Frederick Douglass* (Englewood Cliffs, N.J., 1968), pp. 45–46.
2. Dred Scott v. Sanford, 19 Howard 393, pp. 406–7.
3. For an exploration of this paradox, see below, Ch. 2. Since I first turned my thoughts to this subject, two works have appeared that deeply probe the subject of freedom and bondage in the colonial and Revolutionary periods respectively. They are David Brion Davis, *Slavery in the Age of Revolution* (Ithaca, 1975), and Edmund S. Morgan, *American Slavery American Freedom: The Ordeal of Colonial Virginia* (New York, 1975).
4. Benjamin Quarles, *The Negro in the American Revolution* (Chapel Hill, 1961), is a fine survey of black participation.
5. Ira Berlin, *Slaves without Masters: The Free Negro in the Ante-Bellum South* (New York, 1974). The judgment is my own, based on the excellent account of the process given in the early chapters of Berlin's book.
6. Arthur Zilversmit, *The First Emancipation: The Abolition of Slavery in the North* (Chicago, 1967), p. 124.
7. Berlin, *Slaves without Masters*, pp. 46–47 for tables, text pp. 48–50. For slavery in eighteenth-century Virginia, see Gerald W. Mullin, *Flight and Rebellion: Slave Resistance in Eighteenth-Century Virginia* (New York, 1972).
8. Berlin, *Slaves without Masters*, tables pp. 46–47.
9. Quarles, *Negro in the American Revolution*, pp. 171–72.
10. General Assembly, Petitions from Norfolk, August–October 1792, Virginia State Library, Richmond.
11. William W. Hening, comp., *Statutes at Large; Being a Collection of All the Laws of Virginia, from . . . 1619*, 13 vols. (Richmond, 1809–23), V:8.
12. Will of Richard Randolph, Clerk's Office, Prince Edward County, Va., Will Book of 1797.
13. Berlin, *Slaves without Masters*, p. 50.

14. Unpublished statistics accumulated by Martin Lee Grey at The Johns Hopkins University.
15. See note 6, above.
16. Quarles, *Negro in the American Revolution*, pp. 39, 44.
17. Berlin, *Slaves without Masters*, pp. 33–35, 39.
18. *Ibid.*, pp. 287–303.
19. Zilversmit, *First Emancipation*, p. 106. The process is summarized on pp. 105–8 and 156–67. The cynicism of the Rhode Island law, matched to a considerable extent by New Jersey's similar action, is revealed in the provisions that permitted the Rhode Island slave-traders to continue to bring slaves from Africa to the West Indies, and even hold them over in Rhode Island, provided they were not sold there. And yet, these limitations notwithstanding, by 1787 all the new states from New England south to Virginia had prohibited the importation of slaves as merchandisable property into their own jurisdictions. Donald L. Robinson, *Slavery in the Structure of American Politics, 1765–1820* (New York, 1971), pp. 296–99.
20. Quarles, *Negro in the American Revolution*, pp. 40–42, 195.
21. *Ibid.*, p. 42; Robinson, *Slavery in the Structure of American Politics*, p. 82; Robert McColley, *Slavery and Jeffersonian Virginia*, 2d ed. (Urbana, 1973), p. 170; Winthrop D. Jordan, *White over Black: American Attitudes toward the Negro, 1550–1812* (Chapel Hill, 1968), p. 301.
22. Bernard Bailyn, *The Ideological Origins of the American Revolution* (Cambridge, Mass., 1967), pp. 239–45.
23. *Ibid.*, p. 243.
24. The outstanding study of the intellectual roots of the early anti-slavery movement is David Brion Davis, *The Problem of Slavery in Western Culture* (Ithaca, 1965). See especially ch. 10.
25. Quarles, *Negro in the American Revolution*, noting title of ch. 8.
26. Joseph C. Robert, *The Road from Monticello*, Historical Society Papers of the Trinity College Historical Society, Vol. 24 (Durham, 1941), *passim;* Clement C. Eaton, *Freedom of Thought in the Old South* (Durham, 1940); Stephen B. Oates, *To Purge This Land with Blood: A Biography of John Brown* (New York, 1970), pp. 243–47.
27. William W. Freehling, "The Founding Fathers and Slavery," *American Historical Review* (February, 1972), pp. 81–93.
28. Quoted in Robert Douthat Meade, *Patrick Henry: Patriot in the Making* (Philadelphia, 1957), p. 300.

29. Roy P. Basler, ed., *The Collected Works of Abraham Lincoln,* 9 vols. (New Brunswick, 1953), VIII:333.

2. The Domestication of Domestic Slavery

1. John Hartwell Cocke Diary, January 26, 1848, Alderman Library, University of Virginia, Charlottesville.
2. St. George Tucker, *A Dissertation on Slavery* (Williamsburg, 1796).
3. William Byrd to the Earl of Orrery, July 5, 1726, *Virginia Magazine of History and Biography* (December, 1924), p. 27.
4. Numerous incidents of the sort are recorded in William Byrd's famous secret diaries; the incidents mentioned in the text above, and several others, are reported in Mullin, *Flight and Rebellion,* pp. 65–66.
5. Philip Vickers Fithian, in John Rogers Williams, ed., *Philip Vickers Fithian's Journal and Letters, 1767–1774,* 2 vols. (Princeton 1900), I:145.
6. Quoted in Mullin, *Flight and Rebellion,* p. 22.
7. James S. Schoff, ed., *Life in the South, 1778–1779: The Letters of Benjamin West* (Ann Arbor, 1963), pp. 29–31.
8. Frank Klingberg, ed., *The Carolina Chronicle of Dr. Francis LeJau, 1706–1717* (Berkeley, 1956), pp. 60–137, *passim.*
9. All general studies of slavery since Ulrich Bonnell Phillips, *American Negro Slavery* (New York, 1918), are organized thematically rather than chronologically, dealing with conditions of life, discipline, legal restraints, etc., as though these were the same over time.
10. James Codman Hurd, *The Law of Freedom and Bondage in the United States,* 2 vols. (Boston, 1858), I:42, 45.
11. The state laws governing slavery are summarized in the order of their appearance, state by state, in Hurd, *op. cit.,* II:1–218.
12. Berlin, *Slaves without Masters.*
13. Davis, *Slavery in Age of Revolution.*
14. Mullin, *Flight and Rebellion,* pp. 124–63.
15. Hening, *Statutes,* XI:39–40.
16. John H. Russell, *The Free Negro in Virginia* (Baltimore, 1913), p. 61; Mullin, *Flight and Rebellion,* pp. 124–27.
17. Ben Ames Williams, ed., *A Diary from Dixie by Mary Boykin Chesnut* (Boston, 1949), pp. 533–34.
18. Nathaniel Beverley Tucker, *George Balcombe: A Novel,* 2 vols. (New York, 1836), I:165.

19. For a further discussion of this issue see my "Childhood in Bondage," Ch. 3 below. Support of the idea that slave fathers were dominant family figures is relatively recent. Not many years ago most scholars held that the slave father's position was extremely weak. The truth probably lies between the extremes.

20. Harriet Martineau, *Society in America*, 2 vols. (London, 1838), II:108–9. Eugene D. Genovese's *Roll, Jordan, Roll* is especially valuable for its probing of the ambivalent personal relationships of the plantation world.

21. See, for example, *The Life of John Thompson, a Fugitive Slave* (1st ed., 1856; reprinted New York, 1968); or John A. Scott, ed., *Journal of a Residence on a Georgian Plantation in 1838–9* (New York, 1861), p. 344 (*Fanny Kemble's Journal*). There are illustrations of binding family ties in nearly every slave narrative.

22. Robert Fogel and Stanley Engerman have made a valiant beginning in their *Time on the Cross* (Boston, 1974), which raises conclusions more favorable to slaveowners than any work since Phillips, *American Negro Slavery*. But historians and economists have raised important questions concerning their methods, and it will be some time before some of the scholarly controversies are resolved.

23. Carl N. Degler, *Neither Black Nor White: Slavery and Race Relations in Brazil and the United States* (New York, 1971), p. 72.

24. Fogel and Engerman in *Time on the Cross* stress the extent to which talented slaves were absorbed into the system, often enjoying advancement, remuneration, and emoluments of office.

25. Richard D. Powell to John Hartwell Cocke, August 14, 1857, Cocke Papers, Alderman Library, University of Virginia, Charlottesville.

26. Rupert Sargent Holland, ed., *Letters and Diary of Laura M. Towne* (Cambridge, Mass., 1912), p. 225.

27. Thomas B. Chaplin diary, May 21, 1857, South Carolina Historical Society, Charleston.

28. The following incident is recorded in the letters of Roswell King, the overseer of Butler's estate, to Thomas Butler, then residing in Philadelphia. The letters are of 3 February, 15 February, 22 February, and 1 March, 15 March, and 22 March of 1829, Butler Papers, Louisiana State University Library, Baton Rouge.

29. Scott, ed., *Kemble's Journal*.

30. Robert M. Myers, ed., *The Children of Pride* (New Haven, 1972).

31. William Channing Gannett Papers, 1862, *passim*, University of Rochester.

3. Childhood in Bondage

1. Jacob Stroyer, *My Life in the South* (Salem, Mass., 1898), pp. 17–21, esp. p. 21.
2. For examples, see Lunsford Lane, *Narrative of Lunsford Lane* (Boston, 1842), p. 7; William Wells Brown, *Narrative of the Life of William Wells Brown* (Boston, 1847), pp. 21–22; James W. C. Pennington, *The Fugitive Blacksmith* (London, 1849), pp. 6–7.
3. Although David Brion Davis, in *The Problem of Slavery,* and Winthrop D. Jordan, in *White over Black,* approach their respective subjects chronologically, and upon a broad basis, their works deal more particularly with white attitudes than black ones, and their work does not reach the high period of nineteenth-century slavery in the United States.
4. See Pennington, *Fugitive Blacksmith,* pp. 6–7, 9; and Henry Box Brown, *Narrative of the Life of Henry Box Brown* (Manchester, Eng., 1851).
5. Pennington, *Fugitive Blacksmith,* p. 9.
6. Scott, ed., *Kemble's Journal,* pp. 317, 333; Adolph B. Benson, ed., *America in the Fifties: Letters of Fredrika Bremer* (New York, 1924), p. 11.
7. See, for example, James Henry Hammond Plantation Manual, Hammond Papers, Library of Congress.
8. Frederick Douglass, *My Bondage and My Freedom* (New York, 1855), pp. 102–3; Thompson, *Life of John Thompson.*
9. Fredrika Bremer, *Homes of the New World: Impressions of America,* 2 vols. (New York, 1854), I:449; "Jane Grant Narrative," in WPA Slave Narrative Collection, Library of Congress.
10. Elizabeth Hyde Botume, *First Days amongst the Contrabands* (Boston, 1893), pp. 247–53.
11. Arthur Sumner to Nina Hartshorn, July 19, 1863, Arthur Sumner Papers, Penn Community Center, St. Helena Island.
12. Firm enforcement of deferential manners to all adults, black and white, seems to have been a nearly universal practice of slave mothers. Nearly every missionary teacher commented on this aspect of child-rearing.
13. The editor regrets his inability to determine which fugitive narratives, aside from the ones cited in these footnotes, passed Mrs. Rose's test of authenticity and formed the basis for the argument in this paragraph.
14. Douglass, *My Bondage and My Freedom,* p. 95; Charles Ball, *A*

Narrative of the Life and Adventures of Charles Ball, A Black Man (Pittsburgh, 1854). A striking example of a strong mother was Jermain W. Loguen's, described in *The Rev. J. W. Loguen as a Slave and as a Freeman* (Syracuse, 1859), throughout early chapters.

15. "Mom Peg's" sons are described by Laura M. Towne in Holland, ed., *Towne,* p. 225. For Archie Pope's story see Miss Towne's manuscript diary, Southern Historical Collection, Chapel Hill.

16. Dorothy Sterling, *Captain of the Planter: The Story of Robert Smalls* (New York, 1958). Though semi-fictionalized, this account of Smalls's life, written for young people, is based on family tradition and sound historical sources.

17. Pennington, *Fugitive Blacksmith,* pp. 6–7; Austin Steward, *Twenty-Two Years a Slave and Forty Years a Freeman* (Rochester, 1857), p. 25.

18. Henry Bibb, *Narrative of the Life and Adventures of Henry Bibb* (New York, 1849), p. 14.

19. Ralph Ellison, *The Invisible Man* (Signet ed.; New York, 1953), pp. 19–20.

4. The Old Allegiance

1. "The Background" is taken, in slightly abridged form, from pp. 3, 6–8, 11–12, 15–16, 21, 29–30, 43–44, 47, 76–78 of Rose, *Rehearsal.*

2. Towne ms. diary, November 12, 1862; J A J[ohnson's] account in Beaufort *Republican,* June 26, 1873. Johnson remembered hearing "Yankee Doodle" struck up as he and his fellow Confederate soldiers prepared to retreat from Bay Point.

3. Holland, ed., *Towne,* p. 27; Towne ms. diary, November 17, 1862; Elizabeth Ware Pearson, ed., *Letters from Port Royal* (Boston, 1906), pp. 78–79, 127.

4. Charlotte Forten, "Life on the Sea-Islands," *Atlantic Monthly* (May, 1864), p. 593; Pearson, ed., *Letters,* p. 207.

5. E P in *Second Series of Extracts from Letters Received* (Boston, 1862); Pearson, ed., *Letters,* p. 127.

6. J A J[ohnson] in Beaufort *Republican,* June 23, 1873.

7. Certain of the missionaries who arrived later than the first summer at Port Royal attributed the sack of the town to the soldiers, exculpating the Negroes. All the evidence of those on the spot at the time, including the whilom masters who were clandestinely roaming the region, said the field slaves did the damage. See the New

York *Tribune,* November 20, 1861; Daniel Ammen, *The Atlantic Coast* (New York, 1898), pp. 33–34; Hazard Stevens, *Life of Isaac Ingalls Stevens,* 2 vols. (Boston, 1900), II:354–55.

8. Thomas R. S. Elliott to his mother, Monday night (November 11, 1861), Elliott-Gonzales Papers, Southern Historical Collection, Chapel Hill.

9. New York *Tribune,* November 20, 1861.

10. Samuel Francis DuPont to Henry Winter Davis, December 9, 1861, DuPont Papers, Eleutherian Mills Historical Library, Greenville, Delaware.

11. Thos. R. S. Elliott to his mother, Monday night (November 11, 1861), Elliott-Gonzales Papers.

12. Lewis Pinckney Jones, "Carolinians and Cubans: The Elliotts and Gonzales, their Work and their Writings" (Ph.D. diss., University of North Carolina, 1952), Part I, p. 14.

13. DuPont to Henry Winter Davis, December 9, [18]61, DuPont Papers; New York *Tribune,* December 7, 1861; Holland, ed., *Towne,* p. 27.

14. James Petigru Carson, ed., *Life, Letters, and Speeches of James Louis Petigru* (Washington, D.C., 1920), p. 414.

15. John Berkeley Grimball diary, March 3, 8, 14, 25, 1862; December 17, 1862, Southern Historical Collection, Chapel Hill.

16. William Elliott to his son, William Elliott, August 25, 1862, Elliott-Gonzales Papers.

17. Pierce, "The Freedmen at Port Royal," *Atlantic Monthly* (September, 1863), p. 301.

18. Towne ms. diary, May 23, June 13, 16, 1862; Pearson, ed., *Letters,* pp. 31, 79, 206; William F. Allen ms. diary, January 11, 1864, pp. 90–91, typescript copy in University of Wisconsin Library, Madison.

19. Arthur Sumner to Nina Hartshorn, May 18, 1862, Arthur Sumner Papers.

20. See Vernon L. Parrington, *The Romantic Revolution in America, 1800–1860* (Harvest ed.; New York, 1954), pp. 98–103, for an analysis of and excerpts from Grayson's popular poem.

21. Richard Fuller and Francis Wayland, *Domestic Slavery Considered as a Scriptural Institution* (New York, 1845), p. 158.

22. Nehemiah Adams, *A South-Side View of Slavery: Or Three Months at the South in 1854* (Boston, 1854).

23. Boston *Commonwealth,* October 4, 1862; Scott, ed., *Kemble's Journal.*

24. Scott, ed., *Kemble's Journal*, p. 294; Fuller and Wayland, *Domestic Slavery*, pp. 158–59.

25. H. M. Henry, *The Police Control of the Slave in South Carolina* (Emory, Va., 1914), pp. 10–11.

26. Elkins, *Slavery*, pp. 54–73. Elkins's study probes deeply into the psychological impact of American Negro slavery as a "closed system" offering no recourse to the slave beyond his own master. He explains the servility and childlike qualities of the slave as resulting from the effects of this system.

27. Towne ms. diary, April 28, 1862; William F. Allen diary, December 13, 1863, typescript copy, p. 57. See also Allen's entries in his ms. diary for December 5, 6, 1863, p. 47, and January 19, 1864, p. 102.

28. Fuller and Wayland, *Domestic Slavery*, p. 151. See Whitelaw Reid, *After the War: A Southern Tour, May 1, 1865, to May 1, 1866* (New York, 1866), p. 104, for an account of Dr. Fuller's reception by the Sea Island Negroes in 1865.

29. The territory occupied by federal forces early in the war comprised only a part of Beaufort District. My totals are from the South Carolina ms. Census Reports, State Archives, Columbia. See David Duncan Wallace, *South Carolina: A Short History, 1520–1948* (Chapel Hill, 1951), Appendix IV, p. 710; Guion Griffis Johnson, *A Social History of the Sea Islands* (Chapel Hill, 1930), pp. 36–37.

30. Jones, "Carolinians and Cubans," Part I, p. 52; S.C. ms. Census Reports, Beaufort District, State Archives, Columbia; Johnson, *Social History*, pp. 42–43. Fuller lost no time in inquiring of Secretary Chase about his rights in his slaves and land at Port Royal. See David Donald, ed., *Inside Lincoln's Cabinet: The Civil War Diaries of Salmon P. Chase* (New York, 1954), p. 283, text and note.

31. Donald, ed., *Inside Lincoln's Cabinet*, p. 283, text and note.

32. John Fripp diary, June 19 and July 6, 1857, Southern Historical Collection, Chapel Hill.

33. William Elliot to Mrs. [?] Bayard, January 24, 1846; William Elliott to his wife, August 14, September 11, 1844, August 19, 1845, Elliott-Gonzales Papers; Jones, "Carolinians and Cubans," Part I, p. 32.

34. *New York Times*, February 24, 1862; William Howard Russell, *My Diary North and South* (New York, 1859), pp. 205–6.

35. Pearson, ed., *Letters*, pp. 165–272.

36. Milton Hawks to Esther Hawks, April 30, 1862, Hawks Papers, Library of Congress; Benson, ed., *America in the Fifties*, p. 103; Towne ms. diary, May 23, 1862; Mrs. A. M. French, *Slavery in South Carolina* (New York, 1862), p. 161; Forten, "The Sea-Islands," p. 592; Allen diary, February 4, 1864, pp. 118–19 of typescript; Scott, ed., *Kemble's Journal*, p. 308.

37. McKim to Charles Sumner, January 20, 1863, Charles Sumner Papers, Houghton Library, Harvard University, Cambridge, Mass.; Adams, *South-Side View of Slavery*, p. 37.

38. Fripp diary, July 7, 1857, April 2, 24, 25, 1858; Chaplin diary, January 28, 1845, February 11, 1854.

39. "List of Sick Negroes for 1849," at end of Chaplin diary; *ibid.*, January 10, 1856, April 25, 1857; David Gavin diary, October 18, 1855, Southern Historical Collection, Chapel Hill; Fripp diary, March 27, June 10, 1857, April 2, 1858. Kemble pronounced pleurisy and pneumonia "terribly prevalent" and rheumatism "almost universal." Scott, ed., *Kemble's Journal*, pp. 44–45, 137–38; exposure and improper housing were probably responsible.

40. Scott, ed., *Kemble's Journal*, pp. 45, 232, 241–43, 272, 321; Chaplin diary, January 2, 1852; Hawks to Hawks, May 17, 1862, Hawks Papers.

41. James Hammond Plantation Manual, typescript copy of manuscript, South Carolina Historical Society, Charleston; Fripp diary, November 27, 1857, May 10, 1858; Chaplin diary, October 7, 9, December 25, 1845; Charles Nordhoff, *The Freedmen of South Carolina* (New York, 1863), pp. 5, 6; Stevens, *Life of Isaac Ingalls Stevens*, II:354.

42. William F. Allen, Charles P. Ware, and Lucy M. Garrison, *Slave Songs of the United States* (New York, 1867), p. 48.

43. Fripp diary, October 16, 1858, September 8, 1858; Chaplin diary, October 1, 1852, November 8, 1849, November 6, 1853; Allen diary, December 5, 6, 1863, p. 48, typescript.

44. Lewis Cecil Gray, *The History of Agriculture in the United States*, 2 vols. (Washington, D.C., 1933), II:735; Johnson, *Social History*, p. 64.

45. Chaplin diary, May 3, 1845.

46. Pierce, "Freedmen at Port Royal," p. 300.

47. Botume, *First Days*, p. 96.

48. Holland, ed., *Towne*, p. 9; Elkins, *Slavery*, p. 82.

49. Slave Narrative Collection, XIV, Part II, 198, in Rare Book Room, Library of Congress.

50. Pearson, ed., *Letters,* pp. 206–7; Chaplin diary, May 5, 1850.
51. Isaac Stephens to William Elliott, October 22, 1849, Elliott-Gonzales Papers. Another revealing letter in the same collection is that of Jacob to Elliott, July 3, 1860, showing that Jacob was carrying on the farming operations, borrowing necessary supplies on his master's credit, asking Elliott's advice, and requesting the assistance of a carpenter. Of all the evangels, Edward Philbrick alone gave the "drivers" a poor rating on intelligence and responsibility. See his letter to Edward Atkinson, June 15, 1863, Atkinson Papers, Massachusetts Historical Society, Boston. On a number of Sea Island plantations the drivers served as de facto overseers, for the planters seem to have disregarded freely the statute stipulating the residence of a white person on plantations of more than ten working slaves. See Lorenzo Dow Turner, *Africanisms in the Gullah Dialect* (Chicago, 1949), p. 4; Slave Narrative Collection, XIV, Part II, 88.
52. Johnson, *Social History,* p. 86; H. M. Henry, *The Police Control of the Slave in South Carolina,* p. 80; Fuller and Wayland, *Domestic Slavery,* p. 151.
53. Scott, ed., *Kemble's Journal,* p. 220; "Pat has baby [and] will be out on Monday as it's a month old today," Fripp diary, June 13, 1857; Towne ms. diary, August 25, 1863.
54. Arthur Sumner to Nina Hartshorn, July 9, 1863, Arthur Sumner Papers; Botume, *First Days,* pp. 247, 253; EHP in *Third Series of Extracts from Letters* (Boston, 1863); Towne ms. diary, April 5, 1864. Despite commenting upon severe discipline, Miss Botume thought that with Negro mothers the "maternal feeling was intensified." See her *First Days,* p. 163.
55. Chaplin diary, May 10, 1854; Adams, *South-Side View,* p. 85; Fripp diary, March 3, 1857. Rebecca Grant recalled that the children were given a Sabbath School lesson every Sunday morning on the porch of the master's house, where they were taught the catechism and "to be faithful to the missus and Marsa's work like you would to your heavenly Father's work." Slave Narrative Collection, XIV, Part II, 185.
56. Slave Narrative Collection, XIV, Part II, 179.
57. Chaplin diary, July 10, 1854.
58. Adams, *South-Side View,* p. 85; Elkins, *Slavery,* p. 130; Johnson, *Social History,* p. 137.
59. Melville J. Herskovits, *The Myth of the Negro Past* (New York, 1941), pp. 64–65.
60. Chaplin diary, December 26, 1849. Chaplin's subsequent notation

in pencil is dated "Christmas 1876." This slave wedding no doubt formed a part of the holiday celebration on the Chaplin plantation; Frederick Law Olmsted, *A Journey in the Seaboard Slave States* (New York, 1856), p. 449.

61. Adams, *South-Side View*, p. 88; Scott, ed., *Kemble's Journal*, p. 263, for an indictment of the complaisance of masters and overseers toward promiscuity among slaves.

62. Chaplin diary, May 21, 1857; see also entries May 10 and July 9, 1850.

63. [Gannett and Hale], "The Freedmen at Port Royal," *North American Review* (July, 1865), p. 7. For runaways and their punishments, see Chaplin diary, November 27, 1853; Gavin diary, July 4, 1857; Towne ms. diary, June 13, 1865.

64. Elsie Clews Parsons, *Folk-Lore of the Sea Islands, South Carolina*, Memoirs of the American Folk-Lore Society, XVI (Cambridge, Mass., 1923), p. 62.

65. Bremer, *Homes of the New World*, II:492.

66. Clipping from the Bristol (England) *Post*, October 23, 1865, in the William Channing Gannett Papers, Box XXVIII. The quotation is from a speech Gannett made in Bristol after the war.

67. [Gannett and Hale], "The Freedmen at Port Royal," p. 1.

5. Masters without Slaves

1. Eric L. McKitrick, *Andrew Johnson and Reconstruction* (Chicago, 1960).

2. New York *Nation* (November 30, 1865), p. 682.

3. Joel Williamson, *After Slavery: The Negro in South Carolina During Reconstruction* (Chapel Hill, 1965).

4. Ralph E. Morrow, "The Pro-Slavery Argument Revisited," *Mississippi Valley Historical Review* (June, 1961), pp. 79–94.

5. N. W. Stephenson, "The Question of Arming the Slaves," *American Historical Review* (January, 1913), pp. 295–308.

6. David Schenck diary, n.d., but late 1864, p. 34 of typescript copy of original, Southern Historical Collection, Chapel Hill. See also John T. Trowbridge, *The Desolate South, 1865–1866* (New York, Boston, and Toronto, 1956), pp. 155–74.

7. Bell I. Wiley, "The Movement to Humanize the Institution of Slavery During the Confederacy," *Emory University Quarterly* (December, 1949), pp. 207–20; Z. B. Vance to C. H. Wiley, February 3, 1865, and William E. Pell to [C. H. Wiley], January 30,

1865, Calvin H. Wiley Papers, Southern Historical Collection, Chapel Hill; Calvin Henderson Wiley, *Scriptural Views of National Trials* (Greensboro, 1863), pp. 187–200.

8. Arney Robinson Childs, ed., *Diary of Henry William Ravenel, 1859–1887* (Columbia, 1957), entry of June 25, 1865, pp. 246–47.

9. Williams, ed., *A Diary from Dixie*, entry of May 9, 1865, pp. 531–32.

10. Note, for instance, the confusion in the entry of March 12, 1865, in Childs, ed., *Ravenel*, pp. 220–22.

11. *Ibid.*, pp. 221–22, 246; William H. Trescot, writing about labor conditions, quoted at length in *DeBow's Review* (May, 1866), pp. 551–52. See also the New York *Nation*, September 28, 1865.

12. James I. Robertson, ed., *A Confederate Girl's Diary, by Sarah Morgan Dawson* (Bloomington, 1960), pp. 45–46, 97; Williams, ed., *Diary from Dixie*, p. 531; and Earl Schenck Miers, ed., *When the World Ended: The Diary of Emma Le Conte* (New York, 1957), pp. 41, 46, 49, 53–54, 58.

13. Childs, ed., *Ravenel*, p. 218.

14. Arthur Sumner to Nina Hartshorn, [? February, 1865], Arthur Sumner Papers.

15. Rose, *Rehearsal*, esp. chs. 8, 10, 12, and the Epilogue.

16. Oscar Zeichner, "The Transition from Slave to Free Labor in the Southern States," *Agricultural History* (January, 1939), p. 32; Report of Rufus Saxton, Assistant Commissioner of the Freedmen's Bureau, *Senate Executive Documents*, 39 Cong., 1st Sess., Serial 1238, pp. 140–41.

17. Rose, *Rehearsal*, pp. 346–59.

18. Williamson, *After Slavery*, pp. 98–125; Rose, *Rehearsal*, pp. 353–58; Edwin D. Hoffman, "From Slavery to Self-Reliance," *Journal of Negro History* (January, 1956), pp. 8–42.

19. Rose, *Rehearsal*, pp. 353–54; Williamson, *After Slavery*, pp. 98–100. After 1866, a number of planters began to sell land in the coastal regions. But sharecropping became the usual farming arrangement.

20. Wage labor usually meant working under overseers, identified in the minds of most blacks with slavery. See Oliver Otis Howard, *Autobiography of Oliver Otis Howard*, 2 vols. (New York, 1907), I:239–40.

21. Nothing is more common in the early period of Reconstruction than the expression of this attitude on the part of the one-time slaveowner. It explains the reliance on Black Codes. Most masters

preferred to explain the reluctance of blacks to contract with them on the basis of constitutional laziness than on the basis of ex-slaves' distrust of the planting class.

22. John Edwin Fripp diary, n.d. but late spring, 1865, pp. 121–22 of Vol. III of typescript copy of manuscript diary, Southern Historical Collection.

23. Rufus Saxton in Reports of the Assistant Commissioners of the Freedmen's Bureau, *Senate Executive Documents* 39 Cong., 1st Sess., serial 1238; Stephen Elliott to Lt. Col. W. T. M. Burger, A.A.G., January 15, 1866, Records of U.S. Direct Tax Commissioners of S.C., United States Archives.

24. See, for instance, Childs, ed., *Ravenel*, pp. 250–54.

25. Holland, ed., *Towne*, pp. 163, 167; Rose, *Rehearsal*, pp. 347–49.

26. "We have got to calling them *our* people and loving them really—not so much individually as the collective whole. . . ." Holland, ed., *Towne*, p. 47.

27. Marginal comments made shortly after the war in the manuscript diary of Thomas B. Chaplin. See comments by entries of May 3, 1845, January 28, 1852, January 14, 1854, and the final entry of January 1, 1886.

28. Holland, ed., *Towne*, p. 167.

29. Williams, ed., *Diary from Dixie*, p. 540.

30. Stephen Powers, *Afoot and Alone: A Walk from Sea to Sea* (Hartford, 1872), p. 61.

31. [John Bachman] to Emily Elliott, February 1, 1866, Elliott-Gonzales Papers, and David Schenck diary, June 7, 1865, p. 44 of typescript copy of original.

32. Trowbridge, *The Desolate South*, p. 38; Louis Manigault to Charles Manigault, April 20, 1865, Manigault Papers, Library of Congress; Whitelaw Reid, *After the War: A Tour Through the Southern States, 1865–1866* (Cincinnati and New York, 1866), p. 150.

33. Childs, ed., *Ravenel*, pp. 247–48.

34. *DeBow's Review* (November, 1866), pp. 489–93.

6. Blacks without Masters

1. John R. Lynch, *The Facts of Reconstruction* (New York, 1968), p. 23.

2. Rose, *Rehearsal*, pp. 347–48.

3. *Ibid.*, p. 361.

4. Barrington Moore, *Social Origins of Dictatorship and Democracy: Lord and Peasant in the Making of the Modern World* (Boston, 1966), esp. ch. 3.

5. William E. B. DuBois, *Black Reconstruction in America . . . 1860–1880* (New York, 1935), pp. 389, 411.

6. *Ibid.*, pp. 84, 384.

7. *Ibid.*, p. 55.

8. See especially William A. Dunning, *Essays on the Civil War and Reconstruction* (New York, 1897), and *Reconstruction, Political and Economic, 1865–1877* (New York, 1907).

9. Vernon Lane Wharton, *The Negro in Mississippi, 1865–1900* (Chapel Hill, 1947), pp. 164–65.

10. Williamson, *After Slavery*, pp. 376–77.

7. *Four Episodes in Popular Culture*

1. R. W. B. Lewis, *The American Adam: Innocence, Tragedy, and Tradition in the Nineteenth Century* (Chicago, 1955), p. 1.

2. James D. Hart, *The Popular Book* (New York, 1950), pp. 111–12. 305,000 copies were sold in *Uncle Tom's* first year, almost all in the North, the equivalent of a multimillion copy publication bonanza in the twentieth century. Sales in England were even more astounding.

3. *The Leopard's Spots: A Romance of the White Man's Burden* (New York, 1901); *The Clansman: A Historical Romance of the Ku Klux Klan* (New York, 1905); *The Traitor: A Story of the Fall of the Ku Klux Klan* (New York, 1907). The last book was not as successful as the first two. It detailed the dissolution of the Klan after the founders saw the abuse to which it was put in the hands of unworthy leaders. Needless to say, most modern scholars have recognized that the Klan was never free of political impulses, and Allen Trelease in *White Terror: The Ku Klux Klan Conspiracy and Southern Reconstruction* (New York, 1971) emphasizes the Klan's objectives as being the removal of blacks from political life and the return of the Democratic party to majority status.

4. Richard E. Harwell, in his editorial "Introduction" to *Margaret Mitchell's "Gone With the Wind" Letters, 1936–1949* (New York, 1976), p. xxvii. The figure of 21 million is given for hardback and paperback sales since 1936 in "Why 'Roots' Hit Home," *Time*, February 14, 1977. Other figures deduced from Hart, *Popular Book*, p. 263.

5. BBC radio news bulletin of April 6, 1978.
6. David Gerber, "Haley's *Roots* and Our Own: An Inquiry into the Nature of a Popular Phenomenon," *Journal of Ethnic Studies* (1977), pp. 87–111; "Why 'Roots' Hit Home," *Time*, February 14, 1977.
7. Alex Haley, *Roots: The Saga of an American Family* (New York, 1976), pp. 568–70. Kunta Kinte called the guitar a "ko," and a river in Virginia (probably the Rappahannock) the "kamby Bolongo"—very likely "Gambia" River.
8. Mark Ottaway, "Tangled Roots," *Sunday Times*, April 10, 1977; and personal correspondence from Africanist field workers in author's possession.
9. See below, Chapter 8; "*Roots* Errors Held Unimportant," Baltimore *Sun*, April 10, 1977; "New York Panel Digs at 'Roots'," New York *Post*, April 14, 1977; Israel Shenker, "Some Historians Dismiss Charge of Factual Mistakes in 'Roots'," New York *Times*, April 10, 1977; Walter Goodman, "Fact, Fiction or Symbol?," editorial page, New York *Times*, April 15, 1977.
10. Harriet Beecher Stowe, *A Key to Uncle Tom's Cabin* (Boston, 1853). Raymond Allen Cook, *Fire from the Flint: The Amazing Careers of Thomas Dixon* (Winston-Salem, N.C., 1968), p. 142, quoting the Charleston *News & Courier*, October 19, 1905. See Harwell (ed.), *Mitchell's Letters,* especially Mitchell's letter of July 30, 1937, to Miss Ruth Tallman of Lakefield, Minnesota, pp. 160–2, where eight points are taken up individually, and to Alexander L. May of Berlin on July 22, 1938, where Mitchell lists a bibliography of works on the Civil War and Reconstruction, pp. 215–17.
11. There is another reward too that pleases Haley: black children see him as a model for success. One stiff-braided little girl, brought with her class to meet Haley at a Los Angeles bookstore, said matter-of-factly, "I'm going to write a bigger book than you." Replied Haley: "Come on, honey, and do it." *Time*, February 14, 1977, p. 51.
12. Ibid.
13. Frank Luther Mott recounts the incident without citation in *Golden Multitudes: The Story of Best Sellers in the United States* (New York, 1947), p. 15.
14. Essay-review, "Uncle Tomitudes," *Putnam's Magazine*, I (January 1853).
15. Catherine Gilbertson, *Harriet Beecher Stowe* (New York, 1937),

pp. 140–42. Mrs. Stowe gives this account of her inspiration in her preface to the 1878 edition of *Uncle Tom's Cabin*.

16. *Uncle Tom's Cabin* (Cambridge, Mass., 1962), edited with an Introduction by K. S. Lynn, pp. 422, 424, 425. This edition will be used throughout for citations from the text.

17. Ibid., p. 12.

18. *Uncle Tom's Cabin*, p. 184. The Byronic characteristics of St. Clare have often been pointed out, but nowhere more effectively than by Kenneth S. Lynn in his introduction to the edition used here.

19. *North American Review* (1853), pp. 466–93.

20. Mott, *Golden Multitudes*, p. 122.

21. *American Slavery* (London, 1856), p. 29. This pamphlet is an enlargement and reprinting of an article on *Uncle Tom's Cabin* appearing in no. 206 of the *Edinburgh Review*. The author was Nassau W. Senior.

22. "But it is in England where Uncle Tom has made his deepest impact," wrote the author of "Uncle Tomitudes" in *Putnam's Magazine* (January 1853). "Such has been the sensation produced by the book there, and so numerous have been the editions published, that it is extremely difficult to collect the statistics of its circulation with a tolerable degree of exactness. But we know of twenty rival editions in England and Scotland, and that millions of copies have been produced" (p. 99). Forrest Wilson, *Crusader in Crinoline: The Life of Harriet Beecher Stowe* (Philadelphia, 1941), p. 351, quotes the remark of Charles Sumner, that Lincoln could not have been elected in 1860 without the effect of *Uncle Tom's Cabin* on public opinion.

23. Thomas L. Cripps, *Slow Fade to Black: The Negro in American Film, 1900–1942* (New York, 1977), pp. 16–17. The role as played by James Lowe in 1927 marked the beginning of a more favorable trend toward the restoration of admirable characteristics to the hero.

24. In *Patriotic Gore: Studies in the Literature of the American Civil War* (New York, 1962), Edmund Wilson has a distinguished essay on Harriet Beecher Stowe and her achievement. Kenneth S. Lynn's introduction to the John Harvard Library edition (see n. 16) praises her characterizations, "shockingly believable," and compliments Stowe on her "penetrating and uncompromising realism. . . ." Leslie Fiedler has also taken Mrs. Stowe very seriously. See Edward C. Wagenknecht, *Harriet Beecher Stowe: The Known and the Unknown* (New York, 1965), p. 3, for others. Needless to

say, these tendencies have appeared only in the last two decades.

25. Henry James, "A Small Boy and Others," pp. 92–93, in *Henry James' Autobiography*, ed. Frederick W. Dupré (London, 1956).

26. Reconstructing the acceptance of *Birth of a Nation* by the public is complicated by the fact that some parts were edited out for showing in one locality, while different sections were deleted in others. For the NAACP the most objectionable parts were the original scenes showing blacks running amok in the town of Piedmont, pursuing white women into dark alleys with all too obvious intentions (footage now gone), and the actions of Senator Stoneman's mulatto mistress, writhing in a perfect passion of mingled lasciviousness and anticipated revenge for a social insult, from none other than Senator Charles Sumner! Other objectionable scenes were the attempted rape of Flora Cameron and Silas Lynch's assertion of independence from Senator Stoneman. Kenneth Paul O'Brien, "The Savage and the Child: Images of Blacks in Southern White Thought, 1830–1915" (Ph.D. diss., Northwestern University, 1974), pp. 219–20, 223.

27. Raymond Allen Cook, *Fire from the Flint: The Amazing Careers of Thomas Dixon*, has limitations from the point of view of the social historian, but it is the only biography available, though there are interesting treatments of Dixon in the context of his work in Maxwell Bloomfield, "Dixon's *The Leopard's Spots*: A Study in Popular Racism," *American Quarterly*, 16 (1964), and in O'Brien.

28. C. Van Woodward, *Tom Watson: Agrarian Rebel* (New York, 1938).

29. O'Brien, "Savage and Child," pp. 197–98. Dixon claimed to be a radical and a socialist. Bloomfield points out that Dixon justified his Negrophobia on scientific and humanitarian grounds. "He used liberal arguments to buttress a reactionary creed, and therein lay his appeal to a reform-minded generation." Bloomfield, "Dixon's *The Leopard's Spots*," p. 396.

30. Cook, *Fire from the Flint*, p. 105.

31. *The Leopard's Spots*, the Reverend John Durham speaking, quoted in Cook, *Flint*, pp. 119–20.

32. Cook's biography makes use of family letters in private custody. Brother Clarence's criticisms are described on p. 116.

33. Kenneth T. Jackson, *The Ku Klux Klan in the City, 1915–1930* (New York, 1967), explains the rise of the twentieth-century Klan.

34. Dixon, *Clansman*, p. 149.

35. Thomas J. Pressly, *Americans Interpret Their Civil War* (New

York, 1965), pp. 199–200, quoting a speech made by Wilson at the University of Virginia. Cripps and others have stressed the importance of the Golden Jubilee years of Civil War in promoting the new synthesis of the history of the epoch, and so it is interesting to find Wilson speaking the substance of the quid pro quo so early.

36. Cripps, *Slow Fade*, p. 27: "This metaphor of Southern tragedy which he [Griffith] developed and with which he infused his epic, *The Birth of a Nation*, helped to firmly etch the outlines of Negro character in film long after its fidelity to American realities had passed." This was particularly unfortunate in its consequences for the North, especially the nonurban North, for contacts with blacks were infrequent, and there were few correctives. This accounts for the ready acceptance of the same view as it reappears in less melodramatic form in *Gone With the Wind* twenty years later.

37. W. H. Johnson, reviewing *The Clansman* in *Critic*, 46 (1905), 278.

38. Ibid.

39. Harwell, ed., *Mitchell Letters*, introd., p. xxvii.

40. Margaret Mitchell to Thomas R. Dixon, August 15, 1936, in Harwell, ed., *Mitchell Letters*, pp. 52–53.

41. Cripps, *Slow Fade*, pp. 361–66.

42. In an important letter to Alexander L. May, July 22, 1938, Margaret Mitchell recommends that her correspondent read Robert S. Henry's *The Story of the Confederacy* and his *The Story of Reconstruction* (Harwell, ed., *Mitchell Letters*, pp. 215–17).

43. *Gone With the Wind*, chaps. VIII, XXXVII.

44. Ibid., chap. XLI.

45. Harwell, ed., *Mitchell Letters*, passim.

46. Cook, *Fire from the Flint*, p. 173.

47. Quoted in Cripps, *Slow Fade*, p. 55.

48. Cook, *Fire from the Flint*, pp. 50–53.

8. *An American Family*

1. Philip Curtin, *Economic Change in Pre-Colonial Africa: Senegambia in the Era of the Slave Trade* (Madison, 1975), p. 123.

9. *Killing for Freedom*

1. In all Mrs. Rose's review essays, comprising chapters 8–12, for books identified in her text that have previously been noted in this volume, further citation would be superfluous and has been

omitted. Full bibliographical information about Quarles, *Douglass*, and about any book not noted in these chapters can be found in the notes above.

2. Philip Foner, *Frederick Douglass* (New York, 1948).

3. Philip Foner, ed., *Life and Writings of Frederick Douglas*, 4 vols. (New York, 1950–55).

4. Frederick Douglass, *The Life and Times of Frederick Douglass* (1st ed., 1895; reprinted New York, 1941).

5. Genevieve S. Gray, ed., *The Life and Times of Frederick Douglass* (New York, 1970).

6. Benjamin Quarles, *Black Abolitionists* (New York, 1969).

7. Oates, *Purge This Land.*

8. Louis Ruchames, ed., *John Brown: The Making of a Revolutionary* (New York, 1969).

9. James Malin, *John Brown and the Legend of Fifty-Six* (Philadelphia, 1942).

10. C. Vann Woodward, "John Brown's Private War," in Daniel Aaron, ed., *America in Crisis: Fourteen Crucial Episodes in American History* (New York, 1952), pp. 109–30.

10. Off the Plantation

1. Katherine DuPre Lumpkin, *The Emancipation of Angelina Grimké* (Chapel Hill, 1974).

2. Berlin, *Slaves without Masters.*

3. Jane H. Pease and William H. Pease, *They Who Would Be Free: Blacks' Search for Freedom, 1830–1861* (New York, 1974).

4. Genovese, *Roll, Jordan, Roll*, p. xv.

11. What We Didn't Know about Slavery

1. Gilberto Freyre, *The Masters and the Slaves* (New York, 1946).

2. Frank Tannenbaum, *Slave and Citizen* (New York, 1946).

3. Richard S. Dunn, *Sugar and Slaves: The Rise of the Planter Class in the English West Indies, 1624–1713* (Chapel Hill, 1972).

4. Wesley Frank Craven, *White, Red, and Black: The Seventeenth-Century Virginian* (Charlottesville, 1971).

5. Peter H. Wood, *Black Majority: Negroes in Colonial South Carolina from 1670 through the Stono Rebellion* (New York, 1974).

12. *The New Slave Studies*

1. William A. Shockley has published several articles on the relationship between race, intellect, and environment. His efforts include "Negro IQ Deficit: Failure of a 'Malicious Coincidence' Model Warrants New Research Proposals," *Review of Educational Research* (June, 1971), pp. 227–48; and "Models, Math, and the Moral Obligation to Diagnose the Origin of Negro IQ Deficits," *Review of Educational Research* (October, 1971), pp. 369–79. Arthur R. Jensen is also concerned with the environmental and genetic relationship between intellect and race. His works include *Genetics and Education* (New York, 1972); *Bias in Mental Testing* (New York, 1980); and, with Martin Deutsch, ed., *Social Class, Race and Psychological Development* (New York, 1968).
2. William Styron, *The Confessions of Nat Turner* (New York, 1966).
3. "The Mathmatics of Servitude," *Times Literary Supplement* (May 31, 1974), p. 573.
4. See, for example, Herbert G. Gutman, *Slavery and the Numbers Game* (Urbana, Ill., 1975).
5. David B. Davis, "Slavery and the Post–World War II Historians," *Daedalus* (Spring, 1974), p. 11.
6. John Blassingame, *The Slave Community: Plantation Life in the Ante-Bellum South* (New York, 1972); Gutman, *Black Family*.
7. Philip Curtin, *The Atlantic Slave Trade: A Census* (Madison, 1969).

13. *An Analytical View of the Documentary Sources*

1. James Hasting Nichols, ed., *Force and Freedom: Reflections on History by Jacob Christoph Burckhardt* (New York, 1943), p. 116.
2. The Austin Steward document, like all the documents referred to in this chapter, can be found in Mrs. Rose's *Documentary History*.
3. July 5, 1726, in *Virginia Magazine of History and Biography* (December, 1924), p. 27.

Index

Index

Stowe, Harriet Beecher, 117, 119, 121–24, 135; *Uncle Tom's Cabin*, 127, 134
Stroyer, Jacob, 37–38, 40, 48
Styron, William, 193
Sumner, Arthur, 51, 55, 66
Supreme Court, U.S., 130
Susannah (seamstress), 51–52, 57
Sydnor, Charles Sackett, 223

Taney, Roger Brooke, 4–6, 16
Tannenbaum, Frank, 175–76
Tate, Thad W., 223
Taylor, Joe Gray, 223
Taylor, Orville W., 223–24
Thoreau, Henry David, 151
Times Literary Supplement, The, 195
Tomlinson, Reuben, 107
Tony (Barbaidan slave), 181
Toussaint L'Ouverture, Pierre Dominique, 144
Towne, Laura Matilda, 51, 57, 68
Trescot, William H., 58, 99
Trexler, Harrison A., 223
Trowbridge, Edward, 87
Tucker, Beverley, 28–29
Tucker, St. George, 20, 204
Turner, Nat, 193, 208

United States Census Reports, 219
Upper South: in Constitutional Convention, 13; and end of slave trade, 12; free blacks of, in post-Revolutionary period, 8, 10, 15, 162–66, 199. *See also specific states*

Virginia, 180; black Congressman from, 103; in Constitutional Convention, 13; domestic slavery in, 21–22, 25, 27; eighteenth-century slavery in, 145–46, 182–83, 185–87, 199; and end of slave trade, 12; plantation system's beginnings in, 182–83; Prosser's revolt in, 15, 26, 27; Revolution's impact on slavery in, 7–10
Virginia, University of, Alderman Library at, 219
Virginia Argus, 218
Virginia Gazette, 218
Virginia State Library, 217

Wade, Henry C., 224
Wage labor. *See* Free labor
Wall, Bennett H., 222
Ward, Samuel Ringgold, 167
Ware, Charles P., 51, 216
Ware, Harriet, 51, 64
Warmoth, Henry Clay, 103
Washington, George, 22
Watson, Thomas, 126
Wayland, Francis, 56
Weld, Theodore Dwight, 171, 172
West, Benjamin, 22
West Africa, Alex Haley's research in, 121, 139–41
West Indies, 9, 197–98; rise of planters in, 179–82, 187
Wharton, Vernon, 106
Wheatley, Phillis, 5–6
Whipper, W. J., 95, 107
William Joyner Smith plantation, 56
Williams, Ben Ames, 218
Williamson, Joel, 106
Wilson, Woodrow, 129, 136
Women's rights movement, 161, 170–73
Wood, Peter H., 183–85, 187, 196, 199, 223
Woodman, Harold D., 224
Woodward, C. Vann, 126, 154, 215
Woolman, John, 13–14

Yetman, Norman, 215